European Business

European Business

Text and cases

Ian Barnes and Leigh Davison

BUTTERWORTH
HEINEMANN

Butterworth-Heinemann Ltd
Linacre House, Jordan Hill, Oxford OX2 8DP

A member of the Reed Elsevier plc group

OXFORD LONDON BOSTON
MUNICH NEW DELHI SINGAPORE SYDNEY
TOKYO TORONTO WELLINGTON

First published 1994

© Butterworth-Heinemann Ltd 1994

All rights reserved. No part of this publication
may be reproduced in any material form (including
photocopying or storing in any medium by electronic
means and whether or not transiently or incidentally
to some other use of this publication) without the
written permission of the copyright holder except
in accordance with the provisions of the Copyright,
Designs and Patents Act 1988 or under the terms of a
licence issued by the Copyright Licensing Agency Ltd,
90 Tottenham Court Road, London, England W1P 9HE.
Applications for the copyright holder's written permission
to reproduce any part of this publication should be addressed
to the publishers

British Library Cataloguing in Publication Data
Barnes, Ian
    European Business: Text and cases
    I. Title II. Davison, Leigh
    337.14

ISBN 0 7506 1836 1

Printed in Great Britain by Clays, St Ives plc

Contents

List of contributors	vii
Preface	ix
Acknowledgements	xi
1 Introduction Ian Barnes and Leigh Davison	1

Part One: Introducing the European Business Environment

2 Making the Community work Pamela M Barnes	11
3 The Single Market after 1992 Ian Barnes	34
4 Regulating competition in the EC Edmund Fitzpatrick and Leigh Davison	52
5 The European Community and external relations: the rise of a new trading superpower? Lee Miles	67

Part Two: Case Studies

Case 1 The EC coal industry: into the twenty-first century Colin Turner	95
Case 2 The European Community's Environmental Management and Audit Scheme Pamela M Barnes	115
Case 3 The 'myth' of the level playing field: the case of contested takeovers within the EC Leigh Davison	140
Case 4 Restructuring the steel industry in the European Community Alan Jones	153
Case 5 EC tourism: the case of Euro Disneyland Sue Stacey	176
Case 6 European collaboration in aircraft manufacture Ian Barnes, Derek Chadburn and Rosina Jones	192
Case 7 The European plastics industry: responding to change Debra Johnson	208
Case 8 The European car market David Gray and Gary Cook	227
Case 9 Satellite broadcasting: a missed opportunity for the SEM? Campbell McPherson and Leslie Twomey	259
Index	275

Contributors

Ian Barnes (formerly Associate Dean of the Business School) is Head of Economics, University of Humberside.

Pamela M Barnes is a Senior Lecturer in European Studies, School of Economics, University of Humberside.

Derek Chadburn is International Centre Manager (Pacific Rim), University of Humberside.

Gary Cook is a Senior Lecturer in Economics, School of Economics, University of Humberside.

Leigh Davison (formerly a Senior Lecturer at the Business School) is Senior Lecturer in Economics and European Studies, School of Economics, University of Humberside.

Edmund Fitzpatrick is a Principal Lecturer in Law, School of Finance and Law, University of Humberside.

David Gray is a Lecturer in Economics, School of Economics, University of Humberside.

Debra Johnson is a Senior Lecturer in Economics and European Studies, School of Economics, University of Humberside.

Alan Jones is a Principal Lecturer in Economics, School of Economics, University of Humberside.

Rosina Jones is Dean of the School of International Business, University of Humberside.

Campbell McPherson is a Senior Lecturer in European Studies, School of Economics, University of Humberside.

Lee Miles is a Lecturer in European Studies, School of Economics, University of Humberside.

Sue Stacey is a Lecturer in Economics, School of Economics, University of Humberside.

Colin Turner is a Lecturer in Economics and European Studies, School of Economics, University of Humberside.

Leslie Twomey is a Lecturer in Languages, School of International Business, University of Humberside.

Preface

As the major industrial economies of Western Europe grow more and more interdependent, the integration of a European dimension into most aspects of the Business Studies curriculum has become commonplace. It is increasingly difficult to consider the key influences on the business environment without placing companies in their appropriate European context. The regulations which govern business have been harmonized at a European level or are influenced by European considerations. Business opportunities are assessed more frequently on a European scale and companies perceive their competition as originating in the European, as opposed to the purely national, marketplace. As well as challenging business to improve its competitiveness, Europeanization also provides opportunities for collaboration between European companies to help them meet the challenge of worldwide competition. The recent conclusion of the Uruguay Round of the General Agreement on Tariffs and Trade will lead to a further opening of the global marketplace and demonstrates the need for European business to get its competitive house in order.

This book explores some of the major issues within the European business environment. The first part analyses factors which affect all business sectors, namely the European Community and its operations and its overall influence in a macro sense on business activity. The case studies in the second part of the book demonstrate how the European Community's policies and activities affect individual companies and business sectors and how such companies and sectors are increasingly operating within a European or international, as opposed to national, marketplace.

Ian Barnes
Leigh Davison

Acknowledgements

We would like to take this opportunity to thank each author who has contributed to a case and/or a chapter. Namely, Pamela Barnes, Gary Cook, Derek Chadburn, Edmund Fitzpatrick, David Gray, Debra Johnson, Alan Jones, Rosina Jones, Campbell McPherson, Lee Miles, Sue Stacey, Colin Turner, and Leslie Twomey.

1 Introduction

Ian Barnes and Leigh Davison

European economic and political integration is a process which has been moving forward for some time, predating the European Community (EC) campaign to create a Single Market by the end of 1992. The Single Market campaign was a success, in part because it occurred at a time when the economies of the EC were experiencing a period of consistent economic growth. While a great deal was achieved during this time, there was still much to be done. Also many of the advertised benefits were difficult to recognize when 1993 arrived, in part because of the impact of the recession. This swept through all of Europe, and caused doubts about the future direction of the Community. At the same time the EC was to undergo tensions because of the need to absorb East Germany. Further expansion was on the horizon with the prospect of new members joining from the European Free Trade Area (EFTA). The scope of the Single Market was also to expand for manufactured goods with the creation of the European Economic Area (EEA). To the East, the collapse of the Soviet Union led to a loss of some markets and, in the medium term, the prospect of the former socialist economies of Central Europe joining the Community.

It is within this highly volatile situation that business decisions have to be made and understood. It is easy to believe that the collapse of the European Monetary System (EMS) and the growth of a general Europhobia means that the European dimension does not matter. However, the fact is that around of 60 per cent of all international trade for the EC states, is within the Community. The process of making laws and agreeing initiatives still goes on within the EC and this impacts upon the way business is conducted. This means that there are few areas where business is not without a European dimension. This is not to suggest that we can treat the EC as a homogeneous market place. There are significant differences not only in national legislation, but also in cultures and tastes.

Business needs to take account of the diversity of the European market place, and develop strategies to cope with it. In essence this is the thrust of this book, in that only those who can adjust to open competition within the market will survive. All markets within the EC are now open to competition to some extent. It is no longer the case that firms can rely on the safety of the home market as a basis to build upon for exports. Indeed the impact of recession in the period from 1991 onward, means that competition for the available business is becoming more intense.

There will inevitably be winners and losers in the process of economic integration; however, even within this, the process of competition is not an even one. In a number of states, the state offers help to companies, either in the way that financial aid is offered, or by protection from the most aggressive business mergers. Also the financial strength of successful companies may give sufficient resources to survive and adapt to competition. At the same time there is an ever present threat from producers in world markets, in particular the United States and Japan. Both of these economic powers, along with other emerging rivals, seek to gain ever firmer footholds in the EC market, and compete actively in third markets. In this respect, the completion of the Uruguay GATT Round offers a challenge to EC industry if external access to global markets does improve.

The organization must take a view of the environment it faces when making strategic choices. What it makes of this process depends to an extent on the stake that the various actors have. The need to take account of the concept of subsidiarity, or defend national industrial priorities, is seen as being as essential if national strongholds come under threat. On the other hand, a level playing field is essential to those who are competitive and feel they may gain from the free market. Even if carried through with the greatest care, the evaluation of strategies and the selection of the appropriate way forward, is not a clear cut thing. There is not a definitive right or wrong answer to any of the choices facing business. In part the reason is that even the firmest commitments evaporate in changing circumstances. Also, choices are made against the background of incomplete information. Finally, it should be remembered that implementation of strategy is important. With the variety of cultural perspectives to be found within Europe, it is unlikely that the strategy for implementation in one economy will be the same as in another.

How might this book be used?

This book has two related parts. The first part provides the reader with an analysis of the policy process and decision making of the EC, the Single Market, the management of competition policy and external economic relations. These chapters concentrate on the realities of the policy process and provide a foundation to many of the case studies which follow. For this reason, it is advisable to read the first section of the text before moving on to the cases.

The analysis offered within the cases is limited in order to allow the reader to explore the strategic choices that business has to make. These choices have to relate to the complex cultural, technological, social, economic and political environment which is constantly changing. The cases are designed to stimulate a debate about the strategy that the firm or industry has

Introduction

adopted, or might adopt in the future. To facilitate this a series of questions are offered at the end of each case study, although there will no doubt be other issues which develop.

All the cases are designed to illustrate the problems of operating in the Single Market of the EC, although wider considerations have been taken into account. The cases offer a balance between the sectors of the European economy. The primary sector is examined in the study of the coal industry, the problems of heavy industry are covered by the steel industry, while the development of newer materials is dealt with in the plastics industry. The reality of the competitive process is treated further in the car industry case and the analysis of merger activity. The commercial benefits of environmental awareness are considered in the environmental auditing case, and the impact of technological development is covered in the case on the aerospace case study and that concerning the satellite revolution. Finally the service sector is considered in the case of Euro Disneyland.

Tools of analysis

A number of tools of analysis can be found within economics and strategic management texts which may assist in the analysis of the cases. At a very simple level, strategic choice may be assisted by the use of SWOT analysis. That is the listing of strengths, weaknesses, opportunities and threats. Thought might be given to the application of simple models of rational decision making, so that it is helpful to consider for any organization:

1. Its purpose;
2. The objectives that have been set;
3. The gap between where the organisation is and where it should be;
4. The options that can reasonably be chosen;
5. The implementation of strategy;
6. An evaluation of strategy.

The above headings conceal a range of highly complex issues, and the staged approach to strategy assumes that we live in a relatively simple and rational world. They do not take account of the limited vision of the policy makers, or their lack of basic information. Not all decisions are made by those who have a wider grasp of affairs, and who consider the general interest. Many of the companies find that the best strategy is to be opportunistic given the volatile state of the economic environment. In other cases the realistic range of choices may be limited. Finally, it should be remembered that Europe does not have a homogeneous business culture, and it is not a homogeneous market.

The book has been designed to be used on a range of courses in higher education, ranging from second-year business and economics programmes to postgraduate level students studying for management qualifications.

The structure of the book

Part One: Introducing the European Business Environment

Chapter 2 outlines the roles of the main institutions of the European Community (EC) and investigates their different positions within the decision making process. The decision making process is fully explained. The focus will be on providing an insight into how the leaders of business are able to put their interests forward and influence the decision making process.

The chapter shows that the institutional structure of the European Community is unique amongst international organizations. The presence of the Treaties and the legal framework, based on the European Court of Justice, gives a dimension to the EC which makes it more than an intergovernmental agreement amongst states, but leaves it as less than a federal state.

Chapter 3 critically examines the process of economic integration, in the period after the completion of the initial stage of the Single Market (Internal Market) programme. Not only does it examine the achievements of the Single Market to date, but it also suggests that there is much to be done to fully complete the process. The chapter considers what might have to be done to make the operation of the market more effective in its second stage. Issues considered include: making the legislation effective, the prevention of new obstacles to trade, and the creation of Trans-European Networks.

Chapter 4 explores Brussels' increasing role in regulating the EC-wide competitive environment, particularly with regard to merger, or concentration activity, and the various forms of anti-competitive behaviour that can arise. The new Merger Control Regulation is examined in detail as is the EC Commission's attempt to expand the scope of the Regulation to cover oligopolistic situations.

Finally in Part One, Chapter 5 provides an evaluation of the importance of the European Community to world trade. The chapter analyses the significance of external trade for the European Community and the extent of its influence in shaping the world economy. It discusses four themes. First, the nature of the global trading economy in the 1990s and the importance of the Community to it. Secondly, the character of the European Community as an international trading organization. Thirdly, the role of the

Introduction

Common Commercial Policy (CCP) and the instruments used to govern the Community's external trading relationships. Lastly, an assessment of the challenges the Community faces in the 1990s within the world trading environment is given.

Part Two: Case Studies

1 The EC coal industry: into the twenty-first century

This case study examines both current and future developments within the EC coal sector. Since the end of the Second World War, the coal industry has, in terms of both output and employment, been on a perpetual decline. This decline is expected to continue into the next millennium and it is hard to envisage that coal will continue as a major fuel far into the next century. The case reveals that Member States, to a varying degree, have actively sought to cushion the effects of this decline with various market distorting devices. It goes on to highlight that a number of factors are questioning the continuation of this assistance as the EC as a whole moves to a more liberal energy market that will ensure its security of supply into the next century.

2 The European Community's Environmental Management and Audit Scheme

The subject of this case study is the operation and application of the EC's environmental policy. After outlining the development of the EC's environmental policy, it describes the new Regulation establishing the EC's Environmental Management and Audit scheme. Material is presented so that an evaluation may be made of the likely response of industry to this legislation. The final section of the case study discusses the means by which it is to be implemented in the United Kingdom.

3 The 'myth' of the level playing field: the case of contested takeovers within the EC

Given the objective of establishing the Single European Market, the case study examines to what extent a single market for contested takeovers exists in the EC. Namely, guaranteeing equal opportunities for taking control of quoted companies in every Member State. In particular, it contrasts the UK position on hostile merger attempts with that of Germany, in order to demonstrate that a level playing field has yet to be established. The EC's proposals to bring such into being are also detailed.

4 Restructuring the steel industry in the European Community

This case study examines the difficulties arising from overproduction in the EC steel industry and the approach taken by the EC in dealing with the problem. It illustrates the difficulties of establishing a free market in the European steel industry and the problems of transition to a free market caused by the presence of state aided enterprises. It provides an insight into the Community approach to re-structuring to support the creation of free markets in subsidized sectors. On a broader front, it raises questions about market competition and the politics of the steel production, raising issues relating to the need for intervention and its impact on the industry's performance.

5   EC tourism: the case of Euro Disneyland

April 1992 saw the opening of Europe's largest and most prestigious theme park. Set approximately 23 miles east of Paris, Euro Disneyland seemed ideally placed to take advantage of the European tourist market. The case study traces the development of the resort from the initial signing of the contract with the French government in 1987, to the end of the park's second financial year. It details the many problems faced by the Euro Disney Company since the park's opening, in particular highlighting the failure of the company to adapt both the product and its style of management to meet the requirements of the European market.

6   European collaboration in aircraft manufacture

This case study examines the challenges that face the Airbus consortium in the cyclical downturn of the 1990s. Earlier and continued expansion, which allowed Airbus to gain 30 percent of the global market for large commercial airliners, had come to an end as a result of the stagnation in airline traffic and an overcapacity in the industry. A further factor was the fight back by Boeing, the dominant global competitor, which sought to reduce its manufacturing costs and to enter into new alliances. Along with subsidies, the collaborative model (which was used to organize the industry) was seen by many as the reason for the success of Airbus. This collaborative model has been adopted by the rivals of Airbus as a way of sharing the risks involved in carrying the enormous development costs of new aircraft but, at the same time, its usefulness has been challenged within Airbus. Further, the extent to which subsidies can now be used is limited by international agreement.

7   The European plastics industry: responding to change

This case study examines in detail two of the major challenges facing the European plastics industry in the depth of the European recession in 1993: overcapacity and the increasing demands of environmental regulation. It reveals that the European plastics industry is responding to the problem of surplus capacity by a series of asset swaps, mergers and transnational alliances to reduce the number of players. The case sets out the anticipated

Introduction

benefits for the participants of one particular deal – the proposed merger of the polypropylene and polyethylene assets between Neste of Finland and Statoil of Norway – and its impact on the market.

The second part of this case study assesses the extent and nature of this new environmental legislation and examines the problems which have arisen when one country, Germany, introduces laws which have serious spillover effects in other European countries. This section also examines the response of the European Community to the proliferation of national laws.

8 The European car market

The importance of the western European car market can be seen from the fact that it is the largest car market in the world. This case study documents the major car producers in Europe and reveals that they saddled themselves with a greater capacity than the market required. The case study shows that this problem became apparent while Japanese transplants within western Europe were adding to an already competitive market and has resulted in car makers being forced to adopt strategies that could address this intensified competition: lean production, cooperating in design and pooling R&D resources, changing the relationship between the component supplier and the car builders, and utilizing standard parts over a range of cars.

This case study also focuses upon the Japanese competitive advantage over the European car producers and the lobbying conducted, by certain companies at the European Community level, in an effort to forestall free and open competition within their respective home markets.

9 Satellite broadcasting: a missed opportunity for the SEM?

In this case study, the development of satellite television within the SEM, and the role of the European Commission will be considered. An examination of the potential benefits of satellite broadcasting, both cultural and economic, will be made. The effect on the industry and the consumer of new technological advances is next examined. An overview of technical standards is taken and EC involvement in their commercial exploitation is considered. The case study will also track the EC's role in the development of a common standard for the whole European Community and comment on how far the EC has been successful in developing such a standard. The second section of the study will be concerned with common access and the issues involved in the ability of EC nationals to access programmes broadcast by satellite on an equal basis. Issues are raised, such as which country's jurisdiction prevails in the case of broadcasts involving different European nations.

Part One Introducing the European Business Environment

2 Making the Community work

Pamela M Barnes

Introduction

The European Community (EC) is a political and judicial system which has an impact on the whole of the European business environment. As Europe becomes increasingly a Single Market it is irrelevant whether a business is engaged in export trade or not. The EC is the framework which predominantly shapes the environment in which businesses operate.

It is important that business is able to influence the decisions which are made by the policy makers of the EC. In order to do that the management of a business must understand how the main institutions of the EC interact with one another in the decision making process. Valuable time and money may be lost if management teams approach the wrong institution or person when attempting to ensure that their views are reflected in the different policies of the Community.

The objectives of this chapter are:

1 To identify the unique features of the European Community's institutional framework.
2 To outline the roles of the main institutions involved in the decision making process.
3 To suggest ways in which the management teams of companies may be able to put their interests forward and influence the decision making process.

The EC is not a static organization. The early 1990s were characterized by heated debate about the ratification of the Treaty on European Union (TEU). The TEU will have long-term implications for both the institutions and the way in which policy operate.

The Treaty on European Union (TEU) which came into force on 1 November 1993 consists of 'three pillars'.

1 The European Community is the core of the Union. It will continue the work of economic integration begun under the Treaty of Rome of 1958. This may ultimately lead to a single market supported by a single currency. The use of the term 'Economic' was dropped from the name 'European Economic Community' in the title of the Treaty.

The other two pillars are:

2 Common Foreign and Security Policy (CFSP).

3 Judicial and Home Affairs Policy.

These are the intergovernmental pillars of the 'Union', based on agreements between the Member States. This means that in a strict legal sense, the institutions are the institutions of the EC when dealing with matters relating to the internal market, and the institutions of the Union when dealing with issues relating to areas such as immigration, defence, citizenship of the Union.

The mid-1990s were increasingly dominated by the negotiations for entry to the EC of a number of states from the European Free Trade Association (EFTA). The timetable was set in 1992 for the then applicants to be members of the EC by 1995/1996. At that time the applicants from EFTA included Austria, Sweden, Finland and Norway. Enlargement will make the decision making process more complicated because of increases to be made to the size of the institutions.

The unique framework

The institutional framework of the European Community is unique among international organizations for three reasons.

1 The sharing of the tasks of government

The three branches of democratic government are shared between four main institutions (see Figure 2.1). This has led to a very complex process which requires simplification.

1 The European Commission is responsible for tabling the proposed legislation.

2 The Council of the Union, which is made up of the representatives of the national governments, takes the final decision about the legislation.

3 The European Parliament (EP) has the right to be consulted and pass an opinion on the proposal.

4 The European Court of Justice (ECJ) ensures that the legislation is in keeping with the Treaties.

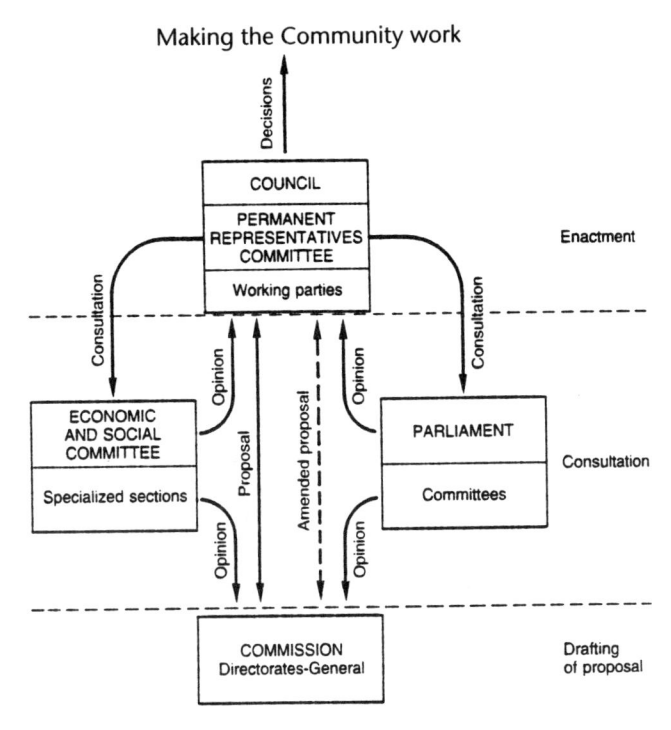

Figure 2.1 The Community's decision making process (source: *Europe in Figures*, third edition, Eurostat, 1992)

2 The allocation of the tasks by the treaties

The institutions have their tasks allocated to them by the Treaties which created the European Community. The European Community brings together the European Coal and Steel Community (ECSC), the European Economic Community (EEC) and European Atomic Agency (EURATOM). The ECSC Treaty was signed in Paris in 1951, the EEC and EURATOM Treaties in Rome in 1957. They were all brought together in a Merger Treaty in 1967 which gave the name the European Communities. Since the three Communities shared one set of institutions the singular European Community came to be the most often used description.

The term European Community has been formally incorporated into the Treaties, as it is to replace the term European Economic Community in the TEU. Although the TEU separates the European Community and the intergovernmental agreements establishing the European Union, the institutions still work for all parts of the Treaty. The European Commission and the European Parliament do not have as much power, however, over CFSP and Judicial and Home Affairs Policy. The officials are employed by the EC and not by the Union.

Other institutions include

1. European Investment Bank. (EIB)
2. The Economic and Social Committee (ECOSOC)
3. ECSC Consultative Committee

All of these were established under the terms of the original Treaty of Rome (1958).

4. The Court of First Instance, which helps with the workload of the ECJ. The Court of First Instance was established by the Treaty amendment in 1986 which is known as the Single European Act (SEA).
5. The Court of Auditors, which monitors the Community's financial management. This was given the status of a Community institution in the Treaty on European Union.
6. The Committee of the Regions (CoR), which was established by the TEU.

The ECOSOC, the ECSC Consultative Committee and the CoR are advisory bodies rather than the decision makers, but according to the Treaties note must be taken of their advice.

As the work of the Community has grown, other organizations have been formed to take on specific tasks needed to ensure that the EC is able to function. These offices and specialist agencies are sited in various parts of the EC, not concentrated in the three main centres of Brussels, Luxembourg and Strasbourg. The decisions about their locations were subject to a lengthy political bargaining process within the EC to ensure that all the states received a share of the Community agencies.

The specialist agencies and their locations are:

1. The European Environment Agency – Copenhagen.
2. The Medicines Evaluation Agency – London.
3. The European Bank for Reconstruction and Development (EBRD) – London.
4. The Trade Mark Office – Madrid.
5. EUROPOL Drugs Agency – The Hague.
6. The Foundation for Training – Turin.
7. European Monetary Institute (EMI) (which is to be the forerunner to the European Central Bank) – Frankfurt.
8. The European Work Health and Safety Agency – Spain (to be decided by the Spanish government).

9 The European Centre for the Development of Vocational Training – Salonika.
10 The Plant Breeder's Rights Office – remained to be allocated at the end of 1993.

3 The recognition of the authority of the European Court of Justice (ECJ)

The presence of the Treaties and the legal framework, including the European Court of Justice, means that the Community does not fit into a recognizable picture of other agreements between national governments. The Court is the supreme judicial authority of the EC. Its function is to act in an independent and impartial way to ensure that the legal framework given in the Treaties is observed both in its interpretation and application in the Member States. Although it is outside the decision making process, it is in the Court's existence and its role and powers that the features lie which separate the EC from other international groupings of states.

The legal instruments of the EC

The Community has the power to make decisions and turn these into legally binding instruments which will affect the population of the twelve individual states who are members of the Community. There are four legal instruments which the Community uses.

1 Regulations

If the legislation is adopted as a regulation it is directly applicable throughout the whole of the EC. See Case 2, The European Community's Environmental Management and Audit Scheme for an example

2 Directives

Directives lay down compulsory objectives, but leave it to the individual Member State how they transfer them into national legislation. This sometimes means that a country which is not particularly committed to a particular directive may try to find ways to circumvent the legislation.

3 Decisions

These are only binding on the Member State, the firms or individuals to whom they are directed.

4 Recommendations or opinions

These are not binding unless they are concerned with measures in the coal or the steel sectors when they become more like directives.

Legal compliance and practical compliance

If a piece of legislation is not put into operation then the Court may take action. There are two areas of compliance the Court may question. The first is legal compliance and the second is practical compliance.

Legal compliance

This simply means that the EC Member States must ensure they have a national law in place to use to apply the EC law. Sometimes countries are slow doing this. The national consultation process may be lengthy and take the introduction of the legislation beyond the timetable set by the EC.

Practical compliance

This means that the countries have to make sure that they have the necessary administrative departments or personnel appointed so that the measures in the legislation are carried out.

The principle of subsidiarity

The European Community has to be very aware of the need to apply the principle of subsidiarity. This was a major point of issue in the period leading to the ratification of the TEU.

The definition of the principle of subsidiarity given in the TEU is that 'The Community shall act within the limits of the powers conferred upon it by this Treaty and the objectives assigned to it wherein' (Art. 3b TEU). Alongside this the Community may take action 'to achieve the aims and objectives of the Treaty if this cannot be done by the Member States'.

Essentially what subsidiarity means is that the Community may only take action in the areas of policy which were agreed by the twelve Member States and outlined for it in the TEU. The areas of policy where Community action is thought to be appropriate are listed at the beginning of the TEU. They include the Common Agricultural Policy, the Common Transport Policy, Competition Policy, policy to ensure the free movement of people, goods, capital and services, social policy, environment policy and then newer areas of concern such as energy policy, consumer and tourism policies.

The division of responsibilities set out in the TEU has two objectives.

1. To maintain the rights of the national governments. Any actions taken, will be the result of the application of the principle that 'Community action is the exception and not the rule'.
2. To avoid excessive centralization of the decision making process in Brussels. The basis of the principle of subsidiarity is that power should be exercised as close to the people as possible.

The institutions of the European Community
The European Commission – initiator and executive

Organization of the Commission

There are seventeen members of the Commission, two from each of the larger states – France, Germany, Spain, Italy and the United Kingdom, and one from each of the other states. Each Commissioner is appointed by the mutual agreement of the twelve governments of the member states. Once appointed, however the Commissioners may not take instructions from their own national government. They are to act in the interests of the Community and are held accountable by the EP.

Following the ratification of the TEU the Commissioners will serve for a term of five years, to coincide with the term of the European Parliament. The President of the Commission also serves for five years. All the appointments are renewable. Each Commissioner is responsible for one area or portfolio, for example, social affairs, industrial policy, foreign affairs.

Administrative staff of the Commission

The administrative staff of the Commission is smaller than that of many of the larger government departments of some states. The work is coordinated by the Secretariat General, which is headed by an influential and experienced bureaucrat. Further subdivision takes place into Directorates-General which deal with twenty-three different policy areas. In total there are about 16 700 officials 15 per cent of whom are translators and interpreters in the bureaucracy. They are normally appointed as the result of competitive examinations, although some national officials may be seconded to the Commission.

Co-ordination between the different Directorates-General to ensure the coherence of policy is difficult. The bureaucratic structure of the DGs is vertically organized and the horizontal linkages between the DGs may be difficult to establish to ensure that policy is coherent. For example the Commission published a consultative Green Paper on Industrial Competitiveness and the Protection of the Environment in 1992[1]. The proposals being made there required coordination of policy objectives being set by no fewer that five different DGs.

It is the responsibility of the Secretariat General to ensure that coordination does take place, but it still remains an area of concern. One method of ensuring these problems may be overcome has been to establish Task Forces for specific issues, which are independent of the DGs and are able to work with officials dealing with more than one policy area.

The work of the Commission

The Guardian of the Treaties.

The primary role of the Commission given to it by the Treaties is sometimes described as to be the 'Guardian of the Treaties' and the 'Motor of Integration'. This means that the Commission is required to perform a number of different tasks.

1 *To initiate the legislation.* It is the role of the Commission to draft legislation, not the Council. The Commission becomes the 'motor of integration' because it has control over the speed at which legislation can be introduced.

The Commission's proposals are the result of a number of influences. Often legislation is the result of an issue being brought forward from discussion by the heads of state or national government officials; on other occasions it is the result of pressure from various interest groups or the European Parliament.

A network of advisory and consultative committees is consulted by the Commission in their drafting of legislation. These range from the Union of Industries in Europe (UNICE) and the European Trade Union Confederation (ETUC) to specialized groups such as the Committee of Transport Unions in the Community (ITF-ICFTU). There are also more than 3000 special interest groups with more than 10 000 employees who are based in Brussels and actively lobby on behalf of their particular interests. Brussels has been called 'the second lobbying capital of the world after Washington'[2]. Because of the complicated procedures to have a piece of legislation adopted which involves the other institutions, the Commission will only introduce legislation which has a good chance of being successful.

There are some areas where the Commission is able to act on its own to make legislation. These are where issues are mainly administrative and concern the effective operation of an area of policy. Most of this work is done in connection with the Common Agricultural Policy. Sometimes it is the result of a particular emergency that the Commission is able to act on its own. Once the agreement had been reached for the timetable to complete the Single Market the Commission was left with a considerable degree of independence over the presentation of the legislation which was needed.

2 *To ensure that the rules of the Treaties are followed.* The Commission has powers of investigation and can impose fines on individuals or companies who breach rules on competition. It has the power to refer cases to the European Court of Justice.

The Commission is heavily dependent on information being given to it in many areas of its supervisory work. Increasingly legislation requires a reporting back procedure to the Commission on its implementation, but the frequent lack of commitment by a member state or an individual company to do this is an ever present problem for the Commission in its supervisory role.

3 *Managing the Community's finances.* The Commission is responsible for drafting the Budget of the European Community. It also has direct responsibility for a number of areas of Community spending.

The Community's resources come from a number of different sources

(a) The collection of tariffs and other duties which are the result of trade between the EC and non EC states.
(b) Agricultural levies, premiums and other duties.
(c) A percentage of value added tax within the Member States. This is based on the application of a 1 per cent rate to the VAT assessment base.
(d) A contribution of up to 1.27 per cent of gross national product.

The Commission takes the general management decisions in the two major spending areas of the Budget – Agricultural Funds and Structural Funds.

The Commission is also responsible for the management and co-ordination on behalf of the Community of a number of environmental and scientific programmes with non-EC states, especially the states of the European Free Trade Association (EFTA) and the assistance to the states of Central and Eastern Europe through PHARE. This is the programme being supported by twenty-four states of the Organization for European Cooperation and Development (OECD) to help in the reconstruction of Poland, Hungary, the Czech Republic, Slovakia, Bulgaria, and Romania.

4 *Negotiator.* The Commission has the responsibility for acting as the external face of the Community in a number of international fora, for example in the negotiations to achieve agreement in the General Agreement on Tariffs and Trade (GATT).

The Commission also acts on behalf of the Community in negotiations for membership of the EC.

Summary of the role of the Commission

1 Initiator of the legislation and rule maker in its own right.
2 Supervisor of the implementation of the legislation.
3 Manager of the Community's financial resources.
4 External face of the European Community.

The Council – the decision makers

The primary role of the Council of the Union is to take the decisions about the proposals, which then become Community law. In 1992 the Council adopted 383 regulations, 166 directives, and 189 decisions[3]. While the Council holds the balance of power amongst the institutions, the roles of the other institutions act as a counterbalance so that it is not possible for the system to work without their input.

The Council does not have the formal right to initiate legislation, that lies with the Commission. However the Council is able to bring pressure on the Commission to propose legislation, but the Commission still holds the right to draft the legislation. The European Parliament then has the right of scrutiny of the legislation. The EP may amend or reject certain legislation if agreement cannot be reached with the Council.

Organization of the Council

The Council is made up of the representatives of the governments of the Member States. Each member state of the EC has a seat on the Council, but the number of votes allocated depends on the size of the state's population. The actual representatives present at the meetings vary with the policy area under discussion. Depending on the subject the Council may be composed of agriculture ministers, education ministers, ministers of the environment, or ministers of transport, for example, These are the 'Technical Councils'. If the meeting is of the Ministers for Foreign Affairs then it is called the General Council. For meetings of the Ministers of Finance the term ECOFIN is used.

The frequency of meetings of the Council varies, there are no set times but the different groups usually meet once a month. It is, however, possible to meet as often as is required. The meetings normally take place in Brussels, but sometimes meetings may be called for Luxembourg. During a period of monetary crisis for example the ECOFIN meetings may occur very frequently. The Agricultural Council also meets more often in the spring when fixing agricultural prices.

Rotating presidency

Each of the Member States of the European Community holds the presidency of the Council in turn for six months. The civil service of the state holding the presidency takes on certain tasks during this period on behalf of the whole Community. The General Council Secretariat numbers only 2200 officials and therefore this assistance from the member states is of vital importance. Providing this administrative support does, however, impose a financial burden on the smaller states of the EC during their presidencies.

Voting procedures within the Council

Traditionally the Council acted on the basis of unanimity. This frequently led to long delays while legislation was debated in order to reach agreement. It also led to a 'horse trading' process of agreements taking place in order to have legislation accepted. To ensure that the Single Market legislation was put into place to meet the 1992 deadline, the Single European Act (SEA) in 1986 introduced the use of qualified majority voting (QMV). The larger states have more votes than the smaller ones.

A total of seventy-six votes are allocated between the members states (see Table 2.1, of which fifty-four are necessary to obtain the majority decision. Voting can be blocked by a coalition of states which carries twenty-three votes. This means that the largest five states cannot outvote the smaller states on a particular issue. They also need to have the support of at least two smaller states to be successful in a vote on legislation. Similarly, the seven smaller states cannot form a blocking vote; they need to have the support of three of the large states in the vote.

Table 2.1 *Allocation of votes in the Council*

Country	Population in millions	Votes
Germany	80.6	10
France	57.5	10
Italy	56.9	10
UK	57.9	10
Spain	39.1	8
Belgium	10.0	5
Greece	10.3	5
Netherlands	15.2	5
Portugal	9.8	5
Denmark	5.2	3
Ireland	3.5	3
Luxembourg	0.4	2

Population figures correct 1 January 1993

The European Council

The main role of the European Council is to direct policy making by providing the broad guidelines for new policy developments. The European Council was not included in the Treaties in 1958. It became part of the institutional framework in the Single European Act in 1986. The membership of the Council is the Heads of State or Government of the Member States and the President of the Commission. Their work is assisted by the Ministers for Foreign Affairs and a member of the Commission. This gives a possible total of twenty-six individuals who have rights to be included in the deliberations of the European Council.

COREPER

The work of the Council of Ministers is supported by the institution, established in the original Treaty of Rome, known as COREPER. This is the Committee of Permanent Representatives of the nation states. It is subdivided into two – COREPER I and COREPER II. The members of this Committee act as Ambassadors for the individual states to the Community and are based in Brussels. The members of COREPER are responsible for preparing the work of the Council.

The whole structure relies on the work which is done in various consultative committees and working groups who feed the views of interested groups and their advice to both the COREPER Committees. The administrative support is given by a secretariat, numbering more than 2000, staff whose work involves them in providing the administrative support for all levels from the Council of Ministers itself to the various specialist working parties.

Summary of the role of the Council

1 To represent the interests of the national governments of the Member States.
2 To provide the broad guidelines of policy.
3 To make the decisions about the adoption of the legislation.
4 To perform the predominant role in the intergovernmental 'pillars' of the European Union where the Commission and the European Parliament are merely consulted about the policy.

The European Parliament – the voice of democracy

The election of the Members of the European Parliament

The Members of the European Parliament have been elected by direct universal suffrage since 1979. Prior to that the Members were nominees from the Member States. The methods used in the elections vary, and depend on the system which is the one applicable in each member state. All the states, apart from the UK, use some form of proportional representation (PR). In

Northern Ireland a system of proportional representation is used. The number of seats in the EP is allocated to the Member States on the basis of population size. But as can be seen in Table 2.2, there are some anomalies, the most obvious of which is the representation for Luxembourg.

Table 2.2 *Number of seats in the EP allocated to the different Member States*

Member State	1989	1994
Belgium	24	24
Denmark	16	16
Germany	81	99
Greece	24	25
Spain	60	64
France	81	87
Ireland	15	15
Italy	81	87
Luxembourg	6	6
Netherlands	25	31
Portugal	24	25
United Kingdom	81	87
EC total MEPs	518	567

The increase in numbers between the elections of 1989 and 1994 was agreed by the Member States during the British Presidency of the Council of Ministers in December 1992. This was the result of German unification and the increase in the population of Germany to over 80 million. The other larger states of the EC were also given the right to elect more MEPs. In the United Kingdom the increase was split so that five more seats were allocated to England and one to Wales (see Figure 2.2).

The members of the European Parliament elect their own president. The presidents serve for terms of two and a half years.

The powers of the European Parliament

These were limited in the original founding Treaty of Rome. The Parliament was known as the General Assembly and consisted of the nominees of the Member States. They tended to be very committed to the ideal of European integration, but the Assembly was regarded as little more than a 'talking shop'.

Figure 2.2 New EP seat allocations for the 1994 elections (source: *Euro Newsletter*, 19 May 1993)

Following the introduction of direct universal suffrage in 1979 the powers of what then became the Parliament were increased to give the MEPs a greater share of the decision making process. The Single European Act of 1986, which amended the original Treaties, was influential in shifting some more of the power towards the EP and the Commission. The TEU has continued this trend by giving more powers to the European Parliament and placing some curbs on the activities of the Commission. These involved an enhanced role in the enactment of legislation, the right of approval prior to the appointment of the Commission, and the power of assent for all major international agreements.

The procedures have become very complex as a result of the adoption of different forms of voting and differing involvement of the EP in the formation of legislation coming from the different Treaties. In some areas of policy the EP may give its opinion of legislation, but the Council does not have to take it into account. This is the Consultation Procedure.

The SEA gave the EP the right to be more closely involved through a cooperation procedure in the formation of legislation based on just ten articles of the Treaty amendment. The EP has two readings of the proposed legislation under this procedure and may propose amendments. If these amendments are endorsed by the Commission, they can be rejected by the Council only if there is a unanimous decision of all the states. This has resulted in much closer working of the two – the EP and the Commission – in some areas, e.g. social policy.

In the TEU these powers of the Parliament were added to by the introduction of the codecision procedure. This extended the right to the EP to have third readings of the legislation. The EP has the right to reject legislative proposals in certain areas, if no agreement can be reached between it and the Council of Ministers. It was also granted the power to ask the Commission to initiate legislation. Time limits have been placed on the procedures in an attempt to speed up what is often a lengthy process from the proposal of legislation to its adoption.

The EP's powers to amend the legislation were also increased to transport, social, vocational training, research, environment and overseas development. The Parliament also gained the right of approval before Treaties with non-EC states could be ratified.

Further developments were made in the EP's powers of scrutiny and supervision in the TEU. The EP was given the right to set up a committee of inquiry to investigate contraventions or maladministration in the implementation of Community law. Alongside this was also the right to appoint an ombudsman to receive complaints from the citizens of the EC about maladministration by the Community institutions. This was part of the ongoing attempt to make the working of the EC more open to its citizens.

Control over the Budget of the EC

This is an important part of the role of the EP. Along with the Council of Ministers the EP is the Budgetary Authority of the Community. It has the scope to amend the spending plans which are proposed by the Commission. If no agreement can be reached with the Council about the Community's spending plans then the EP can reject the whole of the budget. MEPs were also given a much greater influence in the decision about agricultural spending in the TEU.

How to contact an MEP?

The itinerant nature of the institution does make for some difficulties, but it is relatively easy to contact an MEP. Lists of addresses and telephone numbers are available in public libraries, local authority offices, Citizens Advice Bureaux, and the UK EP Office.

What issues is it appropriate to contact them about?

As the role of the EP has grown so too has the range of issues with which the MEPs are involved. The following issues have the most direct impact on the Community's citizens:

- The environment
- Trade
- Transport
- Energy
- Research policy
- Consumer protection
- Equal opportunities
- Regional policy
- Education and cultural affairs

Summary of the role of the European Parliament

1 The right to reject, amend or take steps to initiate legislation.
2 To approve the appointment of the Commission.
3 To act with the Council of Ministers as the budgetary authority of the Community.
4 To approve agreements with non-EC states.
5 To table questions to the Commission and the Council.
6 To receive petitions from the citizens of Europe.
7 To appoint an ombudsman.

European Court of Justice

The organization of the Court

The Court is based in Luxembourg. It has thirteen judges appointed from the Member States. This is done quite deliberately to ensure that the Court is always able to reach a decision in a plenary session. (In the Community of Six[1957–1973] the number of judges was seven for the same reason.) The greater part of the work of the Court is done by groups or chambers of judges. There are four chambers of three judges and two chambers of five judges. It is only for the most serious actions that all thirteen judges sit in plenary session.

Making the Community work

The judges are assisted in their work by six advocates-general. Both judges and advocates are appointed, by the mutual agreement of the Member States, to sit for a period of six years. The practice has been adopted of changing only half of the number of judges at any one time, because of the complexity of the matters with which they deal. This ensures that there is continuity and more experienced judges to work with those who have been members of the Court for only a short time.

All the twelve states of the EC appoint a judge, the thirteenth is appointed by rotation from either Germany, France, Italy the UK, Spain. The six advocates-general are appointed one from each of Germany, France, Italy and the UK, with the other two coming in turn from the other member states. The appointments are renewable. Following enlargement of the EC this will alter to seventeen judges and eight advocates under the present system of appointment.

Although they are appointed by the Member State, the judges and the Court work independently. Their guarantee of independence comes from the Treaties and is ensured by the Member States through their ratification of the Treaties. The independence of the ECJ is further guaranteed as their deliberations are held in secret. The appointment of a President of the ECJ is at the discretion of the Court.

The Court rulings

The different types of legislation which the Community has at its disposal were outlined in the introductory section to this chapter. Articles 169 and 170 of the Treaty of Rome, now incorporated into the TEU, give the Court the right to rule on infringements of the legislation. Actions may be brought by the Commission, individuals or other Member States for failure to comply with the Treaty obligations. The usual procedure is to settle matters before they reach a full session of the Court.

Initially the infringement of the legislation is pointed out in a communication from the Court which gives the Member State concerned the necessary time to take action to comply with the legislation. This is known as an Article 169 letter. Following from this, if no action is taken, the Court may issue its Reasoned Opinion identifying the problem. If the Member State does not implement the measures required then the case is referred to the Court for judgement.

Probably the biggest changes which were brought by the Treaty on European Union to the Court of Justice was the right of the Court to fine member states which did not comply with earlier judgements from the Court (Article 171 TEU). The Commission will recommend the size of the fine which the Court itself will decide is required as a penalty.

This article of the Treaty was based on a UK proposal and is intended to both strengthen the rule of law within the EC and to help British companies. Implementation of legislation is a concern. The record of some Member States on the implementation of the EC's regulations and directives is not as good as in others. This additional penalty was seen as a way of ensuring that the level of infringements of EC legislation is brought under control.

Ineffective or partial implementation of directives may undermine the operation of the Single Market (Chapter 3). It is therefore very important that the Court has both the penalties to ensure the implementation of legislation and also the information to take action.

The ECJ is also available to be consulted by national courts for a ruling on the interpretation or applicability of Community legislation. This must be done if there is no way in which the national legislation can be used to decide on a particular issue. This procedure is known as a 'preliminary ruling'.

The ECJ may be asked to deliver its opinion on agreements which are made between the EC and non-member countries. These opinions are binding. During the period when the EC was negotiating with the EFTA states to form the European Economic Area (EEA) it was the ECJ's concerns about the way in which legislation would be dealt with, which caused delays in the final signing of the agreement.

The Court of First Instance

As the workload of the Court grew at the end of the 1980s with the programme to complete the Single Market legislation, the Court of First Instance was established under the Single European Act. It began its work in 1989 and had twelve members appointed for renewable terms of six years, one judge coming from each Member State. As with the judges of the ECJ, these judges are appointed by mutual agreement of the governments of the Member State. The Court is partially replaced every three years in the same way.

The Court of First Instance rules on various types of cases including those concerning:

1 private citizens of individual companies;
2 competition and dumping measures;
3 cases involving coal and steel;
4 compensation proceedings;
5 actions brought by Community officials.

Its judgements may be submitted to the Court of Justice for appeal procedures.

From the ratification of the TEU it is possible for the Council of Ministers, by unanimous agreement, to extend the jurisdiction of the Court of First Instance. It is hoped in this way that any future extension of the workload of the Court can be dealt with without having to wait for major restructuring and amendment of the Treaty.

Summary of the role of the European Court of Justice

1. To declare void any legal instrument adopted by the Commission, the Council of Ministers or the national governments, which is incompatible with EC law.
2. To pass judgement on the validity or interpretation of points of EC law.
3. To deliver an opinion on agreements with non EC states.

The European Investment Bank (EIB)

The EIB was established in 1958 by the Treaty of Rome. It is based in Luxembourg. Its primary role is to finance capital investment schemes which the EC has identified as being important for balanced growth within the EC. The projects which the EIB supports are in the less favoured regions of the Community, particularly associated with improving the infrastructure of those regions.

It is administered by a Board of Governors nominated from the Member States. The work of the Bank is however autonomous. The Board of Governors appoints its own Board of Directors, which consists of twenty-two administrators and twelve deputies, serving for a renewable five year term. The Board of Directors takes the major decisions about the loans and the day-to-day operation of the EIB. The Management Committee deals with the actual operational side of the running of the Bank, being responsible for the drafting of the contracts and loan agreements.

The Bank can issue guarantees and loans up to a ceiling of 250 per cent of its capital holding. This has been increased several times. In 1993 it was decided that the scope of the then £6.2 billion holding should be extended to include energy, environmental and inner city projects rather than the predominantly transport based projects supported previously.

The Court of Auditors

The Court of Auditors was set up in 1977. It has the very specific role of checking on the financial management of the Community. Its remit covers all the revenue and expenditure of the Community and any agencies it may set up. All the Member States appoint a member, whose independence of action is guaranteed. The TEU requires that the members of the Court of Auditors are people who have belonged to external audit bodies in their own state or who are especially qualified for the office.

The EP has a right to consultation over the appointees. In order to maintain supervision of the work of the Court of Auditors, the Court has to submit a statement of assurance of the validity of the accounts to both the EP and the Council of Ministers.

The Court is required to draw up an annual report on the implementation of the Community Budget. It may also be asked by any of the institutions of the EC to respond to specific questions about the Community's finances.

The Economic and Social Committee (ECOSOC)

Established jointly in the EEC and EURATOM Treaties in 1958, ECOSOC is a consultative committee which brings together different economic and social interest groups. The membership numbers 189 appointees of the Member States, who are based in Brussels and whose appointments are of four year renewable terms (Table 2.3).

Table 2.3 *Membership of the ECOSOC*

Country	Members
Belgium	12
Denmark	9
Germany	24
Greece	12
Spain	21
France	24
Ireland	9
Italy	24
Luxembourg	6
Netherlands	12
Portugal	12
UK	24

Source: TEU Article 194

Three groups are represented on the Committee:

1 Employers – representatives of both the public and the private sector.
2 Workers – predominantly trade union representatives.
3 Various other interests – including small and medium enterprises, consumer groups and environmental organizations.

The primary role of the ECOSOC is to advise all the main institutions in the decision making process. It is organized into nine specialist groups who have the right to be consulted before certain decisions are made. It may also issue its opinion on all aspects of Community legislation.

The deliberations of ECOSOC are not influential in the decision making process. The opinions which they submit are not binding, but the Committee does provide a forum for the various interests to put forward their concerns. The members of the Committee serve only in a part-time capacity and often the proposals which they are being asked to comment on are not forwarded to them until a relatively late stage in the decision making process.

ECSC Consultative Committee

The Commission has considerable rule making powers, given by the 1951 Treaty, over the coal and steel sectors, subject in a number of cases only to consultation with the Consultative Committee. This has not been changed by the TEU. These powers include the definition of what constitutes unfair practices or discriminatory practices. The Commission after consulting with the Consultative Committee may also set both the minimum price during a crisis period and the maximum price. Quotas may be set by the Commission with the assent of the Council.

The Committee of the Regions

The Committee of the Regions (CoR) is a 189 member committee with a consultative role, able to comment on the proposals being put forward by the European Commission. The members are appointed by the Council of Ministers based on proposals made by the national governments. The same distribution of seats on the Committee is used as is used for the ECOSOC. The members are independent of the national governments.

Proposals which have a specific regional implication will be referred to the Committee for discussion. The Committee also has a role in the decisions about projects which are part of the £300 billion trans-European networks (TENS), i.e. investment in transport, telecommunications, energy links between the member states and with the rest of Europe.

Influencing the decision making process

How can a company find its way through this maze of the EC decision-making?

Information is clearly the key. The Commission works very hard to provide more means of consultation and information dissemination. It is important that businesses monitor the growing body of information about what the EC is planning in the various trade association journals which are produced. Based on that information it is then possible for a company to enter the discussion about legislation. It is much easier for the view of business to be incorporated into legislation when it is in the early phases of drafting rather than when it has been through the complicated agreement and adoption procedures within the EC institutions.

It is not necessary to maintain a presence in Brussels to do this. The review of the institutions has shown the importance of the national governments. Remember that the European Community may only take those actions which the Member States have agreed to. It is important for a business of whatever size to ensure that their views are apparent to the national governments.

Membership of the various trade associations is therefore important for a number of reasons.

1 At the national level to ensure that views are put forward to national governments.
2 At the EC level as it is important to make contact with other businesses which may have the same concerns. By extending the use of qualified majority voting procedures to more areas of policy, greater opportunities to influence the decision making process are available for groups who are backed by several countries.
3 While the Commission officials are more readily accessible than national civil servants, they are a relatively small organization. It is not always possible for the Commission officials to be as well informed as they would like. They are reliant on information being passed to them. If a clearly outlined proposal comes from a group of companies then it may be very influential.

Information, consultation and continued pressure on the decision makers are the ways to have influence on the decision making process within the European Community.

Conclusions

There are a number of problems which are the result of the unique nature of the EC institutions and the decision making process for a company which is trying to become involved in that process.

1 The number of institutions which are involved.
2 The way in which these institutions have grown and developed over time. Understanding the most recent changes in the TEU is even more

crucial as these changes will provide the background for the operation of the enlarged Community of a possible 500 million consumers of the twenty-first century.

The pressures for institutional change and reform are continuing. Enlargement of the EC will bring with it an increase in the numbers involved in the decision making process as more states become members of the EC. These states all have their own national concerns and it is very important for companies in the UK to take advantage of the mechanisms of consultation and influence which exist so that their views are fully represented in new legislation which the EC produces.

3   The physical distance between the decision making bodies and the business communities in each of the Member States.

It was decided in the original Treaties which established the EC that a single site would be identified for each of the institutions of the Community. However, the allocation of the institutions which was agreed in 1965 has remained. The Commission is housed in Brussels, the Court in Luxembourg, and the European Parliament is probably the most itinerant of all, moving as it does between Brussels, Luxembourg, and Strasbourg.

4   The existence of differing sets of rules which govern decision making in the different policy areas. There are clearly operational problems which are yet to emerge because of the UK opt out of the Social Chapter of the TEU.

References

1   Commission of the EC (1992) SEC (92) 1986 Final Commission Communication concerning Industrial Competitiveness and the Protection of the Environment. Brussels, 4 November.
2   Thomson I. (1993) Bibliographic Snapshot. *European Access*, 3, June, p. 38.
3   Nugent N. (ed.) (1993) *Annual Review of the Activities of the EC 1992*. Blackwell p. 46.

Some useful sources of information

Butt, Philip A. (ed.) (1991) *Directory of Pressure Groups in the EC*, Longman Current Affairs.

Commission of the EC (1992) *Directory of EC Trade and Professional Associations*. 5th edition. Delta.

Deziron, M.(1991) *A Directory of European Environmental Organisations*, Blackwell.

European Access, published by Hardwick.

Martens, Hans (1992) *A Comprehensive Directory of EC Contacts*, Blackwell.

3 The Single Market after 1992

Ian Barnes

Introduction

The purpose of this chapter is to critically examine the process of economic integration, in the period after the completion of the initial stage of the Single Market (Internal Market) programme. The Single Market is a space without internal frontiers where there is free circulation of goods, services, capital and persons (these are generally known as the four freedoms). The idea of a Single Market was explicitly part of the Treaty of Rome, which came into force in 1958. However, it became an important aspect of the Community's policy agenda in 1985, as a result of the Milan Summit's decision to launch a campaign for its completion. A programme of important measures was set out in the White Paper 'Completing the Internal Market',[1], with a target date for completion of 31 December 1992.

The Community's programme suggested nearly 300 measures which were considered to be of importance. However, the original list was reduced to 282, because some of the measures were not needed, or were consolidated. (Other measures were included to support the programme so, that in total 500 Single Market measures were actually passed in the period to the end of 1992.) Approximately 95 per cent of the White Paper directives had been agreed at the Council of Minister level by 1 January 1993. However, so many of the directives had still to be incorporated into national law in 1993, that the Commission felt obliged to initiate legal proceedings.

The 1992 Programme reflected the political realities of the time when it was launched in 1985, in that many of the measures were essentially compromises, which took account of what was felt was achievable at the time. So, for example, the completion of the energy market was not even to be attempted until 1995. However, there can be no doubt that the EC made considerable advances in achieving the four freedoms, that is freedom of movement of goods, services, capital and people. The completion of the Single Market is a project which is closely linked to almost all EC policy areas, in that they effect the four freedoms. So, for example, the Common Agricultural Policy (CAP) had to be reshaped to take account of the need to remove the artificial price differences between the the member states. Similarly, the move towards Economic and Monetary Union, was seen as being an essential underpinning to a Single Market.

Once 1993 had arrived, the nature of the debate concerning the completion of the Single Market changed. The White Paper became a reference point in the history of the development of the market, rather than being the blueprint for action. The Community then needed to build upon the success of the Single Market. In November 1992 the Sutherland Report was published, which proposed a strategy to ensure the Single Market operated effectively after 1992[2]. This was followed in June 1993, by a communication from the Commission to the Council of Ministers and to the European Parliament, entitled 'Reinforcing the Effectiveness of the Internal Market'[3]. This Report further developed the Sutherland Report's conclusions, and laid the foundation for the future. While this document did not carry the authority of the White Paper of 1985, it did set out a number of practical steps. Its existence also acknowledged the fact that there was still more to be done in order to complete the Single Market.

The process of economic integration

The purpose promoting the integration of the European economies is that it is hoped that material welfare will be improved as a result of the process. There is, however, a political rationale, because it is hoped that economic integration will cement liberal democracy and promote peaceful coexistence within Europe. While it was possible to discuss the issue of integration within Europe, almost exclusively on the basis of the European Community (EC) until the late 1980s, it is now important that we look beyond the boundaries of the Community, and take account of the lengthening queue of potential members. These include members of the European Free Trade Area (EFTA), the states of Southern Europe including Cyprus and Malta, and the Central European States such as the Czech Republic, Hungary and Poland.

The process of expansion from six to twelve states has meant that the EC has become more heterogeneous in its structure. While in 1958, only Italy could be described as being significantly behind the rest of the Community in terms of development, now there is Portugal, Spain, Greece and Ireland. In addition to this, the unification of the two Germanies further complicates the situation.

Economic integration will affect the rules by which the economy is being governed. However, it is not likely to overcome the diverse regional traditions that are a feature of European society. The maintenance of regional identities with regard to social values, the kinds of food consumed, or the style of housing and consumer goods, should be regarded as a source of strength, rather than something to be concerned about. These diversities will still mean that there is a role for smaller firms in all sectors of the economy.

Instruments to promote economic integration

Left to the free market, many of the artificial barriers to trade would disappear. However, there is a need for a common framework for commercial relations within an economy to ensure that business transactions take place efficiently and that the consumer is protected. The EC has attempted to move to this point through a series of steps.

1 The completion of the customs union

The customs union was completed when the member states agreed to create an area of free trade, so that once goods enter into it, or when they were produced within it, they could circulate freely, without paying tariffs. The main features of the customs union are;

1. Tariff barriers are eliminated between Member States.
2. A common external tariff (CET) is established. Within the EC, this is known as the Common Customs Tariff (CCT). This ensures that import duties are charged at the same rate regardless of the point of entry.
3. The customs revenues are distributed amongst the members according to an agreed formula.

Customs unions discriminate against non-members on a common basis. The degree of discrimination varies depending on individual trade agreements that the customs union has with external trading partners. As a consequence of this, the EC allows more generous trading terms to less-developed countries than to Japan.

Goods may enter the EC at any point, and this created problems of distributing tariff receipts. The Netherlands for example receives a significant amount of cargo destined for Germany, and if they had been allowed to keep the tariffs for their own use, they would benefit at the expense of the Germans. To overcome this problem the EC uses the customs receipts to finance its activities. Imports into the customs union pay the same level of tariff regardless of the point of entry.

Jacob Viner pointed out that customs unions cannot always be assumed to operate in a way that will improve economic welfare. This is because of the need to trade off the benefits of trade creation, against the loss due to trade diversion. He suggested that only if the benefits of trade creation are greater than those of trade diversion, is membership of a customs union worth considering from a trade point of view.

Trade diversion is the loss a country suffers due to the switching of supply of a particular good from a cheaper source outside the customs union to a more expensive one within it. Spain, for example, could purchase agricultural products at world market prices prior to joining the EC in 1986. After becoming a member, the Spanish were obliged to buy their food within the confines of the more expensive CAP.

Trade creation is the gain that a country enjoys as a result of being able to purchase goods at lower prices because tariff walls have been removed.

2 The establishment of a common market

This is a further step along the road towards greater economic integration. It incorporates the existence of a customs union with features such as free movement of capital and labour. The harmonization of business laws and some agreement as to non-tariff barriers are required. Finally, there should be common policies to deal with areas such as transport, energy, industry and taxation. The EC had gone a long way to reach this goal, with the completion of the Single Market legislation.

3 Economic union

This would mean the abolition of differences in economic policy based upon nationality. If the European Community countries ever reach this stage, they would have achieved the same degree of integration as a national economy. In an economic union, there must inevitably be a considerable loss of individual national economic sovereignty, so, for example, there would be a common currency as suggested in the Treaty on European Union, which was agreed at Maastricht.

The impact of a larger market

The process of economic integration has helped to create a larger market within the EC–12 of 340 million people, with significantly reduced barriers to trade. This has created a dynamic business environment, with the following results:

1. An improvement in the competitive environment, which helps to get rid of marginal firms, and rewards those businesses which are efficient. Competition is an incentive to modernize and improve the quality of products and the production process, but it can cause problems where firms are forced to close down in areas of high unemployment.
2. Greater economies of scale, which allow larger production units to be created. This can result in considerable cost advantages. Where the quality of the product counts, the more efficient producer can still gain

because of the resources that can be put into improving product development.
3   Greater economic power as a result of belonging to a larger trading group. Membership of the EC gives many states a greater say in international negotiations, although some members do regret their loss of independence.

A period of rapid economic growth helped the EC to make significant progress towards the completion of the Single Market in the early years. Tariffs between member states were abolished on 1 July 1968, some eighteen months ahead of schedule, and trade between member states grew rapidly. Economic growth slowed in the 1970s due to a period of high oil prices, after which the progress became much more difficult. It was soon realized that the removal of tariffs did not assure that there would be free trade.

The development of the Single Market was hampered by a whole layer of non-tariff barriers, that is national regulations and bureaucratic processes which either by accident or design make trade either difficult or impossible. In many cases these have proved to be a far greater obstacle to trade than tariffs, because they cannot be overcome by a simple cut in the price of a product. The addition of the new member states added new barriers, on top of those existing within the founding members. This led to a situation where some exporters were to complain that it was often easier to send goods to countries outside the Community, than to those within it.

Calculating the benefits

Many of the non-tariff barriers only come to the notice of the EC if there are complaints. For this reason, the cost of the barriers is difficult to calculate. However, an attempt to quantify the known costs was made by the EC Commission with a series of surveys commissioned into the monetary value of the opportunities being missed by the member states. The summary of these findings was published in a popular form in the Cecchini Report in 1988[4]. This showed that the cost of not completing the Single Market as being as high as £140 billions, therefore that was the size of the potential benefits to be gained from pushing ahead and removing the technical, physical and fiscal barriers to trade. The welfare gain from removing the barrier was estimated as being as being between 5 and 7 per cent of the EC's GDP, and there would also be benefits in terms of creating a large number of new jobs. In the short term, the consumer would gain from being able to buy goods and services at cheaper prices.

The Cecchini Report was essentially a political document, designed to support the process of completion of the Single Market. The estimates of the benefits were therefore not as assured as the report suggested. What the researchers produced for the Cecchini Report, were the most favourable estimates that were likely to materialize from the process if all barriers are removed. Many of the reforms suggested reflected the need to win agreement, rather than being ideal in terms of removing barriers to the internal market. In addition, the survey was not able to take account of the ways in which producers are currently able to overcome the barriers. That is, the potential nuisance value of many restrictions could well be far less for those firms already well organized for trade.

The benefits of the completion of the Single Market are unlikely to be evenly spread. There are winners and losers, unless measures were taken to compensate those regions which have less efficient industrial structures. Although it was thought that some 1.8 million jobs will be created in the long-term from completion of the market, more than 500 000 people will actually lose their jobs as a result of deregulation. Sectors like telecommunications, mechanical engineering and pharmaceuticals were set to grow, even against the strong external pressures of Japan and the United States, while there will be contracting employment in sectors like the glass industry, textiles, railway equipment, clothing and furniture. It has been suggested that countries like Portugal, with low labour costs, could gain a competitive advantage. However, the availability of even cheaper labour either in Central or Eastern Europe, or even outside of Europe, may cast doubt upon this. Also, in many cases success will be related to existing industrial competitiveness and the ability to attract future investment rather than lower labour costs. When industries do start to face severe job losses, and because of competition from other EC states, then there will be significant pressure for financial support from member governments. An example of this is the pressure to maintain the structure of a number of national steel industries, despite massive losses in the early 1990s, despite evidence of considerable overcapacity.

The Single Market campaign saw a return by the Community to its core economic role and it was able to move forward in a positive way because it coincided with a period of economic success. In the period from 1984 to 1990, industrial output in the EC had grown by 20 per cent, 8.5 million jobs were created, and inter-community trade had grown back to the levels it enjoyed in the early 1970s. In the early 1990s this economic success started to evaporate, with the problems associated with German unification and a slow down in the global economy. By the time the Treaty of European Union was finally ratified in 1993, there was only a limited enthusiasm for taking the process of integration further.

The Commission proposes that there will be a further study of the impact of the Single Market which will commence in 1994, and will report in

December 1996. This will test the extent to which the benefits set out in the Cecchini Report have been realized. In order to do this the EC will need to have adequate information as to the activities of firms and the way that their activities have changed. This is easier in the case of larger enterprises, but could be difficult for the small and medium-size company sector.

The Single Market issues

Three broad areas of reform were considered to be of importance in achieving the initial stage of the Single Market.

1 The removal of physical barriers

Significant physical barriers to trade existed at the customs posts throughout the Community, until many were removed in 1993. These posts existed as a convenient point to check on the compliance of national rules with regard to indirect taxation, and allowed the fixing of differing prices for agricultural products. Britain, Denmark and Ireland kept minimal border controls in place after 1992, for a variety of national reasons, including the wish to deter terrorism and to help the fight against drugs. The UK also wished to check the spread of rabies to the island.

One of the most important developments towards removing the physical barriers has come about as a result of developments outside the formal structure of the EC. This is the Schengen Agreement between all the member states with the exception of the UK, Denmark and Ireland. It has a limited effect on the Greeks because they do not have a land border with other EC states. From 1987 onward there have been only spot checks on the borders between the Schengen countries, where 400 million people cross in the course of the year. The Agreement was due to be fully in place in February 1994, when the national police forces were able to exchange information about fugitives. Because the movement of people between the Schengen countries will be even freer than elsewhere in the Community, there will be need for even greater vigilance at the external frontiers. This led to the creation of the Schengen Information System, to exchange vital information concerning cross border criminal activities. The existence of the Schengen has led to the creation of a two-tier system of movement of people within the EC, and the need to create procedures within the Schengen states to deal with the non-member EC states.

2 The removal of technical barriers

The existence of differing technical standards in each of the member states arose from differing national priorities and historical traditions. In the past the EC had been the subject of a great deal of ridicule when attempts were made to try to ensure that the technical standards applying to all products were the same. This is called the 'old approach' to technical harmonization. It failed in many areas because new products were being developed far faster than the Community's ability to keep up with them. The old approach still applies in areas where important health and safety issues are concerned, and it is in these areas where progress has been slowest because of the detail work that is involved.

In contrast, the 'new approach' calls for agreement only on essential technical requirements, and non-essential items are subject to the principle of mutual recognition. This was based upon a principle established by the Cassis de Dijon case of 1979, when the European Court of Justice held that there must be mutual recognition of products. Products were to be allowed to circulate freely throughout the EC, unless they threatened the health or safety of the consumer, damaged the environment or other aspects of the public interest. This was even to be the case if the technical or quality requirements differed from those imposed on domestic products.

The role of developing detailed technical standards by the European standards bodies; the European Committee for Standardization (CEN) and the European Committee for Electrotechnical Standardization (CENELEC), has been much enhanced.

3 The removal of fiscal barriers

The setting and collection of taxes is an issue which is very close to the heart of national sovereignty. For that reason, the Single European Act did not have a provision for majority voting on fiscal matters. Progress on fiscal harmonization has been slow, although at the very early stages of development the EC was able to agree to the setting of common customs duties for goods entering the customs duties. The use of value added tax dates back to the first VAT directive of 1967, which required the member states to introduce the tax by 1972. While VAT is a major source of revenue for the member states, and a portion of it is donated to the Community budget, the rates which applied throughout the Community varied considerably until 1993, when customs-based formalities at the borders relating to the documentation and payment of VAT were removed.

As of 1993 there was an agreed minimum standard rate for VAT of 15 per cent throughout the Community, with special lower rates and exemptions for particular countries, for example the UK retained a zero rate on children's clothes. The very high rates of luxury tax were also to be phased out. For the individual, once goods are purchased and VAT is paid, those goods can be moved around the Community without paying further VAT on entering another member state.

Duty free sales are to be retained at ports and airports until 1999, but there are limits to the extent of purchases. The agreement to retain duty free sales was designed to help producers of luxury items such as perfumes and whisky. They feared that without the duty free sales their businesses would suffer. Also the sales are profitable for the owners of the shops and they are popular with travellers. It is a concession which has been criticized, the sales need to be monitored, and they offer tax breaks to the travelling public, which is generally made up of the more affluent members of society.

Excise duties on alcohol and tobacco products have presented much greater harmonization problems. Social attitudes vary considerably in relations to these kinds of products. In countries like the UK, excise duties are set at higher rates in order to discourage smoking and drinking to excess. If indirect taxes on these items are reduced, many would feel that public health was being threatened. While rates of taxes, and therefore prices to consumers do differ, the free movement of people should ensure that the differences are not so significant that the trade becomes difficult to monitor.

The achievements of the 1992 Single Market campaign

The results of the Single Market campaign were impressive. The image of bureaucrats simply developing a mindless series of directives, such as those concerning the shape of a cucumber or the Euro-coffin has given way to a recognition of the benefits that have emerged. The volume of directives fell sharply once the Single Market was in place, so that there was also a period when greater emphasis could be placed on making the Single Market work. The achievement was that:

1 Most of the restrictions on goods crossing borders had been removed.
2 Individuals could move freely, especially in the case of the countries which participated in the Schengen Agreement.
3 There was mutual recognition of professional and higher education qualifications which made it easier for professionals to operate across frontiers.
4 There was freedom to provide many services across the EC, although some work needed to be done in areas like financial services.
5 Road and air transport services were liberalized. So that, for example, road hauliers could compete for business outside their own states.
6 There was harmonization of technical regulation.
7 Public sector contract became more open to bidders from outside the home state.
8 Indirect taxes were sufficiently in line, so that there was not a need to restrict individuals from taking their purchases into another state.

Gaps in the Single Market programme

The free movement of goods within the Single Market was almost assured for most sectors in 1993, however, there were significant gaps in a number of areas. These included:

1 Services

The Single Market for the services sector is unlikely to be fully in place until the end of the century. This is despite the fact that most measures concerning telecommunications, energy and transport are of importance not only in their own right, but also to assist the production and movement of goods.

2 Consumer needs

Criticism of the Single Market also emerged from consumer groups. The Bureau of European Consumers (BUEC) was to declare that 'The Single Market will not exist for European consumers on 1 January 1993 and will not be implemented for many years yet'[5]. They listed a multitude of sectors where the situation was far from satisfactory. These included the fact that at that time lists of authorized food additives had not been approved, and rules for labelling were incomplete. There were no Community regulations banning furniture filling materials which emitted toxic fumes when they burned. Television standards were still different. Consumers were not protected against aggressive sales of insurance policies and air transport would not be fully liberalized until April 1997.

3 The system of payments

The virtual collapse of the European Monetary System's (EMS) Exchange Rate Mechanism (ERM) in August 1993, meant that the payment for goods and services became more subject to the whims of the foreign exchange markets. It made worse a problem that had already been seen as a significant disincentive to trade. In an ideal world the solution to many of the problems of cross border payments would have been the adoption of a single currency. This was a pillar of the Treaty on European Union, but few seemed to believe that it was a realistic possibility within the time span proposed within the Treaty.

In the absence of EMU, the Commission has sought to pressurize banks within the EC, to stop profiteering at the expense of the consumer and small business. There are only 200 million retail cross-border payments every year within the EC, which is small in relation to domestic transactions. Cross-border payments are only 0.8 per cent of domestic business in the UK, and even in an open economy like Belgium, they amount to only 4 per cent. The

Commission blames this on the high level of charges, which can be twenty times the equivalent national rates. An example cited by Leon Brittan is of a British company charging ECU 42 to collect a French cheque to the value of ECU 67, also of a Belgian who was charged ECU 12.5 handling charges for a book costing only ECU 5 in Luxembourg [6].

The Commission wished to ensure that such payments are both as rapid, reliable and inexpensive as payments made within the domestic economy. They proposed that there be closer cooperation between the banks and their customers. The Commission proposes the first European-wide 'Users Charter', which would set out customer service targets. This would give customers the right to have full information about the cost of services in advance, a breakdown of charges and the right to legal protection. It was also proposed that payments should take no more than six days. If the cost of payments can be cut by half, it was estimated that those savings would be ECU 1 billion per year, a benefit which would go predominantly to small and medium enterprises[7].

The situation with regard to monitoring the progress of payments has continued. A survey in 1993, showed that the quality of service offered to business had improved, although charges were still significantly higher for cross-border payments. The average time for payments was found to be 4.6 working days, with 87 per cent of all transactions within the Community being completed within 6 working days. There were however, cases where payments had taken seventy days to complete[8].

4 Price differences

The issue of price differentials within the single Market has proved to be controversial. With a wide geographical spread, differences in tastes, national taxation regimes, and variability in the national distribution systems, it might be that prices do vary. This is a situation which is made worse by exchange rate movements and differences in wage rates and inflation rates. Some of these factors will become less important over time, however, there are price differences which are significant, and which are maintained by state or EC support. An example which is commonly quoted is that of car prices, where prices have varied by as much 30 per cent. While individuals can go to another EC state to buy a car to import it into his own country, the automobile manufacturers were able to persuade the EC that the maintenance of an adequate service network required that bulk imports by unauthorized dealers was not acceptable. A similar situation has arisen with regard to drug prices. As Table 3.1 illustrates, prices vary considerably, although there are no significant differences in production costs, and the costs of transportation are only a minor consideration.

Table 3.1 *Drug prices in EC states 1992: average = 100*

France	64
Spain	84
Italy	96
Belgium	101
Germany	111
UK	125
Netherlands	134

Source: *Financial Times*, 11 October 1993, p. 2

The explanation for the differences of Table 3.1 can be ascribed to national prescription habits, which result in French doctors handing out seven times more prescriptions per capita, than the average for the UK. However, the price differences shown above can only exist, if there are barriers to trade which sustain them, and national governments prepared to operate price controls. If the Single Market had been fully in place in 1993, these differences would not be as significant.

5 Standards

There are some significant gaps in the range of EC standards. To tourists, the most significant failure, is the absence of a European standard for electrical plugs, although attempts have been made to agree one. In 1993, there were over twenty plug configurations, with a number of differing types of socket. There is a wide range of overlap between national, European and international standards bodies. Influencing the setting of standards can confer important strategic advantages. Europe has gained internationally from its move towards the adoption of common standards, because of the size and importance of the market in which they operate. Where companies have products which fail to match up to standards, they may have to consider if the cost of complying with the new standards is really worth while. For example the European Toy Directive put a number of small toy manufacturers out of business.

The move to complete the Single Market led to a rush to agree EC standards. There were complaints that some of the standards had been poorly drafted, and were subject to misinterpretation, especially between the differing national certification and testing bodies who confirm that a standard has been met. To try to overcome some of these problems, the European Organization for Testing and Certification (EOTC) was set up in January 1993, to ensure that the differing national bodies recognize each other's work. There are in the region of 10 000 independent testing laboratories and a large number of certification organizations within the EC. The mutual recognition of test certificates will mean that many of these will go, which should cut costs for industry over a period of time.

The second stage of the Single Market

Once the Single Market legislative programme came near to completion, the EC started to think through a strategy to take the process beyond 1992. In March 1992 a high-level group was formed under the former Commissioner, Peter Sutherland, with a brief to identify ways of securing the benefits of the Single Market on a long-term basis[9]. The group presented its report to the European Council held in December 1992. The report recognized the unprecedented legislative achievement of the initiative which left only eighteen proposals outstanding. The report called for the EC to make the rules to have the same effect everywhere. This meant that there needed to be greater mutual confidence between the Member States. It would therefore be necessary to:

1 explain to business the new laws and how they operated. The consumer would also need to be satisfied that mutual recognition would not result in a reduction in the safety of the products they purchased, and that in the case of anything going wrong there would be adequate redress;
2 ensure that business could fully participate in the market, and that the new trend towards subsidiarity did not lead to creation of new trade barriers;
3 accelerate the development of practical cooperation between national and Community institutions.

Objectives of the next stage

The Commission built upon many of the ideas in the Sutherland Report, when it set out its aspirations for the next stage of the Single Market in the publication, 'Towards a strategic Programme for the Internal Market'[10]. The objective of the next stage of the Single Market programme was to continue with the process of improving the living conditions of the citizens of the Community. The framing of the programme reflected the sensitivity of the Commission to the situation in the Community post-Maastricht, where a number of member governments, felt that there was a danger that the EC was becoming too federalist, and the rights of the member governments were being eroded. In order to counteract this, the concept of subsidiarity became further refined, so that the Community attempted to ensure that policy was to be implemented at the most appropriate level. In particular, the Commission's programme proposed to:

1 support job creation and economic growth, while at the same time ensuring that social and environmental protection remains in place, so that the citizen is not exposed to new risks as the programme is implemented;
2 intervene only in those cases where mutual recognition cannot guarantee an adequate result;
3 legislate in a coherent way, which did not result in a refragmentation of the Community, because of national initiatives[11].

In terms of the role of the Community, there is a need to ensure that in future the existing legislation is fully utilized and applied. This is important in order to prevent new barriers appearing, and to enable the existing barriers to be removed. In this respect the process of transposing Community legislation into national legislation in a clear and transparent way is of particular importance. Also that there is a common interpretation of regulations. In addition to this the effect of regulation and directives needs to be monitored. The fact that the Community has legislated in a particular area is no guarantee that it will be effective, and there may well be a need to return to the issue at a later date.

New legislation was inevitably a feature of the Community's future programme. As the market gains a dynamic of its own, there will inevitably be new problems to solve. Also, existing problems become more pressing; for example, in 1993 the Commission turned its efforts towards addressing issues related to intellectual property and data protection, which were outside the existing programme.

An example of an issue which was resolved in 1993 was that books and films should benefit from copyright protection for seventy years after the author's death, while musical recordings could receive royalties for fifty years from the date of recording. This measure was agreed by a majority vote, and meant that it was not possible to exploit the position where certain states had lax rules. Thus, the Beatles' early recordings which were not due royalties in Germany because of a twenty-five year copyright rule, will be entitled to a payments from July 1997. The owners of the Beatles copyright will then be able to receive royalties, because a fifty year rule comes into effect[12].

Making the market work

As the Single Market became a legislative reality, so the need arose to make the legislation work. The first stage was to ensure that when directives were passed, they were transposed into the law of the nation states. This was more difficult than might be imagined because of the need to frame appropriate national legislation. In addition to this, the national parliaments had to have their say. The Commission had the task of ensuring that the 2000 pieces of legislation which were passed, in each of the Community's nine official languages, were monitored to ensure that they complied with the original directives.

The Commission is responsible under Article 155 of the EEC Treaty, for ensuring that the legislation is then enforced, and in this respect it has relied not only on its own resources, but also of those of a number of different pressure groups, and the complaints from business and the general public. The Commission has tended to receive a large number of complaints about aspect of the Single Market, most commonly about the free movement of goods.

It is the national administration which usually has the task of administering the legislation concerning the Single Market. This decentralization means that there has to be a degree of control over the activities of national administrations, because without such a system, distortions can creep into the mechanisms. In this respect, there needs to be a regular audit of the activities of those who are responsible for implementing the legislation. If there is a failure, then the first point of access for complaint must be to the national administration. In the UK, the Single Market Compliance Unit was set up to:

1 advise those who have evidence of a breach of EC Law;
2 research and verify cases where breaches have occurred;
3 act as a focus for complaints from outside the UK.

The normal practice is for member states to deal with complaints on a bilateral basis. After this, there are national courts, and finally there is the European Court of Justice. Generally legal action is very time consuming and expensive. It can take up to three years to bring a case to the European Court of Justice. The only case where the Community takes a specific view as to the remedies available to complainants is the case of public procurement. In some areas there is a provision for judicial review, for example with regard to the Customs Code or the mutual recognition of qualifications, however, in most cases there has not been thought a need to have a specific remedy. This however, may be an area which needs to be developed further.

Preventing new obstacles to trade

Changing the structure of the EC market to permit free movement means that there has had to be an improvement in the control over goods entering into the market from outside the EC. Indeed this also applies to areas like migration, because individual nations borders are also in place to protect the whole of the Community. There has to be a recognition of the following:

1 National authorities are now acting on behalf of the whole of the Community. This means that national authorities need to be aware of a whole range of Community rules.
2 National laws need to be transparent (easily understood and have a clear meaning), especially as the Community has adopted subsidiarity. Devolving governmental tasks downward to the most appropriate level is desirable, in the sense that the citizen can feel closer to the instruments of government. However, it does mean that there are opportunities for national law makers to diverge in the way that rules are set, and so they may create new barriers within the market.

The Commission has a range of tools which it can employ to promote mutual recognition and ensure that barriers to trade do not reappear. The prospect of the Community regressing to the point where a range of new and significant barriers could be a significant new obstacle to trade led to the Community taking positive action in the form of Directive 83/189/EEC, which has applied to goods since 1988. Member States are required to inform the Commission of any planned rules or regulations. Once the Commission has been informed a process of vetting then takes place. Action can be taken against Member States who refuse to recognize the technical standards of others. However, the process needs to be more transparent than at present, with the onus being on Member States to declare which products they refuse to accept and the basis on which this is done. Animal health is a good example of this, where it is possible to create a major public reaction against certain products. However, these kinds of problems could well be best resolved by joint Community action taken to resolve the overall problem rather than discrimination against the products of a particular Member State.

Trans-European networks

If the European economy is to operate as a Single Market, the infrastructure needs to be fully in place to ensure that trade, production and communications are not hampered. The natural tendency for most states is to think in terms of their own domestic needs rather than those of other states whose activities pass through their territory. This can lead to a situation where areas of the European economy are left remote from the main stream of economic development. The coordination of infrastructure should ensure that competition is maintained throughout the Community, that transport times are faster, and that capacity is fully utilized. Also it should help to avoid significant bottlenecks, such as those in the road network.

The establishment of trans-European networks in the fields of energy, transport and telecommunications, is a question of the Member States combining with the Community in order to achieve an overall coherence. This should promote economic growth, cohesion and integration within the European area, reaching well beyond the geographical limits of the present European Community. Not only should the volume passing through the networks increase, but there will be efficiency gains via interoperability and interconnectability of the networks.

There is a general recognition that the development of networks will be a medium to long-term task. The Commission has helped the process along by drafting plans for the three key sectors. The road network is an example of where EC planning has been relatively advanced[13]. The plan for this sector recognized that road transport is the major way of moving both goods and people throughout the Community. The problem is that road transport has been a victim of its own success, with worsening congestion, and an inability to provide an adequate service not only within the EC but also a linkage with the EFTA states and the states of Central and Eastern Europe. However, the provision of an adequate road network should also be linked to the need to try to reduce dependence on road transport for environmental reasons. This means that the Community needs to fully link this strategy with that for rail and multi-mode transport.

Associated with the provision of adequate networks, is the problem of financing. The provision of road networks will not provide many benefits for those states which use transport corridors to other markets. So, for example, Germany within the EC and Switzerland within EFTA, have both expressed dissatisfaction at being used as transit states. Even more pressing is the problem of the Central European states, which simply lack the resources to provide adequate links. To compensate for this an acceptable method of charging for the services provided has to be found, while at the same time investment funds need to be made available.

To assist the development of networks, the EC has made structural funds available in certain cases. The Cohesion Fund, which was introduced as a result of the Maastricht Agreement, offered funds for this purpose to the four poorest members of the EC. Funding is also available via the European Investment Bank.

Conclusion

The success of the completion of the Single Market campaign was marred by a recession and the collapse of the Exchange Rate Mechanism. The 1992 campaign was a highly visible attempt to promote the benefits of Community membership. Moving onward to the next stage where the achievements could be consolidated and built upon is inevitably a lower profile task. However, if the process of economic integration is allowed to stagnate as it did in the 1970s, it is easy to envisage a situation where new barriers come into place and the achievements of the 1992 campaign are eroded.

As a priority for the future, the issue of the tax environment of companies was seen as being important, along with the promotion of quality products within European industry, external aspects of the internal market, and developing trans-European networks. Underlying these priorities there is a need to ensure that the European economy is efficient and flexible. The high levels of unemployment which came with recession in the 1990s caused pressures on public finances and raised a debate about the extent that there was a need to liberalize labour markets. The difficulty for the Community is how to increase the flexibility of labour markets without damaging social protection. If states compete within the market on the basis of lower social protection, competitive exchange rate devaluations or lower environmental standards, then the basis of the Single Market may be challenged. This may undo the benefits of much of the legislation now in place. However, without greater flexibility throughout, it may be difficult for the European economy to compete effectively in global markets.

References

1 Commission of the EC (1985) *Completing the Internal Market.*
2 Sutherland, P., (1992) *The Internal Market After 1992 – Meeting the Challenge*, Commission of the EC.
3 Commission of the EC (1993) *Reinforcing the Effectiveness of the Internal Market,* COM (93) 256 final.
4 Cecchini, P. (1998) *The European Challenge 1992*, Gower.
5 *Europe* (1993) 6 January, No 5891, p. 15.
6 *Europe* (1992) 26 March 5697 (new series), p. 8.
7 *Ibid.*
8 Europe (1993) 2 October, No. 6034, p.7.
9 Sutherland, P. (1992) *The Internal Market After 1992 – Meeting the Challenge,* Commission of the EC.
10 Commission of the EC (1993) *Reinforcing the Effectiveness of the Internal Market,* COM (93) 256 final.
11 *Ibid.* p. 4.
12 *Financial Times* (1993) 15 June, p. 2
13 Commission of the EC (1993) *Towards a Master Plan for the Road Network and Road Traffic,* Directorate General for Transport.

4 Regulating competition in the EC

Edmund Fitzpatrick and Leigh Davison

Introduction

Competition policy and regulation is one of the key areas of European Community activity. Under the original EEC Treaty, and more recently under an important Council Regulation, the Commission has powers to act against anti-competitive behaviour. This chapter will examine how the Community deals with anti-competitive agreements, the abuse by firms of dominant market positions, potentially harmful mergers and states' aids to their industries.

Single European Market and the particular need for a concentration regulation

The movement towards a common or single European market goes back to the original Treaty of Rome. The first step towards implementing this came when the abolition of tariffs between Member States was completed on 1 July 1968, eighteen months ahead of schedule. The next stage – now known as the Completion of the Single European Market (SEM) – required the removal of non-tariff barriers that existed between Member States. This was agreed at the Milan Summit (June 1985) by the then EC heads of government, the target date for completion being 1 January 1993. Research funded by the EC Commission (resulting in the Cecchini Report, 1988) estimated the cost of **not** completing the SEM at £140 billion. Viewing it from a slightly different perspective, this figure can be seen as an estimate of the potential benefits that might accrue from the completion of the SEM.

In the long term, it is envisaged that the removal of non-tariff barriers will lead to a more competitive business environment in the EC as a whole. For example, a firm will now have a possible domestic market in excess of 320 million, thereby giving it the opportunity to exploit potential economies of scale. However, the SEM also opens up the opportunity for anti-competitive behaviour as firms may be tempted – through merger activity – to increase their market power or dominance. This prospect helped to galvanize EC governments into agreeing upon legislation specifically designed to control concentrations (mergers) with a Community-wide dimension; the original Treaty of Rome being without such a provision.

Regulating competition in the EC

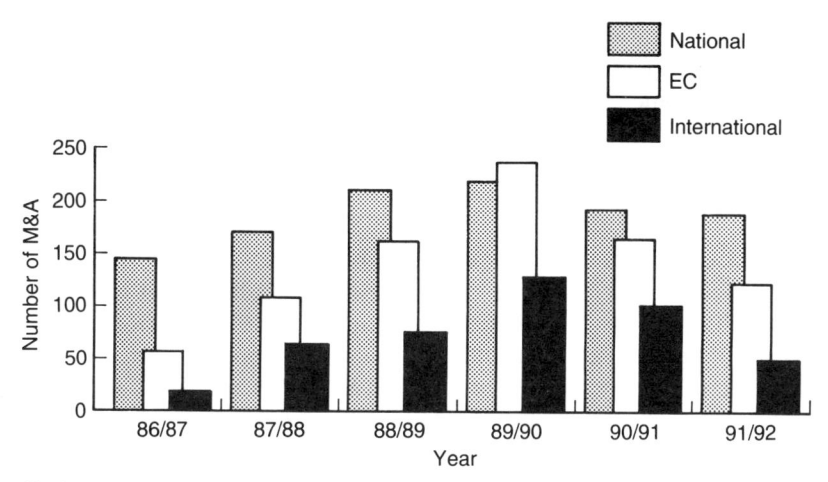

Figure 4.1 Acquisition activity involving EC firms: combined turnover above ECU 1 billion (source: EC competition report 1992)

National: acquisitions and mergers involving firms from the same member state
EC: acquisitions and mergers involving firms from different member states
International: acquisitions and mergers involving firms from the EC and third countries

Figure 4.1 shows an overall increase in all three categories of merger activity during the period covered. This is not surprising given the economic boom conditions that prevailed for much of the period. What is particularly noticeable is the rapid growth in the number of Community mergers from 1986/87 up to 1990/91. Indeed, in 1989/90 the number of Community mergers exceeded, for the first time, the level of national mergers. To a certain degree this can be attributed to firms anticipating the completion of the Single European Market. Moreover, firms would have appreciated that the proposed Merger Control Regulation was increasingly likely to become a legal reality. This would have encouraged firms to achieve concentrations in advance of the new regulatory system, which eventually came into force in September 1990.

Principal EC competition measures

Below are the major Community provisions controlling competition:

1 Treaty of Rome Article 85: controls anti-competitive agreements.
2 Treaty of Rome Article 86: controls the abuse of a dominant market position.
3 Council regulation (EEC) No 4064/89, 'The Merger Regulation': controls certain mergers and certain joint ventures with a community dimension.

4 Treaty of Rome Article 90: subjects state owned enterprises to the same competition rules as private enterprises.
5 Treaty of Rome Article 92: restricts the ability of Member States to give aid to their own industries.

Article 85

Article 85 controls restrictive practices, having as its target cooperative market behaviour. It prohibits collaboration by undertakings which may affect trade between Member States where the collaboration distorts, prevents or restricts competition within the common market. Article 85 gives specific instances of the kind of activities that will amount to infringement. These activities include price fixing, market sharing and agreeing production quotas. Although certain conduct can be exempted from Art. 85, the consequence of operating an infringing agreement is that the parties involved are liable to a fine, imposed by the Commission, of up to 10 per cent of their worldwide turnovers.

In order for enterprises to be liable under Article 85, the Commission must be satisfied that there was some agreement, decision or concerted practice by the organizations concerned. The agreement does not have to be a formal contract; in the **Quinine Cartel** (1969) case, a group of European producers had entered into what they described as a 'gentlemen's agreement' to fix prices and exports. Although the agreement was not to be legally binding, the Commission still decided that it was contrary to Article 85.

This willingness on the part of the Community to examine the substance of parties' conduct rather than its strict legal form can be seen from its prohibition on concerted practices. In **Dyestuffs** (1972), the European Court of Justice (ECJ) had to deal with the situation where dyestuff producers, without entering into any form of agreement, had imposed uniform price increases on three occasions. The ECJ ruled that parallel conduct can be an indication of the existence of a concerted practice, the latter it defined as being the substitution by organizations of practical cooperation for the risks of competition.

Article 85 is concerned to protect normal competition. It may be that although an agreement has the potential to increase trade it also distorts competition. In **Consten & Grundig** (1964), the European Court of Justice had to consider the following situation. Grundig, the German electronic goods manufacturer, had granted Consten, a French firm, the sole distributorship of its goods in France. Grundig also promised that it would obtain undertakings from its distributors outside France that they would not export Grundig products to France. Consten discovered that another French firm was importing Grundig goods which had been sold to its German dealers.

These imports were being sold for less than the prices charged by Consten. Consten tried to prevent the sales in France of the goods imported by its competitors. It was argued in the ECJ that the effect of the original agreement with Grundig would be to increase the sales of Grundig products in the Community. The Court held that, even if trade in the goods was increased, the effect of the agreement was to eliminate competition at the wholesale level and that the agreement would have to be amended to avoid this effect.

If Article 85 were given a blanket application to all agreements falling technically within its scope, the benefits of certain kinds of collaboration which, strictly speaking, are contrary to the article, would be lost. It is consistent with the policy of flexible application of competition rules and policy that some agreements are eligible for exemption from Art. 85. There are a number of so-called 'block exemptions' which cover agreements relating to such things as exclusive distribution, exclusive purchasing, patent and know-how licensing, motor vehicle distribution and research and development.

It is also possible for parties to an agreement not covered by a block exemption to apply for exemption on the grounds, for example, that the agreement contributes to the improvement of the distribution of goods or promotes economic progress. So, an agreement may be exempted if it results in economies of scale being achieved, provided that a fair share of this benefit is passed on to consumers.

Article 86

Article 86 complements Article 85. While the latter deals with anti-competitive agreements, the former regulates, broadly speaking, what would be regarded under the United Kingdom's competition rules as unacceptable monopolistic behaviour. Where one or more organizations abuse a dominant market position within the Common Market so as to affect trade between Member States the Commission may intervene to prohibit this conduct.

As with Article 85, enforcement of Article 86 requires the Commission to undertake a degree of economic analysis. **United Brands** (1978) is a good illustration of the issues that have to be considered. In that case, a number of fruit distributors who were supplied with bananas by United Brands complained to the Commission about some of United Brand's practices which they considered unfair. Among other things, distributors were charged – for no objective reason – different prices, while United Brands (UB) refused to supply one distributor after it had taken part in an advertising campaign for a competing brand.

The first issue to be considered when deciding whether UB was in breach of Article 86 was which was the relevant market to be considered? Discerning the relevant market, both in terms of geographical scope, product and any temporal considerations, is important as this will provide the basis for assessing the effects of an organization's economic power. UB, not surprisingly, argued that as a banana producer it is part of the fresh fruit market as a whole, and that that should be treated as the relevant product market. The Commission, however, maintained that bananas were a separate market. It alleged that for certain consumers, particularly the very young and the very old, bananas formed an important part of their diet and were not substitutable with other forms of fruit. There was little cross-elasticity of demand in relation to these consumers. This argument was accepted by the ECJ.

The second matter was the question of dominance. This is not decided purely by reference to the size of an organization's market share. UB had a market share of about 40 per cent, but its dominance was determined by its ability to behave 'to an appreciable extent independently of its competitors, customers and ultimately of its consumers'. In other cases, the Commission and the ECJ have looked at other indicators of market dominance. These have included how difficult it is for new competitors to enter the market, the existence of stable competition in the market, the size of individual market shares of an organization's competitors and the ease of access of an organization to financial resources such as the international capital market.

Once UB's market dominance was established, the matter of abuse had to be determined. UB's conduct fell within the list of abuses set out in Article 86, although the ECJ did not accept a third complaint against UB concerning its prohibition of the resale of certain products.

The Commission has the power, as with Article 85, to impose a fine for infringement of 10 per cent of turn-over.

The merger regulation

The Treaty of Rome did not provide specific rules for the control of mergers. However, in two landmark decisions, **Continental Can** in 1973 and **BAT** in 1987, the ECJ held that Articles 86 and 85, respectively could apply to mergers. It was reasoned in **Continental Can** that the acquisition of a competitor by a dominant firm could prejudice the competitive structure of a market and thus constitute an abuse by a dominant firm of its market position. **BAT** concerned an agreement under which the tobacco company Rembrant undertook to transfer a 30 per cent holding in Rothmans International to Phillip Morris. Although a firm's acquisition of an interest in a rival may not necessarily restrict competition, the ECJ took the view that where such restriction was a possibility the Community had the power to intervene.

Despite these decisions the Commission pressed for specific EC-wide merger rules that would obviate reliance on Articles 85 and 86. The Mergers Control Regulation, the first attempt at such a regulation having been made as long ago as 1973, was finally made law in 1989 and came into force the following year.

It was felt that the control of concentrations with a Community dimension could not be adequately left to the regulatory procedures of individual Member States, on account of their marked lack of consistency and varying effectiveness. Without control at the Community level, this fragmented approach would effectively undermine the SEM.

An advantage of the new Merger Control Regulation is that it allows the Commission to intervene before a merger has taken place; under Articles 85 and 86 the Commission was able to act only once a merger had occurred. In addition, the application of both these articles was unpredictable, creating uncertainty for organizations that wanted to plan and undertake lawful mergers activity within the Community.

The scope of the Regulation

The Regulation empowers the Commission to declare a 'Concentration with a Community Dimension' (CCD) incompatible with the common market. A CCD will be incompatible where it creates or strengthens a dominant market position so as to impede effective competition in the common market, or a substantial part of it. As there are circumstances where it is possible for a joint venture to occupy a position of market dominance, the Regulation makes specific provision for such collaborations. (The application of the Regulation to joint ventures is considered below.)

The Regulation defines a concentration as occurring where two or more previously independent undertakings merge, or where one or more persons who already control at least one undertaking acquire such securities or assets control of another undertaking or undertakings. The concentration will have a community dimension where the combined aggregate worldwide turnover of all the undertakings concerned is more than ECU 5 billion **and** the aggregate Community-wide turnover of each of at least two of the undertakings involved is more than ECU 250 million, **unless** each of the undertakings concerned derives more than two-thirds of their Community-wide turnover within one and the same Member State.

Where a merger meets the criteria set out in the Regulation, it must be referred to the Commission for a decision. The Commission is given, on competition grounds, exclusive jurisdiction to deal with CCDs and where one exists, national competition authorities must stand aside. The decision of the Commission is final and if a CCD is cleared at Community level it cannot then be blocked at the national level, unless the merger involves certain limited and clearly identified public interest concerns (some of these are discussed below). It has been asserted that major European businesses would benefit from the certainty of having to deal with only one competition body – the so-called 'one stop shop' regulation. The Merger Regulation procedure is detailed in Figure 4.2.

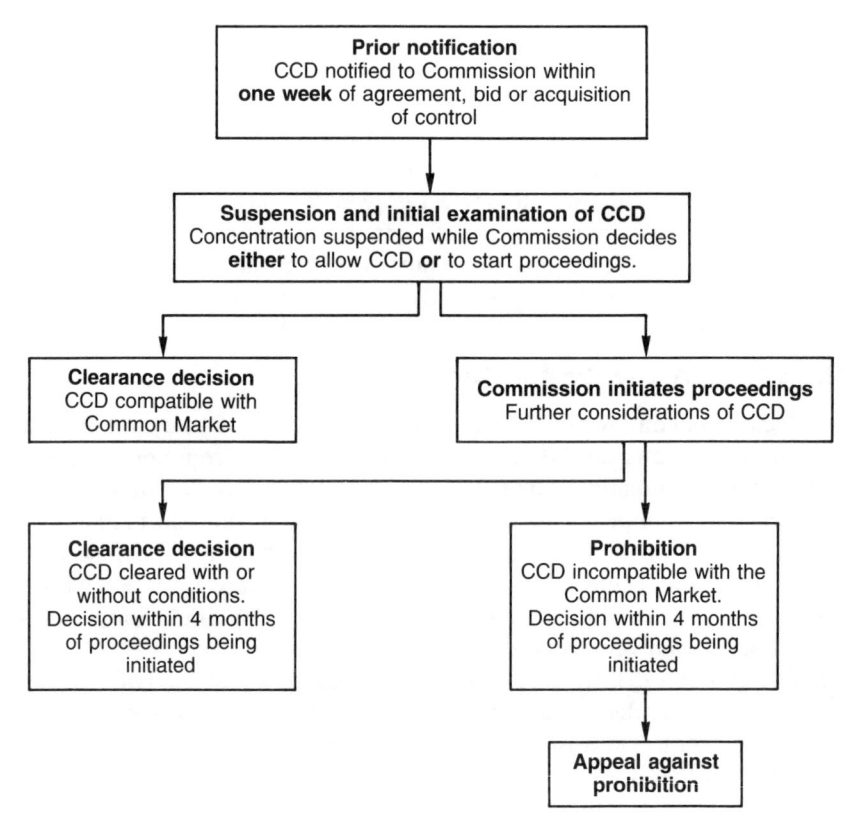

```
┌─────────────────────────────────────────────┐
│              Prior notification              │
│    CCD notified to Commission within         │
│  one week of agreement, bid or acquisition   │
│                 of control                   │
└─────────────────────────────────────────────┘
                      │
                      ▼
┌─────────────────────────────────────────────┐
│    Suspension and initial examination of CCD │
│  Concentration suspended while Commission    │
│  decides either to allow CCD or to start     │
│  proceedings.                                │
└─────────────────────────────────────────────┘
          │                        │
          ▼                        ▼
┌──────────────────┐    ┌──────────────────────────┐
│ Clearance decision│   │ Commission initiates     │
│ CCD compatible   │   │ proceedings              │
│ with Common Market│   │ Further considerations   │
│                  │    │ of CCD                   │
└──────────────────┘    └──────────────────────────┘
                            │            │
                            ▼            ▼
                  ┌──────────────────┐  ┌──────────────────┐
                  │ Clearance decision│  │ Prohibition      │
                  │ CCD cleared with │  │ CCD incompatible │
                  │ or without       │  │ with the Common  │
                  │ conditions.      │  │ Market.          │
                  │ Decision within  │  │ Decision within  │
                  │ 4 months of      │  │ 4 months of      │
                  │ proceedings being│  │ proceedings being│
                  │ initiated        │  │ initiated        │
                  └──────────────────┘  └──────────────────┘
                                              │
                                              ▼
                                        ┌──────────────┐
                                        │ Appeal against│
                                        │ prohibition  │
                                        └──────────────┘
```

Figure 4.2 Merger regulation procedure

The Commission's competence to deal with CCDs is based on competition grounds. There are two areas where Member States retain jurisdiction. The first – of which Germany was the main proponent – is when a concentration threatens competition in a **distinct market** within a Member State. It was anticipated the exception would apply to local markets; the Commission's examples being retailing or the hotel sector. The distinct market procedure was first used in **Steetly/Tarmac** (1992), where the Commission allowed the UK authorities to consider a merger in the brick and clay tile industry where significant barriers to entry meant that the merger would have little impact on the rest of the Community.

The other exception to the principle of the Commission's exclusivity is the power the Regulation gives to Member States to consider **legitimate interests**. Public security, the plurality of the media and the supervision of financial bodies are all grounds where a Member State may intervene as of right. This could lead to the possibility that a merger cleared by the Commission on competition grounds might, under the legitimate interests provision, be scrutinized by national authorities. Such an eventuality would be counter to the 'one stop shop' approach, which was claimed to be one of the Regulation's major advantages.

The Commission's application of the Regulation

The Commission estimated that the Regulation was likely to produce about fifty cases a year. By September 1993, the Commission had dealt with 178 notifications, the vast majority of which were cleared within the required four-week time period. Indeed, all notified mergers, with only the one exception of **de Havilland/Aerospatial/Alenia** (1992), have been cleared, although in some cases clearance was subject to a condition such as divestment or restructuring.

The way the Commission dealt with the de Havilland acquisition raises important questions about the way it operates merger policy. The American aircraft producer, Boeing, wanted to sell its Canadian commuter aircraft subsidiary, de Havilland. By 1991, it was agreed that de Havilland would be sold jointly to Aerospatiale of France and Alenia of Italy. These two European enterprises saw the acquisition as an opportunity to strengthen their position in the troubled world commuter aircraft market. In effect, they would go some way to creating a 'European champion' in this field.

At the beginning of October 1991, the Commission blocked the takeover. The decision was reasoned on the competition grounds that the new enterprise would have 50 per cent of the world market and 70 per cent of the Community market in commuter aircraft with 20-70 seats. Sir Leon Brittan, then the Competition Commissioner, believed – and managed to persuade a majority of the Commissioners – that the accumulation of market power in this form would be prejudicial to competition. He felt that, unlike other mergers, the new group's market dominance could not be reduced by the Commission requiring divestments or restructuring.

The decision, however, has its critics. The Merger Regulation gives the Commission the authority to take into account industrial and social factors –

as well as purely competition considerations – when examining a CCD. The critics have advocated that Community industry policy must be directed towards producing European champions, who, given the globalization of business, must be of sufficient size to compete effectively with American and Japanese rivals. This would require a certain tolerance of approach when considering the competition implications of alliances between large corporations. Such a view was behind the comment made by the French transport minister at the time of the de Havilland decision that the Commission, by blocking the merger, had gone against the interest of the European aerospace industry, thereby weakening it in the face of world competition.

In July 1992 the Commission made another key decision – in the **Nestlé/Perrier** case – on the application of the Regulation. The effect of the decision is to extend the Regulation's scope to mergers which would create not just a simple monopoly, but an oligopoly, in which several producers jointly dominate a market. The **Nestlé/Perrier** notification involved Nestlé's proposed acquisition of Perrier for £1.6billion. Nestlé had received tactical assistance in the takeover from the largest food group in France, BSN. It had been agreed between them that once the purchase of Perrier was complete Nestlé would sell Perrier's second largest brand, Volvic, to BSN. If the merger and sales had gone ahead as planned, the transactions would have given BSN and Nestlé 94.1 per cent of the mineral water market in France. Eventually the Commission allowed the acquisition to proceed on condition that Nestlé sold some of its businesses. The divestment of the sources and brands which this required amounted to around 20 per cent of the total capacity formerly held by the three companies involved. (Even so, after compliance with the condition, Nestlé and BSN's combined market share still totalled about 68 per cent).

The Commission's stance in this case showed that it was prepared to consider how the balance of a market's structure as a whole may be affected by the takeover instead of simply looking at the position of the companies directly involved. However, Juan F Biones Alonso, of the Commission's General Competition Merger Task Force, has stated that the Commission will not automatically assume that oligopolies created by merger activity are undesirable. Nevertheless, the Commission will guard against shared market dominance where there is the possibility of either tacit or overt collusion between the major players.

In reaching the Nestlé decision, the Commission looked at a number of factors which, taken together, they concluded could pose a threat to competition. These included the following:

1 If allowed in its original form, the suppliers – Nestlé and BSN would jointly control over 90 per cent of the French bottled mineral waters market.

2 The number of national water suppliers would be reduced from three to two, thereby creating a duopoly.
3 After the proposed merger, a symmetric duopoly would be left. With Nestlé and BSN having similar capabilities and shares of the market, the two companies would have a strong inducement to act in parallel to achieve profit maximization.
4 If the original merger had been allowed, the fact of both low, cross and price elasticity of demand for the brands of mineral waters owned by Nestlé and BSN could make it possible for the two companies to impose significant price increases without suffering losses of revenue. The Commission recognized this as a possibility because since 1987 Nestlé, BSN and Perrier had, acting in parallel, constantly increased their prices.
5 The absence of a significant cost advantage for either Nestlé or BSN reduced the likelihood of effective competition between the two.
6 Because of the high degree of market transparency, which would make it relatively easy for the supposed competitors to monitor each other's behaviour, the scope for parallel conduct would be further increased.
7 Real competition from imports would be unlikely as these accounted for only 1-2 per cent of the French market.
8 There existed barriers and risks to entering the French bottled water market which were likely to deter potential competitors, for example, the established reputation of existing brands owned by Perrier, BSN and Nestlé.

As noted above, the Nestlé development amounts to a considerable extension of the Regulation's scope. The Regulation does not refer to joint dominance and at present there remain doubts about the Commission's entitlement in law to interpret the Regulation in this way. The legal uncertainty will have to be resolved by the ECJ and currently there is no pending legal action relating to this matter. Mr Alonso has acknowledged that there are good legal arguments for saying that the Commission exceeded the jurisdiction of the Regulation. Allowing for the probability that the Court would support the Commission's interpretation of the Regulation, there remains the uncertainty about how the Commission will decide cases that are similar, but not identical, to the Nestlé/Perrier merger. It is not clear what weight the Commission gave to the individual factors which it regarded as pointing to the likelihood of collusion in the Nestlé/Perrier merger. Would the absence of any of these factors lead the Commission to conclude that an oligopoly would not threaten competition, or alternatively, is the presence of one of these factors highly probative of market dominance likely to lead to market collaboration? The lack of specific guidance on the relative importance of these factors obscures the Commission's decision making process and creates concerns about the transparency of competition policy.

The Merger Regulation and joint ventures

Another area where the Merger Regulation has been concerned with the issue of oligopoly is that of joint ventures. Certain joint ventures may fall within the scope of the Regulation as they might create a new concentration. For example, two independent vehicle manufacturers may agree to establish a third business, which they jointly own, to manufacture spare parts. The creation of the new third company might have the potential to distort competition within the Community, and if this is the case, its creation would need to be considered by the Commission.

The Regulation's provisions dealing with joint ventures are fairly technical and had to be supplemented with explanatory information by a Commission Notice. Article 3 of the Regulation provides that the 'creation of a joint venture performing on a lasting basis all the functions of an autonomous economic entity, which does not give rise to co-ordination of the competitive behaviour of the parties amongst themselves or between them and the joint venture, shall constitute a concentration'. It is important to note that if the joint venture is short term, or is not economically autonomous of its parents or exists for the purpose of allowing the parents to co-operate in areas where they would normally compete, then the joint venture would not be a concentration; rather it could constitute an agreement covered by Article 85 of the EC Treaty.

The Commission Notice identified certain considerations that might be used to assist in dealing with the question of whether a joint venture is 'concentrative' (thus potentially falling within the scope of the Regulation) or cooperative (thus potentially falling within the scope of Article 85). These include:

1. Will the joint venture take over pre-existing activities of the parent companies?
2. Will the joint venture undertake new activities on behalf of the parents?
3. Will the joint venture enter the parents' market?
4. Will the joint venture enter upstream, downstream or neighbouring markets?

In addition, the Notice stresses the importance of the ideas of economic autonomy from the parents and the long-term nature of joint venture in identifying a joint venture as concentrative. Moreover, if a joint venture is to be used as a vehicle for the coordination of competition it cannot be treated as concentrative. So, in **Flachglas/Vegla** (1992), the Commission decided that a joint venture set up by the parents to process scrap glass was not concentrative as it would not become an independent buyer and seller in the recycled glass market but would remain an auxiliary of its parents. On the other hand, in **Elf Autochem/Rohm & Haas** (1992), a joint venture by two companies to take over the production of acrylic glass amounted to a new concentration. In addition to the joint venture having its own research facilities and distribution network, the parents had transferred to the new undertaking the human and physical resources necessary for the production of acrylic glass. Moreover, irrevocable licences had been issued to the new venture, there were plans to build a separate factory for the production of glass and the joint venture would be free to choose its suppliers. The fact that the agreement between the parents was to last for 99 years was also an important consideration.

As with the **Nestlé/Perrier** decision, which relates to straightforward mergers and takeovers, the Commission will not restrict its consideration of concentrative joint ventures to the single issue of whether the new undertaking occupies a position of market dominance. Even if a new joint venture does not become a dominant company, the potential, resulting from the implementation of the new venture, to create an oligopolistic market will need to be examined. This kind of analysis was undertaken in **Rhône Poulenc/SNIA** (1992).

A new joint venture was established by Rhône Poulenc and SNIA to produce the carpet, textile and industrial fibres which had formerly been made by the two companies. The Commission decided that the new joint venture was concentrative, but was not the dominant firm in the fibres market. However, the presence of important competitors meant that there was a possibility that the major players might substitute a relationship of oligopolistic interdependency for the competitive relationship that ought to exist between them.

Accordingly, the Commission examined the markets where there were significant risks that the presence of the joint venture could create an oligopolistic abuse of market power. In the market for carpet fibres, the joint venture had about a quarter of the market share, while the two other major competitors, ICI and Du Pont, held about two-thirds of the market. In the markets for textile and industrial fibres the joint venture would have a share of between 40 and 50 per cent. However, in both of these markets, there was at least one strong competitor with a market share of between 20 and 30 per cent.

The Commission held that in each of these three markets oligopolistic interdependency was unlikely. The reasoning the Commission employed in respect of the textile and industrial fibre markets illustrates the kind of economic assessment that the regulator will undertake when confronted with a joint venture that can alter existing market structures. In addition to taking into account the existence of at least one major competitor in each of the markets, the Commission examined how competitors might respond to an increase in price introduced by the joint venture. The technology used in the production of the different types of fibre was in fact very similar. It would take less than a day to change production from one type of fibre to another. This would mean that the competitors could react very quickly to an increase in the price of one type of fibre by increasing their output of that particular fibre. Thus the potential for product substitution was strong and would make anti-competitive price increases – because they would be unprofitable – less likely.

Although the Commission's analysis in **Rhône Poulenc/SNIA** lead it to conclude that the creation of the joint venture would not distort competition, the real importance of the decision is that it signals the Commission's willingness to examine the oligopolistic implications – and their consequences in terms of market abuse – inherent in the creation of a new joint venture.

Merger Regulation: an important current issue

Article 1 of the Regulation lays down that the financial criteria for determining a CCD would have to be reviewed by the end of 1993. A single European market requires a uniform EC-wide merger Regulation which covers the majority of cross-border acquisitions. The question raised is, does the current Regulation satisfactorily meet this objective? In at least one respect it clearly fails as the current 5 billion ECU worldwide turnover threshold means that a majority of mergers are dealt with at the national level. Given the differing approaches to policing concentrations in the Member States, the outcome can only be a fragmented as opposed to a single European market.

State aids

All Member States take great interest in the economic health of commercial ventures operating within their national frontiers. Part of the wealth created by industry can be redistributed and the presence of strong industry can help to achieve social goals such as improved standards of living and high levels of employment. Therefore, there is frequently a temptation on the part of Member States to give their industries a helping hand. This kind of state aid prevents unaided industries in the same sector from doing business on equal terms with their aided counterparts and may result in deleterious effects on competition within the common market. On this issue, Karel Van Miert, the current European Commissioner for Competition has said, 'if "beggar my neighbour" aid schemes that merely export unemployment and try push problems (sic) onto other Member States are not stopped, then these other Member States will only retaliate with countervailing aid schemes, resulting in a redivision of the common market and a general reduction in wealth'.[1]. He added, 'the Commission must be very careful with its role as a referee of aids to be granted by Member States – an aid to prop up a job in one Member State can easily cause the loss of an equivalent job in another Member State'[2].

The Treaty's principal state aid measures

The Treaty of Rome requires Member States to notify the Commission of any intention to give aid. The Commission can block the aid, or, where it has already been given, can require it to be repaid.

The key provisions here are Articles 92, 93 and 94. Articles 93 and 94 deal with the procedures for the regulation of state aids, while Article 92 establishes the kind of state assistance which is prohibited. Aid will be incompatible with the common market where it distorts or threatens to distort competition by favouring certain undertakings – or the production of certain goods – to the extent that this affects trade between Member States.

The obvious form of state aid is a subsidy. However, the Commission considers the following as potentially incompatible with the common market: exemptions from tax or other duties, the deferred collection of taxes, the provision of goods and services on preferential terms (for example, cheap energy), preferential public ordering, guarantees of loans on favourable terms, indemnities against losses and preferential interest rates. In the **British Aerospace** Sweeteners (1991) case, the UK Government's writing off of £44 million Rover Group debts – on top of an approved write-off of some £469 million – was considered by the Commission to be unacceptable aid.

In identifying aids in their different forms, the Commission and the ECJ have adopted a kind of lateral thinking based on market criteria. For example, in **Intermills** (1984), the Belgian authorities had assisted a paper business. In particular, the Walloon Regional Executive had provided capital for the firm in return for a controlling interest. Although many states have holdings in private sector organizations, the acquisition of capital can be an aid where the firm would not have been able to raise that scale of investment on the money markets. The test is whether a private investor, having assessed the likelihood of a return on the investment, would have subscribed to the aided firm's capital?

The Treaty does except certain aid from the prohibition under Article 92. Aid to make good the effects of a natural disaster is treated as compatible with the common market. The Commission also has the discretion to allow aid to promote economic development in an area where the standard of living is exceptionally low or where there is serious underemployment. However, to be eligible for this exception, the level of deprivation must be measured on a Community rather than a national scale. It is also possible for aid to be allowed where it is necessary to carry out a project of important European interest or to develop certain economic activities and areas in a way that does not prejudice existing trading conditions. This last exception allows the Commission to consider aids to industrial sectors and regions.

State aids and restructuring

Restructuring of industries within the EC can be seen as a response to at least four major factors; the current economic downturn, global shift, technological change and completing the internal market. Such restructuring can lead to considerable pressure on Member States to aid ailing industries, as is demonstrated by the current position of steel production in the EC (see relevant case study). On the issue of state aid for restructuring, the Commission believes that the main responsibility is with the companies involved to take the appropriate measures to ensure their long-term viability. State aid may be acceptable to assist this process, but not simply to prop up a failed industry.

References

1 Van Miert, Karel Analysis and guidelines on Competition Policy in *AGENCE EUROPE* 15 May 1993, no. 1834, p. 5.
2 *Ibid.*, p. 6.

5 The European Community and external relations: the rise of a new trading superpower?

Lee Miles

Introduction

The European Community (EC) is an important regional trading power in the world economy today. At present, the EC represents the world's largest trading bloc, with a market of some 325 million consumers. Consequently, the EC has a major influence on world trade because of its size and the extent of its external relations. The purpose of this chapter is to analyse the significance for the EC of external trade and the role the European Community has in shaping the world economy. The chapter will discuss four issues. First, the nature of the global trading economy in the 1990s and the importance of the Community to it. Secondly, the character of the European Community as an international trading organization. Thirdly, an evaluation of the EC's Common Commercial Policy (CCP) and the instruments used to govern its external trading relationships. Finally, an analysis of the Community's future challenges will be undertaken.

The importance of the European Community to the global trading economy

The first point is that the Community's effect on world trade is intrinsically linked to the nature of the world economy and the role of GATT in world trade. Since the end of the Second World War, the global trading economy has been based on one guiding principle, namely that international economic relationships ought to be based on free trade[1]. The principle of free trade became the governing concept for the revised post-war international trading system. This framework became known as the Bretton Woods System, named after the place where it was first established in 1944. Its three main institutional pillars were the International Monetary Fund (IMF), the International Bank for Reconstruction and Development (IBRD or `World Bank') and the General Agreement on Tariffs and Trade (GATT). This system has faced many problems and had to be greatly modified in the early 1970s when universal fixed exchange rates were abandoned.

Nevertheless, this system was mainly responsible for the huge expansion in international trade in the post-war period. Throughout the 1980s, world trade and output have continued to grow (see Figure 5.1). The GATT framework is still the dominant global vehicle for international trade liberalization. It is the environment against which the European Community's performance must be judged.

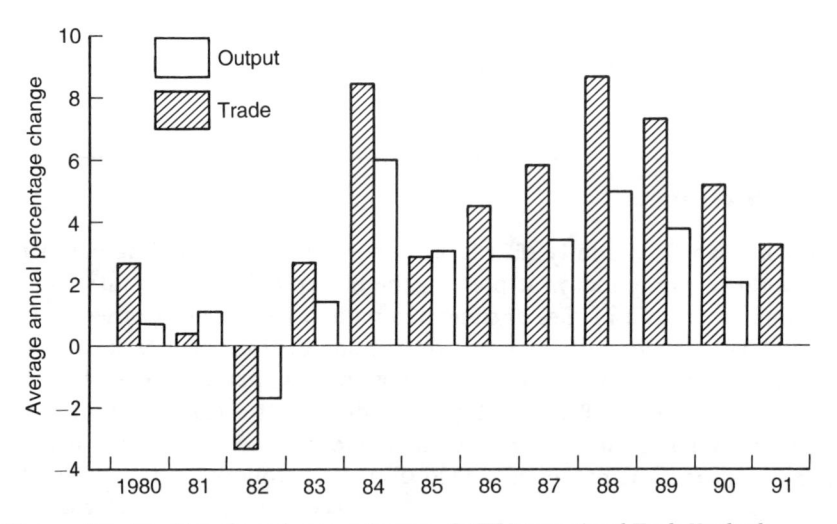

Figure 5.1 World trade and output (source: *GATT International Trade Yearbook* 1991-1992)

Regional economic cooperation has generally become a major feature of global trade. Regional economic groupings, such as customs-unions and free trade areas are exempt under GATT rules (Article XIV) on the pre-condition that the creation of such regional groupings will not lead to a raising of reduced tariff barriers agreed universally under GATT. The European Community is the largest of these regional groupings at this time (see Table 5.1 and Figure 5.2). It can be argued that the EC presently represents the world's only true trading bloc[2]. There are four basic characteristics for a trading bloc: relatively similar levels of per capita gross domestic product, geographic proximity, compatible trading regimes between Member States and a political commitment to regional organization. The EC alone seems to meet all these requirements. Yet, the EC has been committed to the principle of freer trade. It is notable that all of the EC Member States are signatories and members of GATT. Both the EC and its Member States subscribe to GATT rules.

The European Community and external relations

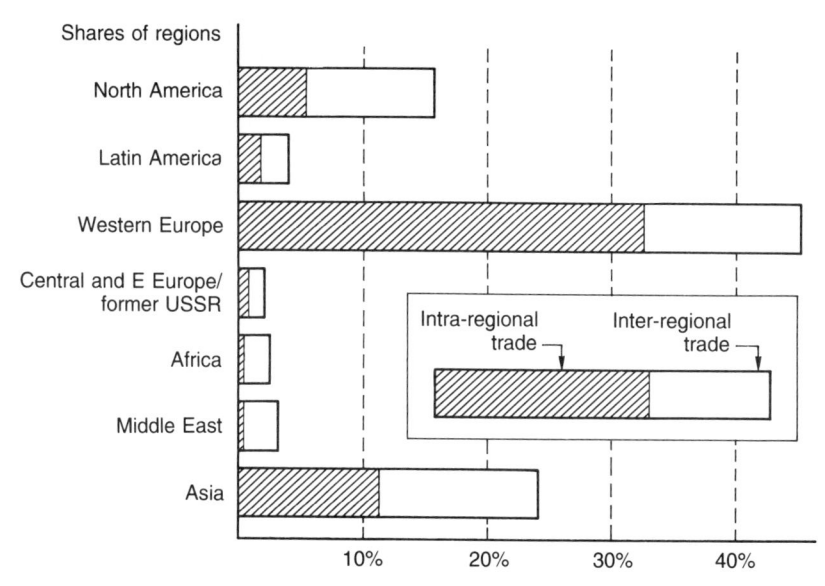

Figure 5.2 World exports 1991 (source: *GATT International Trade Yearbook* 1991–1992)

Table 5.1 *Emerging trading blocks?*

	1980 $bn	%	1986 $bn	%	1989 $bn	%
EC-12						
Total imports	826.5	100	781.4	100	1,165.8	100
of which: Intra-regional trade	399.5	48	44.5.4	57	677.2	57
Imports from ROW[1]	427.0	52	336.0	43	498.6	43
from East Asia	49.0	6	63.9	8	104.5	9
from North America	85.8	10	66.0	8	104.2	9
NORTH AMERICA[2]						
Total imports	335.7	100	481.9	100	635.9	100
of which: Intra-regional trade	107.5	32	150.5	31	210.4	33
Imports from ROW	228.2	68	331.4	69	425.5	67
from East Asia	64.2	19	159.4	33	202.0	32
from ED-12	50.1	15	90.6	19	105.8	17
EAST ASIA						
Total imports	294.5	100	308.7	100	558.2	100
of which: Intra-regional trade	92.8	32	117.9	38	224.5	40
Imports from ROW	201.7	68	190.8	62	333.7	60
from North America	59.6	20	69.9	23	123.8	22
from EC-12	29.2	10	40.4	13	77.0	14

1 Rest of the world. 2 US, Canada and Mexico.
Source: IMF, *Direction of Trade Statistics Yearbook*

The EC's influence has been extended due to several factors. First, the actual size of the European Community has progressively grown from six states to twelve, due to successive EC enlargements in 1973 (UK, Ireland, Denmark), 1981 (Greece) and 1986 (Spain and Portugal). The Community now constitutes the largest regional grouping in terms of population size. In 1989, the total population of the EC registered 325.243 million.

Secondly, the EC encompasses most of Europe's industrially developed states, including a large number of OECD states. The Community has a disproportionately large influence on world trading matters as it includes a majority of the world's developed exporting nations. The EC held 22.4 per cent of the world market for goods and services in 1991 (excluding intra-EC trade), with external trade representing 41.2 per cent of total EC trade[3]. This is larger than both the United States share at 15 per cent and Japan's at 9 per cent[4]. The EC is both vulnerable to world trade trends and a major influence in shaping them.

The implications have been two-fold. First, the EC's larger size and relative importance have enabled it to constitute a greater voice in international trading relations. Secondly, EC trade has displayed distinctive trade patterns and a local geographical basis. The majority of the EC's trading partners are close geographical neighbours, such as Sweden and Switzerland. They are extensively integrated and form a major element of EC external trade relations. In 1991, for example, imports from the geographically close European Free Trade Association (EFTA) states represented 22.7 per cent of EC external imports.

Ironically, although the EC remains an important player in international trade, EC external trade has become less important to the Community due to EC enlargement and deeper integration. As Figures 5.3 and 5.4 illustrate, between 1961 and 1991, the twelve current EC members increased their exports to one another from 43 per cent of total exports to 63 per cent. In the 1980s, the divergence between the increase in trade within the EC (intra-EC trade) and that with the rest of the world (extra-EC trade) became particularly marked (see Figure 5.4). The share of intra-EC trade in world exports rose from 15 per cent in 1961 to 24 per cent in 1991. Over the same period, the share of EC exports to third markets in world exports fell from 20 per cent to 15 per cent (see Figures 5.3 and 5.4). In 1992 alone, the value of intra-EC trade rose by 2 per cent while the value of extra-EC imports fell by 1.3 per cent[5].

The impact has been trade diverting. Many companies that might have exported to the EC have invested locally and have chosen to supply the EC market from within the Community. It can be suggested that further enlargement to include most EFTA states will further increase intra-EC trade, while reducing the importance of extra-EC trade. The EFTA states which are

The European Community and external relations

presently large external trading partners will be included in intra-EC trade in the future. External relations will become less rather than more important to the EC. External trade policy will change in emphasis and will be internationalist and less focused on Europe. External policy will be increasingly centred on non-European partners.

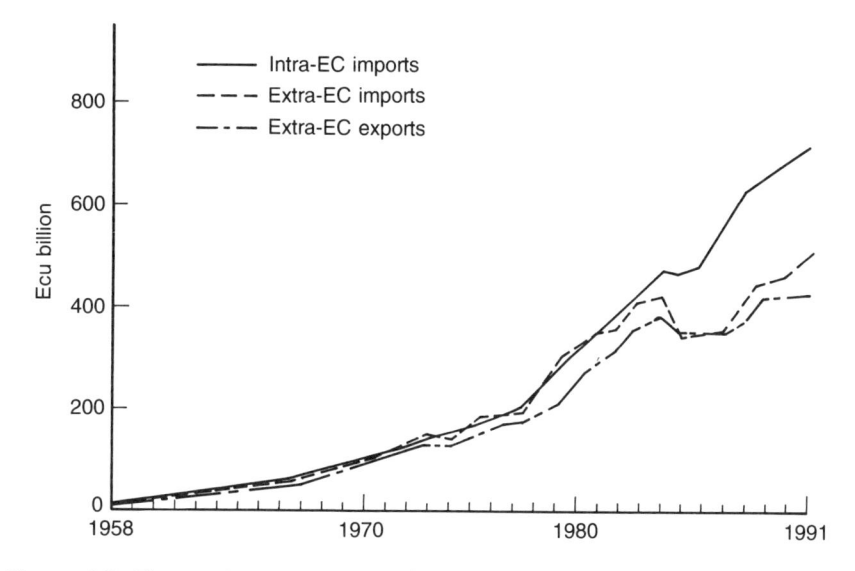

Figure 5.3 The growing introspection of EC trade (source: GATT secretariat)

At the same time, the Community is also a dynamic trading bloc. Its commitment to greater economic integration has grown significantly since the development of the Single European Market (SEM) programme. The SEM has revitalized the EC and with it the extent and nature of relations with non-Member States[6]. Non-member states have become increasingly aware that the EC integrationist policies have repercussions for their own trading relations with the Community. The SEM raised the issue of whether the EC would become a 'Fortress Europe', discriminating against non-member states and excluding them from Community markets through protectionist measures. This became a major issue in international trade diplomacy in the late 1980s, illustrating the EC's presence within international trade.

Ironically, just as economic trends have meant that external trade is less important to the EC, its integrationist policies have caused a strong external reaction from third countries. Consequently, the EC has developed a network of preferential agreements, which both increases its influence and its profile in international trade. The European Community has become a major economic component of global trade and a substantial political influence upon it.

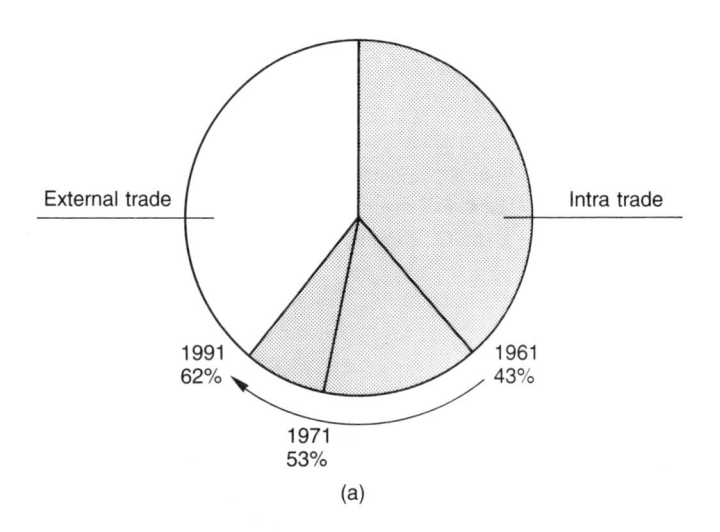

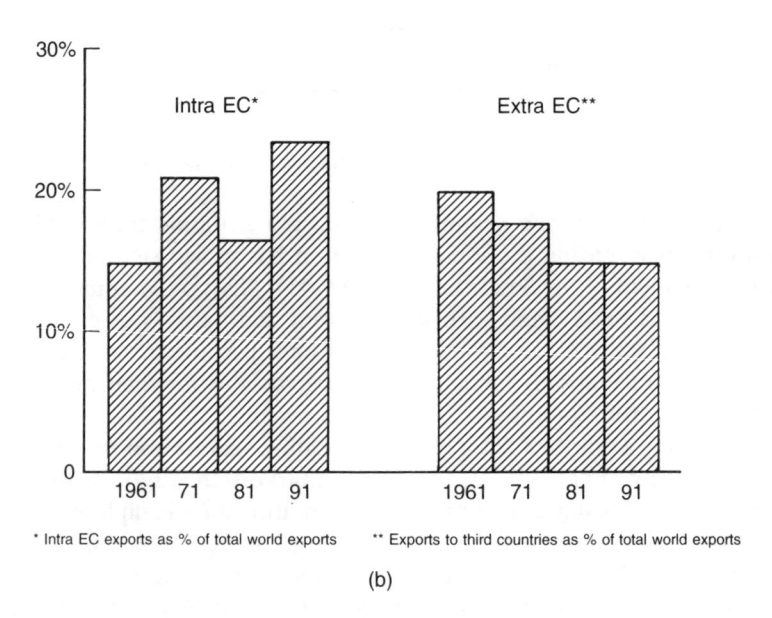

Figure 5.4 Share in (a) EC and (b) world exports (source: GATT secretariat)

The special nature of the European Community as an international organization

The European Community constitutes a unique institution. It does not fall easily into established categories or definitions of international organizations. International organizations have been defined as formal, continuous structures established by agreement between members with the aim of pursuing the common interests of the membership[7]. In addition, many scholars have also tried to categorize the EC as a 'civilian power', devoid of any military or political role[8]. The Community is, after all, built upon the concept of a customs-union, discriminating against non-Member-State trade and including an integrated external trade policy.

The EC is rather more than any of these. It is not just an international trading organization. The Community has an overt political agenda, committed to achieving further integration between its Member States and supported by various theories of European integration. The EC's strategy has been to formulate selected economic policies to achieve the wider objective of political integration.

The EC is increasingly also more than just a 'civilian power'. Since 1 November 1993 and the ratification of the Maastricht Treaty, the Community has become part of a wider European Union. This development into a European Union necessitates a strong and clear external trade policy, centred around the Common Commercial Policy (CCP). The CCP should be distinguished from the EC's wider international relations[9]. The Community has many levels and tiers of relations with other states and groups of countries. At the political level, the EC attempts to present a united European voice in international relations on areas outside the realms of the CCP. The Member States, for instance, established European Political Cooperation (EPC) in the 1970s. The Maastricht Treaty introduces the concept of a Common Foreign and Security Policy (CFSP), reiterating the Community's intention to be more than just a 'civilian power'[10]. In the future, the EC may even assume a limited political and defence role.

Evaluation of the Common Commercial Policy (CCP)

Nevertheless, the EC is primarily a customs union. According to customs union theory, the Community must maintain an external trade barrier to non-customs-union members. This external barrier is the Common Customs Tariff or Common External Tariff (CCT or CET). This is governed by a common commercial policy in order to ensure that the CET is coherently operated between the custom union members. The Common Commercial Policy (CCP) is essential to any successful customs union. It is the central element in defining the EC's trading relationship with non-Member States.

The legal basis of the Common Commercial Policy (CCP)

The Common Commercial Policy's simple purpose is to achieve uniform and amicable trading relations between the EC and non-Member States. The Preamble to the 1957 Treaty of Rome outlines the desire of the EC to 'contribute by means of a common commercial policy to the progressive abolition of restrictions on international trade'. Article 3 of the Treaty of Rome specifies that the EC's activities shall include both a CET and a CCP with third countries.

Articles 110–116 of the Treaty of Rome provide the legal basis for the EC's CCP and detail its parameters. The aspirations of the EC's CCP are set within the global free trade environment and the EC's conformity with GATT principles. Article 110 stipulates that by establishing a customs union, member states aim to contribute to the common interest and `the harmonious development of world trade'[11]. Considering the discriminatory purpose of the CCP in its role of defending the customs union, the CCP has unusually been consistently shrouded in the language of trade liberalization and free trade.

Rationales for developing the CCP

There are four major reasons for developing a Common Commercial Policy (CCP).

1 Raise international profiles and bargaining power. By Member States adopting one collective EC trade policy, then member states' bargaining power in international trade negotiations is increased. A collective common commercial policy helps to make the world trade environment compatible with EC interests.
2 Avoids damaging competition between Member States. The 'spillover' effects of national trade policies need to be reconciled. The CCP avoids destructive competition between Member States for third countries' markets, for example subsidies given by one Member State government for exports to third countries may affect the competitive position of another Member State's companies in external export markets.
3 Increases the effectiveness of the trading bloc. A technically uniform CCP should ensure that trade and aid policies will be more effective if coordinated at the EC level. A CCP lessens the possibilities of duplication between national policies[12].
4 Leads to greater consensus between EC Member States. From the EC perspective, a coordinated CCP should theoretically increase political homogeneity between EC Member States. The CCP allows member states to cooperate together in the field of external relations. It is a potential foundation for wider integrated foreign policy actions as envisaged in the Maastricht Treaty.

The European Community and external relations

The objectives of the CCP

It can be argued that the EC Common Commercial Policy (CCP) encompasses three main objectives.

1 *A uniform CCP*. The CCP must ensure that uniform trading relations are applied by member states to third countries. Article 113 declares that the CCP shall be based `on uniform principles' especially regarding tariff rates, trade agreements and measures to protect fair trade from dumping or subsidies.
2 *A supranational CCP*. Trading relations covered by the CCP should be conducted at the Community level. Implicit in the CCP is the acceptance by member states of a limited loss of freedom of action. The CCP should be a supranational policy conducted by supranational institutions. Trading relations between Member States and third countries in areas covered by the CCP are mainly handled by the EC Commission. The EC Commission under Article 228 can conduct international trading negotiations and sign international treaties under Articles 237 and 238. General guidelines are set by the EC's Council of Ministers for the Commission in practice.
3 *A comprehensive CCP*. The EC has developed a host of instruments to govern and direct the CCP. In 1975, the European Court of Justice ruled that the CCP should cover all trade instruments[13]. The Court established the CCP's 'principle of parallel powers' whereby the EC's external treaty making powers with non-Member States are equal to its internal competencies in any given policy area. In other words, the Community's external trade powers in dealing with non-Member States are similar and equal to the elements of trade policy that the EC governs between the Member States. The CCP contains the same elements as the external trade policy of a state.

The mechanisms of the Common Commercial Policy (CCP)

1) The Community's Common External Tariff (CET)

The Common Commercial Policy began operating from the end of the transitional period in 1968. The main instrument of the CCP is the CET, being in place from 1 July 1968. The CET is the general level of duty or tariff that an importer must pay to import his goods into the EC market. The Community's CET is defined in Article 29 of the Treaty of Rome. The impact of having a uniform CET is that the level of EC protection has been gradually reduced. However, the overall effect of the reducing the CET is hard to gauge. It is difficult to differentiate between the specific role of the EC and the wider context of GATT in determining trade liberalization. The

EC has participated in the successive GATT Rounds and reduced tariff barriers. The EC's participation in the 1961 Dillon and the 1963–1967 Kennedy GATT Rounds, resulted in the CET being cut by half on most products[14]. The 1973–1979 Tokyo GATT Round instigated a further CET cut of approximately 35 per cent. The EC's CCT has been progressively reduced, symbolizing the EC's commitment to GATT principles and reflecting its claim of liberalizing international trade.

The level of the CET is now very low, being on average only 3.5 per cent on most products imported into the Community[15]. The resulting trade liberalization has in reality been an effective mixture of both Community and GATT initiatives. Nevertheless, although the EC has effectively worked towards freer trade, the scope of this commitment has been restricted. The EC's tariff reductions have generally only applied to industrial products. The CCP and CCT have failed to unify the structure of protection. Certain sensitive products such as, agriculture, textiles, steel and chemicals remain highly protected.

2) Accompanying common procedures

Agreement on a common rate of duty is only one step towards a uniform CET and alone does not constitute a common commercial policy. A common regime for categorizing the treatment of EC imports is necessary if the CCP is to be effective. The CCP includes a range of procedures for applying the CET:

(a) *Customs nomenclature:* a common classification for goods being imported into the EC for customs purposes.
(b) *Customs valuations:* a common system of deciding the level of imposing duty on imports.
(c) *Uniform duty suspensions and reductions:* a common system of enforcing limited reductions or suspensions of duties as determined by the EC.
(d) *Common Rules of Origin:* These rules are vital to the EC's trade policies. Rules of Origin ensure that only states with preferential trade agreements with the EC benefit from duty reductions or suspensions. Rules of Origin are necessary in order to prevent producers from non-preferred states from sending their goods to EC markets via states claiming preferential trading condition under EC trading agreements.

3) Commercial policy trade rules

The CCP also contains instruments to protect EC trade. The EC has a complex set of rules for protection against unfair trading practices. These rules supposedly subscribe to GATT rules, although in practice they do break the 'spirit' of GATT. The main elements of CCP's trading rules are:

(a) *Anti-dumping measures:* According to Winters (1991) and Article VI of the GATT[16], dumping occurs when countries sell products abroad `at less than normal value'. Normal value being defined as the price of home sales. Dumping is not completely prohibited. Only if it can be proved that dumping causes material injury to domestic producers in the importing Member State or the overall EC market, will the EC have the power under GATT rules to implement anti-dumping duties to counteract their effects. The only proviso is that the anti-dumping duties must not be greater than the difference between the price of the import and the price of home sales. The effect of anti-dumping duties can be easily illustrated. In September 1993, the EC doubled an existing anti-dumping duty of 34.45 per cent imposed in March 1993 on imported Chinese mountain bikes, increasing the price of Chinese bikes by 30.6 per cent in the EC market[17].

(b) *Countervailing measures and duties against subsidized imports:* Countervailing duties aim to neutralize the practice of foreign governments of subsidizing the production and/or export of goods, so as to maintain an artificially low price for their exports. If it can be proved that the government subsidy causes domestic injury to EC producers then a countervailing duty may be imposed. The EC may impose a countervailing duty not greater than the incidence of the subsidy.

(c) *Surveillance measures against foreign firms or governments' suspected malpractice:* The EC has also developed a number of surveillance measures to provide evidence and gauge damage to EC domestic producers, such as issuing import licences.

(d) *Safeguard measures against serious injuries to domestic producers.* The EC has also incorporated into its trade agreements the right to impose safeguard measures. Safeguard measures are designed to defend against surges of imports which are alleged to damage EC domestic producers. They usually take the form of quotas or Voluntary Export Restraints (VERS), which numerically restrict imports. Safeguard measures may be imposed regardless of whether the importer is dumping or benefitting from illegal subsidies.

With these measures the EC has tried to ensure that they subscribe to Article 113 and are based on `uniform principles'. The EC Commission has assumed that the EC must sanction their usage and has adopted four approaches. First, all CCP actions should be legitimized at the EC level. EC trade agreements incorporate articles allowing for the usage of these measures under limited circumstances so that power is not deflected by member state actions.

Secondly, the EC Commission aims to abolish or harmonize national quotas on imports in order to impose EC-wide quotas to match the Single European Market. All national measures and quotas are progressively being replaced by EC ones due to the emergence of the SEM. This is a large task as national quotas number around 6500. The importance of the CCP to Member States will increase. The EC external barrier will become the sole major obstacle to damaging imports once the SEM has been completed. Member States will find it difficult to control intra-EC trade in a free single market.

Thirdly, the Treaty of Rome itself remains ambiguous and ambivalent about the feasibility of creating a CCP. The Treaty includes Article 115 which provides for the possibility of Member States imposing their own protective measures. The only condition was that Member States should notify the Commission and seek its approval. This allowed Member States to retain a measure of autonomy in external trade policy by operating their own lists of products subject to national import restrictions. The Commission and the European Court of Justice have sought to interpret Article 115 narrowly in order to limit the ability of Member States to deflect EC trade[18]. Actions under Article 115 have been slowly limited but have been used frequently in the textiles area. Article 115 should become redundant with the advent of the SEM.

Finally, EC powers under the CCP are flexible in order to be effective to threats to EC domestic producers. In 1984, the EC introduced the New Commercial Policy Instrument to both legitimize its actions in the CCP and make the EC more flexible in responding to unfair trading practices of non-Member States. The EC has also introduced fast-track 'anti-absorption' procedures in 1988, allowing the Community to increase anti-dumping duties without a new inquiry, if it believes that existing anti-dumping duties are being 'absorbed' by the importer and not leading to price increases. This has been sparingly used as it is suspected that it infringes GATT rules; for example, the EC Commission in August 1993 doubled the anti-dumping duties on Chinese plastic sacks raising the duty to 85.7 per cent, which is only the second time it has been used since 1988.

However, the CCP remains complex and cumbersome. It has failed to maintain its three main objectives in several respects. Despite the Community's official aspiration of leading to the harmonious development of free trade, the Community has in practice openly countenanced the use of discrimination. The Community has also interpreted GATT rules inconsistently to suit its own interests. Thus, the CCP has not operated cohesively on uniform principles and power has only been grudgingly given by Member States to the EC supranational level, for example, Germany appealed to the European Court of Justice over the Community's new banana regime in 1993.

Indeed the banana regime is an interesting case. The Community's banana regime was introduced in February 1993 aiming to create a single market for bananas by protecting the EC's traditional high cost suppliers in the Third World. The regime imposed a quota of two million tonnes and a further duty of 170 per cent on non-preferred bananas above this quota from Latin America[19]. The German government argued that it was protected by a 'banana protocol' in the Treaty of Rome, guaranteeing it unrestricted access to Latin American fruit, expecially as Germany had no duty on bananas and in 1991 imported some 2.4 million tonnes of these 'dollar bananas' from Latin America. The European Court of Justice ruled against Germany in June 1993.

The harmonious development of free trade or an EC hierarchy of trading relations?

In theory, both the global free trade environment and GATT operate under certain guiding principles. The most important of these are the principles of transparency and non-discrimination. This is embodied in GATT's Most Favoured Nation (MFN) clause (Article 1), which requires that every trading country should be treated as well as the most favoured partner. All trade concessions given to one GATT member should be extended to all GATT members. Preferential trading arrangements designed to favour one nation over another are theoretically prohibited.

However, the EC openly discriminates between third nations. In fact, the EC offers strict MFN treatment only to the US, Japan, Canada, Australia and New Zealand. The economic weight of these five countries and limits on the coverage of EC preferential schemes ensure that 60 per cent of EC external imports do not receive MFN tariff treatment. The EC has formally established a hierarchy of trading relations with non-Member States. This discrimination partly arises out of the EC's own treaty-making powers under Article 228 and 238[20]. The vehicle for setting the level of trading relations being various trading agreements that the EC can sign with third states. One of the features of the EC's external relations which determines the ranking of a country in this hierarchy is the degree of access it is allowed to Community markets. These trading agreements formally record and define the level of access to the EC market. In 1991, 40 per cent of all EC imports entered the EC market under preferential arrangements. Generally, there are three types of international agreements that the Community signs with third countries (see Table 5.2).

Table 5.2 *Types of European Community Agreements with third countries*

Type of agreement	Legal basis	Main points	Examples
Cooperation Agreement	Art. 238 (EEC)	Grant MFN status	1988 Gulf States States Agreement (UAE, Bahrein, Oman, Kuwait, Qatar, Saudi Arabia)
			1988 Czechoslovakia
Trade and Co-operation Agreement	Art. 238 (EEC)	Grant MFN status	Maghreb States 1977 (Morocco, Algeria, Tunisia)
		Preferential special trade liberalization (one way, no reciprocity)	
		Restrictions maintained on agriculture, textiles	
	Art. 238 (EEC)	Grant MFN status	1988 Hungary 1989 Poland 1990 Romania 1990 USSR 1990 Bulgaria
		Preferential trade liberalization. Removal of quantitative restrictions	
		Agenda for future cooperation	
		Safeguard measures	
Association Agreements	Art. 238 (EEC)	Political dialogue	1991 Europe. Agreements, e.g. 1991 Hungary 1991 Poland 1993 Bulgaria
		Free trade area	
		10-year preferential asymmetrical trade liberalization (reciprocity)	
		Safeguard measures	
		Future economic cooperation	

The European Community and external relations

1 *Cooperation Agreements:* These are usually restricted to infant relations between the EC and the third country. Co-operation Agreements only usually reaffirm the MFN principle of GATT. They open further avenues for negotiation, which may or may not include trade liberalization. The EC signed a limited Cooperation Agreement with Slovenia in 1993, as the first step in relations with a new Central European state[21].
2 *Trade and Cooperation Agreements:* These represent the next 'rung' or level in closer relations for third countries with the EC, for example, the EC initially signed a Cooperation Agreement with Czechoslovakia in December 1988, due to its limited programme of economic reform; this was however quickly replaced by an EC Trade and Cooperation Agreement in May 1990, once this process of reform had speeded up[22]. These agreements usually include limited trade concessions on quantitative restrictions to third parties. Reciprocity may be part of the agreements. The Community signs these types of agreements with economically weaker states, allowing for asymmetrical trade liberalization to occur. The EC progressively liberalizes its quantitative restrictions facilitating gradual open access to its markets, but excluding certain sensitive products, such as steel, chemicals or agricultural products. The only usual reciprocal requirement is the recognition of MFN status on EC exports. These agreements also include a wider agenda for future cooperation. The EC has signed these types of agreements with Eastern European and the Mediterranean Maghreb and Mashreq states.
3 *Association Agreements:* The EC may offer or sign an Association Agreement under Article 238. These aim to strengthen relations between the Community and the third country through long-term trade liberalization. The Association Agreements normally establish a free-trade area between the EC and the non-Member State and usually include an asymmetrical long-term reduction in tariffs and quantitative restrictions. The Community usually plays the leading role in making concessions first. Examples of these agreements are the 'Europe' agreements between the EC and Hungary and Poland, the Czech and Slovak Republics, and Bulgaria. They provide for a ten-year programme of trade liberalization with the EC removing all its restrictions in the first five years. This type of agreement is concluded with states wishing to join the Community in the future. The signing of the Association Agreement does not however guarantee EC membership in the short term, but is usually seen as a positive step towards it.

The European Economic Area (EEA): The Community has also developed closer formal relationships than even Association Agreements. The EC signed a unique and comprehensive agreement in 1991 with the EFTA states, which created the 'European Economic Area' (EEA) on 1 January 1994. The EEA has been widely regarded as the EC's most ambitious agreement with non-Member States. It establishes an advanced free trade area between the EC and the EFTA states (excluding Switzerland) allowing for 'the fullest possible realization' of the free movement of goods, services, persons and capital[23]. Crucially, the EEA allows the EFTA states (excluding Switzerland) to gain greater access to the EC's Single European Market programme, short of membership. It has also been widely seen as an `ante-chamber' or waiting room for the EC's most eligible future applicants, for example, Sweden, Finland, Austria and Norway.

The Lomé Conventions: The EC has established special generous arrangements with the developing world. Trading relations between the EC and its original former colonies were recognized as important right from the Community's inception. The previous colonies of France, Holland and Belgium received special recognition in the Treaty of Rome and generous arrangements were made in the original Yaounde Conventions (I 1963; II 1969). Today, EC relations with the developing world (which are otherwise known as the ACP (African–Caribbean–Pacific) states) are governed by the Lomé Conventions. The Lomé Conventions (I 1975; II 1979; III 1984; IV 1989) have been seen as a 'symbol of continuity, renovation and innovation', despite the ACP states accounting for only 3.9 per cent of EC external imports.

The Lomé Conventions provide for an asymmetrical relationship in which the ACP states gain open access to EC markets. These are the most generous agreements financially offered by the EC to non-Member States, with Lomé IV funding amounting to some ECU 12,000 million for the period 1990–1995[24]. Lomé includes systems such as SYSMIN and STABEX which are special support measures for minerals and commodities and go beyond normal trade liberalization[25]. Both the EEA and the Lomé Conventions are specialist, tailor-made agreements, based not on the limited array of EC formal powers, but are responses to dynamic political relations with these regions of EC trade.

It can be concluded that there are several overriding factors which dictate what level and generosity of agreement the EC signs with non-Member States. Although the EC claims to support GATT principles of non-discrimination, it has been active in establishing a hierarchy of trading relations between itself and non-Member States. It can be argued that this is based on six factors, which operate collectively.

1 *The degree of 'economic threat':* In other words, the level of competition that the third country provides against the EC. This is usually dependent on the third country or groupings level of economic development. The

The European Community and external relations

EC offers the ACP states preferential concessions as these are a weak grouping economically and do not pose a substantial economic threat.

2 *The degree of leverage the EC enjoys in trade negotiations:* This depends on whether the EC is the 'senior' or dominant partner in the negotiations. The EC can be generous with the ACP states as it sets the Lomé agenda mostly on its own terms due to the donor–donee relationship. The EC is cautious in dealing with the USA or Japan where it could be viewed as an economically weaker partner in the trading relationship.

3 *Geographic proximity and trade significance.* The EC's largest trading partners are usually the closest geographically. The EC was willing to conclude the EEA agreement with the EFTA states as they are geographically close, collectively represent the Community's largest trading partner and form a logical extension to the Single European Market. Equally, the EC was able to offer the `Europe' Agreements to the Central European states, partly because of their geographic proximity and status as promising export markets.

4 *The legacy of existing or past trading patterns:* The EC has also consistently addressed the problems of the ACP states as key member states have historically close ties and trade links with some of their former colonies. The Lomé Conventions must be understood in terms of Europe's post-war imperial legacy[26].

5 *Wider EC political priorities.* The extent of EC political interest in that region of the world. External trade policy does not operate in a vacuum and trading relations are part of a wider political agenda. Terms and application of agreements have been influenced by wider EC concerns for human rights or democracy; for example, the 1963 EC-Turkish Association Agreement was suspended in the early 1980s due to Turkey's return to military rule. The EC's initial reaction to the reforms in Eastern Europe was to immediately allocate it a high place in the EC's hierarchy of external relations, reflecting the Community's priorities.

6 *Sectoral discrimination.* The nature of the non-Member States' main trade with the EC. The EC has faced heavy criticism that the 'Europe' Agreements with Central and Eastern Europe were too restrictive. It has maintained restrictions on Central Europe's main exports of steel, textiles, agricultural products and chemicals, despite these products representing 45 per cent of all the exports to the EC. For example, the Commission slapped provisional anti-dumping duties on Polish and Czech steel tubes and in April 1993, the EC agreed to limit imports of six types of Czech and Slovak steel to 1991 levels, adding 35 per cent in 1994[27]. These are sensitive EC industries facing existing problems of oversupply and rationalization, and demanding protection.

Hence, the Community maintains sectoral discrimination and ignores 'uniform' attitudes to trade liberalization. Although the EC has progressively reduced its general level of protection through constant reductions in the CET, the Community has also been careful not to radically change the structure of protection that it enjoys. Generally, the EC has maintained high levels of protection and restrictions on chemicals, textiles, steel and agriculture. Some areas, textiles for example, have been specifically regulated by restrictive international agreements, such as the Multi-Fibre Agreement (MFA). Yet, this sectoral protection has generally been common to all states in the GATT framework. Nevertheless, the Community has come under intense pressure to liberalize these sectors due to its disproportionate influence on world trade and its emphasis on long-term trade liberalization as the main corner-stone of trade policy.

Overall, despite the rhetoric, the EC has been more concerned with maintaining an international and sectoral hierarchy of trading relations rather than seeking the harmonious development of world trade. This hierarchy is actually proving to be a growing source of friction for the EC and an ironic contributor to international trade disharmony. The disputes in the GATT Uruguay Round have forced the EC to be more conciliatory and subtly to reconsider certain aspects of its discriminatory policy.

A uniform and supranational Common Commercial Policy?

The Community's intention of achieving a comprehensive and supranational CCP has not proved a complete success either. The EC Commission's ability to exercise measures under the CCP has been restricted in practice. Despite the Commission being the official negotiator for the EC in international trade negotiations, it has still faced problems of internal disunity within the Commission and from Member States. The Commission has failed at times to maintain a united voice. In the GATT negotiations, the Commission was openly divided in 1992 with the its President, Jacques Delors and the EC agricultural negotiator, Ray MacSharry, differing on the Blair House accord.

The Commission has also found it difficult to reconcile international pressure with the national interests of the Member States. The EC Commission has faced resistance from Member States in certain trade negotiations. The supranational cohesiveness of the CCP has proved illusive and has been challenged by Member States; for example, France threatened to veto the 1992 EC–US Blair House Accord on oilseeds in GATT in 1993 (see Appendix 5.2). The inability of the EC Commission to persuade individual Member States to maintain EC policy lines has undermined the EC's credibility in external relations.

The operation of an effective CCP is intrinsically linked to the Member States implicit recognition of limitations on their freedom of action in trading relations. Member States must enforce the CCP universally. This has not entirely proved the case in practice. Member States have consistently sought to limit the supranationality of the CCP where it conflicts with national interests and traditional trading relations. The issue of Member State bilateral agreements with non Member States is illustrative. The German government in 1993 refused to impose token trade sanctions against the US on telecommunications, citing that the EC policy conflicts with a 1954 German–US non-aggression pact on telecommunications[28].

THE EC's Common Commercial Policy and sources of possible friction

The CCP is not completely uniform or comprehensively governed at the supranational level. This causes concern as there are six major challenges that will dominate EC's trading relations into the 1990s.

1   *Reconciling the CCP and GATT:* One of the themes of this chapter has been the intrinsic relationship between the EC's CCP and the role of GATT. The Community's relationship to and role within the GATT framework remains the greatest challenge that the EC faces today. It is notable that most important GATT initiatives have coincided with significant events inside the EC. The adoption of the SEM programme by the EC coincided with GATT's Uruguay Round being launched at Punte del Este in September 1986. European integration is linked to international trade liberalization[29].

    Within the GATT Uruguay Round, the Community faced a number of problematical issues (see Appendix 5.1). Although the GATT deal will bring considerable benefits and reached agreement in many areas (see Appendix 5.3), there are still several aspects of its agenda, such as financial services, telecommunications, audio-visual equipment and maritime transport, where consensus was only partially reached. These issues will remain areas of contention in international trade. In particular, the GATT deal envisages the agreement being implemented by a new World Trade Organization (WTO). One of the major challenges the EC faces is progressively reconciling its international role as a trading bloc with the traditional global role of GATT and its new WTO successor. The preferential hierarchy of EC external relations needs to be more firmly legitimized within the GATT structure. The EC must endeavour to provide realistic solutions.

2 *Reconciling the Community's Common Agricultural Policy (CAP) with world agricultural trade:* The CAP has wider implications for a harmonious CCP with non-Member States. The Community's CAP is clearly protectionist aiming to maintain high prices and security of supply of agricultural products through price support and restricting foreign agricultural imports. The Community has provided export subsidies for farmers leading to allegations of the 'dumping' of agricultural products on world markets and the depressing of world market prices.

The CCP does include the external aspects of the CAP. This was traditionally a minor issue within the CCP as agricultural products were mostly excluded from progressive trade liberalization. However, the CAP became a major issue in the Uruguay Round, as it placed agricultural questions firmly on the agenda. An agricultural arrangement was agreed with the Blair House Accord. The following 1993 deal and farm trade reform represents 90 per cent of the suspected $213 billion a year increase in trade from the Round. Yet, this agreement is still rather minimal and has not placated all US concerns on agricultural questions. It will remain a problematical area for world trade. Ironically, the major beneficiary from the agricultural deal will initially be the EC gaining the majority of its estimated increase in trade ($80 billion a year, World Bank/OECD, 1993) from a reduction in agricultural prices. Yet the external implications of the CAP's protectionism have increased friction with non-Member States, bordering at times on open trade wars. The challenge for the EC will still be to reconcile the CAP's role in world markets with CAP internal reform, providing a clearer definition of its place within the CCP framework. In practice, the EC should ensure that the MacSharry CAP reforms agreed in 1992 are compatible with the GATT deal.

3 *Improved trading relations with the USA and Japan.* The third challenge for the EC will be to redefine the EC's relations with key non Member States. EC relations with the USA have been preoccupied by the problems of agriculture and the Uruguay GATT agenda. The Community must be cautious in placating US fears of the EC's rising profile in international trading relations and its protectionist tendencies to develop a `Fortress Europe'.

4 *Managing the progressive liberalization of sensitive sectors of EC trade.* The Community faces the dilemma of appeasing external pressure for further trade liberalization and access to EC markets while managing the internal problems of declining industries and over supply within EC domestic markets. This will dominate EC relations especially with Central Europe. Poland, Hungary, the Czech and Slovak Republics, Romania and Bulgaria sent 75 per cent of their exports to the EC in 1992, only half of which

The European Community and external relations

entered duty free. The EC faces intense pressure to liberalize steel and textile quotas to facilitate the regeneration of central Europe at a time when the EC faces problems in rationalizing its own steel industries.

5   *EC relations with emerging regional trading arrangements:* The 1993 deal has raised the profile and expectations of GATT within the global economy. Yet, there was frustration at the protracted Uruguay Round negotiations, which ran from 1986 to 1993. The problems of the Uruguay Round led to crisis in confidence within the GATT framework. Probably the greatest success of the GATT deal is that it has avoided the possibility of further regional trade wars between regional associations. However, there has been a growing tendency for states to seek alternative ways of guaranteeing freer trade with their closest neighbours. There has been a shift from global free trade towards a system of managed trade within regional trading arrangements. It was estimated in 1988 that 41.4 per cent of world trade fell within existing regional trading arrangements, with another 4.9 per cent falling within new arrangements between the EC and Eastern Europe and NAFTA[30]. There has been a proliferation in the number of major regional trading organizations, for example NAFTA, Caricom and the Asia Pacific Economic Co-operation (APEC) Forum. The success of GATT has averted initial future trade wars, but has not removed the desire of states to seek further free trade through managed regional organizations.

Since these regional trading arrangements are discriminatory, there is also a likelihood that the EC may encounter trade friction with other regional groupings. A major challenge in the 1990s will be to develop EC relations with these new blocs and avert potential trade wars. Greater usage of 'peace clauses' may provide a temporary answer (see Appendix 5.2).

6   *Maintain EC relations with the developing world.* As the stature of the EC has grown, so has the expectation of the developing world that the EC should provide more generous arrangements for economic development. The Community has maintained a sound trading arrangement with the ACP states through the Lomé Conventions. Friction between the EC and the developing ACP states has increased as the EC has progressively become more cautious in financing the economic problems of the ACP states. The EC will need to placate ACP fears that they are a lesser priority now that Eastern Europe is a pressing issue for the EC.

The EC faces the problem that if it claims to be a world trading entity, it must develop better relations with other parts of the developing world. The Community has faced criticism in 1993 for discriminating against poor Latin American states, such as Ecuador, in favour of more expensive trade with its traditional ACP partners. The Lomé Conventions new preferential banana 1993 regime was heavily criticized by GATT for breaking international trade rules as it discriminated against high-quality Latin American bananas in favour of more expensive ACP bananas. The Community will need to readdress these issues and ensure that the Lomé Convention is legitimized through the GATT framework. Indeed, the Community has announced a renegotiation of Lomé IV in September 1993 in order to take account of these concerns[31].

Conclusion

The EC does have a dramatic influence on international world trade and has developed into a trading power in its own right. The Community maintains a somewhat complex and comprehensive CCP and has a clear hierarchy of trading relations with third countries. Yet, the EC is still not an economic superpower in the sense that has been predisposed to the USA in the past. The CCP has been restricted by national interests and internal tensions in practice. The EC is an important but not dominant element within the GATT framework, able to flout GATT rules, but unwilling and unable to replace it. However, the EC may become more influential if the trend towards regional trading arrangements continues. It will be a leading arbiter in any future negotiations on the nature of the global trading economy. The European Community may not be a trading superpower yet, but will remain a major player in setting the international trading agenda.

References

1 Griffiths, A (ed.) (1992) *European Community Survey*, London: Longman, p. 33.
2 *The Financial Times* (1993) IMF World Economy and Finance Survey, 24 September 1993, p. IX.
3 Commission of the ECs (1993), *Eurostat Statistical Yearbook 1992*, Brussels, p. 132.
4 Commission of the ECs (1992), *Europe in Figures*, Third Edition, Brussels: Eurostat. p. 17.
5 *Agence Europe* (1993) No.6049, 25th August 1993, Brussels, p. 7.
6 Redmond, J. (ed.) (1992) *The External Relations of the European Community*, London: Macmillan, p. 2.
7 For a more detailed critique see Archer, C. (1992) *International Organisations*, Second Edition, London: Routledge, pp. 38–70.
8 The concept of 'civilian power' is more deeply analysed in Bull, 'Civilian Power Europe: A Contradiction in Terms?' in *Journal of Common Market Studies (JCMS)*, 21, 1982.
9 McDonald, F. and Dearden, S. (eds.) (1992) *European Economic Integration*, London: Longman, 1992, pp. 146–147.

10 Lodge, J. (ed.) (1993) *The European Community and the Challenge of the Future*, Second Edition, London: Pinter, pp. 227–251.
11 Article 110 states that 'By establishing a customs union between themselves Member States aim to contribute, in the common interest, to the harmonious development of world trade, the progressive abolition of restrictions on international trade and the lowering of customs barriers.'
12 For more detailed analysis see Hine, R.C. (1985) *The Political Economy of European Trade*, Hemel Hempstead: Harvester Wheatsheaf, pp.74–99.
13 See *Opinion 1/75 ECR 1355* or further details in Shaw, H. (1993) *European Community Law*, London: Macmillan, pp. 238–257.
14 For a more comprehensive discussion see Hitiris, T. (1991) *European Community Economics*, Second Edition, Hemel Hempstead: Harvester Wheatsheaf, pp. 207–215.
15 Molle, W. (1990) *The Economics of European Community Integration*, Aldershot: Dartmouth, p. 443.
16 Winter, A. (1991) *International Economics*, Fourth Edition, London: Harper Collins, pp. 140–145.
17 The *Financial Times*, (1993) *China Faces Steep EC Duties on Bikes*, 9 September 1993, p. 4.
18 This was analysed in greater detail in the EC Commission's *Fifth Report on the Implementation of the White Paper on the Internal Market*, COM (90) 90, or see Shaw, J. (1993) *op. cit.* p. 251–256.
19 *The Financial Times* (1993) Court Turns Down German Challenge To Banana Regime, 30 June 1993, p. 34.
20 See McDonald, F and Dearden, S (1992) op. cit. pp. 149–150.
21 Commission of the ECs, (1993c) Week In Europe, 11th September 1993, Brussels, p. 1.
22 Commission of the ECs, (1991) *EC-Eastern Europe Relations DGX Background Brief*, Brussels, p. 4.
23 European Free Trade Association, *The EEA Agreement*, 2/92, Geneva: EFTA, p. 1.
24 Commission of the ECs, (1992) *European Development Cooperation Policy Background Report*, ISEC/B32/92, 8 December 1992, p. 1.
25 Hewitt, A. (1993) 'Development Assistance Policy and the ACP' in Lodge, J. (ed.) *The European Community and the Challenge of the Future*, Second Edition, London: Pinter, pp. 301–311.
26 See Cosgrove, C. and Laurent, P.-H. (1992) The Unique Relationship: The EC and the ACP, in Redmond, J. (ed.) p. 120.
27 *The Economist*, The Two Europes, Poor Relations, Vol. 327, No. 7806, 1 May 1993, pp. 46–47.
28 *The Financial Times*, (1993) Brussels Goes To Court In Dispute Over Trade

Policy, 6 July 1993, p.4.
29 For a more detailed critique, see Tsoukalis, L. (1993) *The New European Economy*, New York: Oxford University Press, pp. 278–332.
30 De Le Torre, A. and Kelly, M. (1992) Regional Trade Arrangements, Occasional Paper 93, Washington D.C.: International Monetary Fund, p. 2.
31 Commission of the ECs, (1993f) *Week In Europe*, 16 September 1993, Brussels, p. 1.

Appendix 5.1: The European Community and the GATT Uruguay Round

The GATT Uruguay Round issues at stake in the negotiations in 1993

Agricultural trade

Liberalization of farm sectors.
Issue of open access to agricultural markets.
Transparency of governmental support for agriculture.
Removal of export subsidies.

Comprehensive tarification

Removal of easily manipulated forms of protection, e.g. quotas.
Transparency in, and eventual removal of, non-tariff barriers.
Agree new GATT market access package.

Textiles

Phasing out of quota restrictions under Multi-Fibre arrangement.

Steel

Dealing with global over-capacity and complex series of subsidies to sector.

Trade in services

Liberalization of banking, insurance, securities, construction, distribution, tourism, software and computer services and professional business services. Opening up financial services markets across the developing world.

Maritime services

Port and on-shore facilities to be liberalized.

Audio-visual services

Abolition of national limits on sales of films and TV programmes.
Removal of local-language minimum programming requirements.

Intellectual property rights
Global protection of copyright and patents.
Uniform enforcement of intellectual property protection from books to music and computer software.
Concessions on royalties to pharmaceutical companies for usage of drugs in developing world.

Dispute settlement
GATT dispute procedures presently slow and weak.
Strengthen GATT authority.
Introduce GATT trade weapons and sanctions.
Remove bilateral trade weapons, such as US Section 301.

Subsidies, dumping and procurement
New and modified GATT 'Codes' on subsidies, dumping and procurement procedures.
Greater number of signatories to agree to 'Code' disciplines.

Appendix 5.2: 1992 'Blair House' Agreement: US–EC Accord

Main points

Subsidized farm exports to be cut by 21 per cent in volume over six years. Value to be cut by 36 per cent, with internal price supports trimmed by 29 per cent.

EC land for oilseeds production limited to 5.128 million hectares.

Oilseeds for industrial use limited to 1 million tonnes.

10 per cent of EC oilseeds land to be 'set aside' permanently.

Compensation allowed to EC farmers for taking land out of production.

A six-year 'Peace Clause' agreed on outstanding disputes.
Prevents either the US or the C from taking unilateral action against each other on trade and reduces chances of future trade wars.

Extension to EC agreement to curb exports of subsidized beef to Asian countries.

(Modified from *Financial Times*, 20 September, 1993, p. 3)

Appendix 5.3 Overview of the 15 December 1993 GATT Uruguay deal

Area	Agreement
Industrial tariffs	Tariffs on industrial goods cut by more than a third. 40 per cent of imports enter duty-free. Scrap duties on specific areas, e.g. pharmaceuticals, steel; beer.
Agriculture	Subsidies and import barriers cut over six years. Farm support reduced 20 per cent. Subsidized exports down 36 per cent in value and 21 per cent in volume. Japan and South Korea open rice markets.
Services	Non-discrimination framework special provisions for air transport. Further talks on telecommunications and financial services.
Intellectual property	Agreements on patents, copyright, trademarks. International standards of protection and enforcement.
Textiles and clothing	Multi-Fibre Arrangement quotas dismantled over ten years and tariffs cut. Developing countries lower trade barriers.
Anti-dumping duties	Rules for investigations and criteria on dumping. Duties lapse in five years.
Subsidies and safeguards	Define legal types of subsidies. Leeway for developing states. Rules for Safeguards. Not exceed four years and then liberalized.
GATT rules	Revised codes on customs valuations, licensing, state aids, waivers on customs unions and FTAs.
Technical barriers	Rules on technical norms, testing and certification.
Government procurement	Separate accord on services, public works, procurement by regional/local governments.
World Trade Organization	GATT now permanent world trade body (goods, services, rights). WTO implements GATT deal.
Dispute settlement	Rules on adoption of reports. Binding arbitration and appeals.

Part Two The Case Studies

Case 1 The EC coal industry: into the twenty-first century

Colin Turner

Introduction

Coal was the foundation stone for the development of the modern European Economy. It was the energy source that propelled many of these countries to greatness. Yet since the end of the last war, coal has been on a seemingly inexorable decline. The heart of this piece is how this decline is being managed by the EC and the major coal producing Member States. This has to be seen in the light of a noticeable shift in energy policy, within the EC, as decisions in this sector are increasingly taken out of the hands of planners and left more to the market. The purpose of this case study is, therefore, not about the history of the sector, but about its recent past and prospects for the future.

The first section of this study will note the challenges and processes of change within the EC coal sector. The second section will note EC's policy towards this sector and how it is likely to evolve in the future. The final section seeks to analyse recent and future trends for the industry within the major coal producing Member States.

The EC coal industry

The purpose of this section is to set the scene for later parts when the specific countries and companies involved will be examined in greater depth. This section will seek to point out general themes and policies that will have an inevitable bearing upon the development of the coal industry over the next few decades. What is important to recognize in institutional, political and economic terms, is that it is the EC that sets the framework within which national coal producers operate. The coal sector itself is managed by the ECSC (European Coal and Steel Community) which, despite its original objectives, has evolved to control the decline within this industry.

Solid fuels

Recent trends

Solid fuels (that is hard coal and lignite) account for some 22.5 per cent and 29.7 per cent of EC energy consumption and production respectively (1991). In 1980 the share, in terms of production, was some 40 per cent. In 1991 some 59.3 per cent of the EC's consumption of coal was met by indigenous sources; in 1980 the figure was well over 80 per cent. Linked with this decline in the use of indigenous coal there has been a reduction in the level of employment within the sector. In 1991, the sector employed over a quarter of a million fewer people than it did a decade before. A decline in employment of some 57 per cent over the period. True to this picture, coal production across the EC has declined by a quarter since 1980.

Coal production across the EC is, on the whole, concentrated in four main states; of these the UK, Germany and Spain account for some 93.4 per cent of total production. Within all of these Member States there has been a significant decline in the level of coal production over the last decade or so. The relative extent of this decline will become apparent in later sections. The decline in the use, and hence the production, of coal has been hit by rising imports and changes in the relative price of other fuels, especially hydrocarbons. The competitiveness of EC coal has been hit by the fact that a large proportion of it (some 90 per cent) is deep mined and, thus, as resources dwindle, mines have to get deeper and operating costs soar. This position is compounded by the fact that the EC's major competitors in coal production obtain the majority of it from cheaper open cast mines (50 per cent – Australia; 60 per cent – USA; 85 per cent – Canada). Compare this to the fact that German coal is, on average, mined at a depth of some 900 metres.

Over time, due to persistent price differentials, EC-produced coal has lost competitiveness with the imported product. This has provoked a spate of rationalization within the EC. In the UK, for example, the number of mines has fallen by some 45 per cent in the eleven years to 1991, and as the recent coal review showed, this is likely to continue. As a result of these changes some 40 per cent of the EC's coal consumption is imported. The ECSC has sought to achieve a single market in coal but the discretion allowed to Member States in this sector means that attempts to achieve this have, on the whole, proved fruitless and intra-EC trade remains marginal.

The market for coal

Demand

Of the coal demanded in the EC, some 62 per cent is used in power generation; its other major use is in the production of coke for the steel industry. This area has declined over the last decade or so as steel production in the EC has fallen by 30 per cent. Over the decade up to 1991 there has been a rise in the demand for coal in power generation, but world recession and technological changes have offset this by reducing its demand in other areas, most notably industrial and domestic uses. As these have declined so the importance of power generation to the coal industry has risen and is now vital to the future of the sector. As a result governments across the EC

The EC coal industry: into the twenty-first century

have been keen to offer incentives to power producers to use domestically produced coal. But due to the high nature of fixed and sunk costs involved in the use of coal, producers would only tend to switch if there was a sufficient incentive, be it a preferential price or a subsidy. As the price of hydro-carbons has fallen so there has been pressure to substitute towards these away from coal.

Supply

Obviously the supply of coal into the EC can come from imports or from indigenous production. At the moment it is estimated that EC reserves stand at some 33 billion tonnes (1989) which, it is estimated, will last some 170 years at current rates of production. But due to the relatively costly nature of coal production in the EC the economic viability of these reserves cannot be assured.

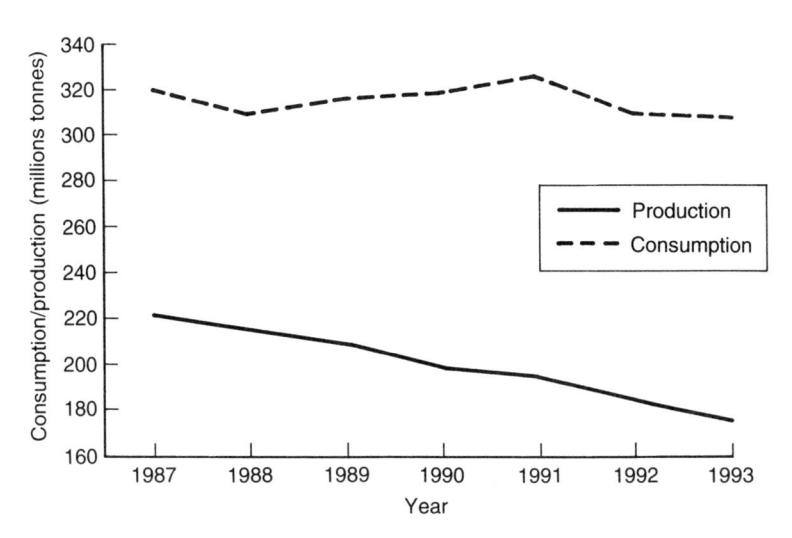

Figure C1.1 EC coal production and consumption 1987–1993 (est.) (source: Eurostat)

Processes of change

Over the past decade there has been a general process of rationalization within this sector right across the EC. The major threat has been to the marginal pits which have been sacrificed to put the industry in a position where it will be able to compete on more effective terms with imports.

The level of coal that is used in industry has been on an inexorable decline, and its use is mainly limited to large consumers. On the whole, coal's use within European industry is limited due to:

1. high investment cost of coal plant and long pay back times,
2. high operating costs,
3. price and regulatory uncertainty,
4. an image problem,
5. a lack of clean coal technology for small consumers.

As a result, in this sector of the market, there has to be a significant and persistent price differential between coal and its substitutes, if any uptake in its demand is to occur.

From what has been said it is clear that in general across the EC, the future for coal is not bright and one can see the recent trends continuing into the future.

DRI, a consultancy group, estimates that by the year 2000 there will have been a decline in the production of EC coal by some 35 per cent, while the level of consumption is estimated to rise by approximately 23 per cent. As a result one can only expect the level of imports of coal within the EC to rise even further. It estimates some 71 per cent of consumption will be met by imports by the year 2000. In addition, DRI expects the competitiveness of EC coal to deteriorate as the price differential with imports is maintained or even widens. As a result, it is likely that if the industry is to survive, it will have to battle harder to win favours from the governments and their main customers or it will have to cease the resistance to change and rationalize at a quicker rate.

Figures from the EC suggest a bleaker trend between 1990 and 2000; coal consumption is estimated to fall by 4.4 per cent while consumption for other fuels over the period is expected to rise markedly (gas 46 per cent; oil 13 per cent). In terms of production the EC expects a fall of around a third while, on the whole, other fuels will see their production rise by an average of 13 per cent. As a result of these changes, it is expected that coal imports will rise by 78 per cent over the period. Though the coal input into power generation is expected to rise by some 9.5 per cent, this rise is overshadowed by the expected rise in gas as a form of power (a rise of 141 per cent over the period). This coupled with a fall in the use of the fuel in industry means that the overall coal consumption will fall by 29 per cent while the other fuels will see a rise of somewhere in the order of 22 per cent. In terms of electricity generation capacities, it is estimated that there will be a net expansion of coal of 1.966 GW'S, this is poor compared to the rise in the use of gas (some 76 GW's).

A final factor that seems to reinforce the bleak future for EC coal is an estimate by the EC that up to the year 1994 (and probably beyond) the competitive advantage of imports will increase as the price of EC coal rises by 2.8 per cent, while the price of the imported product declines by an estimated 5 per cent.

The role of the EC

The coal sector is covered by the Treaty of Paris and the industry is thus coordinated by the ECSC. Over time the ECSC's function has altered in that it now has to seek to manage the decline of this sector in a way that does not create a great deal of social upheaval. Thus it has allowed the sector a degree of protection from the market and has encouraged (unsuccessfully) a number of initiatives to promote the consumption of coal. However, with the EC's lurch towards liberalization, both internally and externally, the assistance given to the sector looks increasingly anachronistic.

Energy is an important cost to EC firms and having to pay inflated prices because of the protection afforded to this sector could put them at a competitive disadvantage. Hence the EC faces a problem of how to reconcile the conflicting aims of a more efficient energy sector with the social and economic problems caused by coal's decline. This is not only a problem for the EC but also for the Member States who may seek to blame and use the EC as an excuse for such politically unpopular but economically necessary decisions.

EC state aid policy towards coal

State aid, for example, subsidies and low interest loans, have been a traditional form of assistance given by Member States to their coal producers. Despite them being on the whole against EC law. Despite the treaty of Paris prohibiting most forms of aid the problems of the coal sector mean the EC allows, subject to its approval, some forms of assistance. However, the EC's attempts to enforce the spirit of its treaties have been resisted by the major coal producing Member States. To get around the conflict of the Member States desires and the provisions of the Treaties, the EC has sought to justify aid in terms of security of supply. This is particularly true in the 1970s. In the 1980s the EC has sought to get tougher, stressing economic viability as the major concern of the coal sector. The policy has evolved to stress transparency of procedures (that is the ability to detect illegal aid more easily) and a decline of aid in real terms. To an extent, these have been achieved.

Currently state aid to the sector is governed by the decision 2064/86/ECSC. Under this, aid is deemed to be compatible with the common market if it contributes to one or more of the following objectives:

1 improvement of competitiveness of the coal industry which contributes to assure a better security of supply;
2 creating new capacities provided they are economically viable;
3 solving the social and regional problems related to developments in the coal industry.

In seeking to achieve these aims the level of aid in general should not exceed that which is deemed necessary to achieve the above objectives. To be an effective judge of the level of subsidies that are being granted, the EC needs a high degree of transparency and greater information so that all forms of assistance can be included, and their appropriateness with EC law assessed. Under this scheme some of the types of aid that are considered admissible are:

1 aid to cover losses (if not doing so would mean closing a big part of the sector);
2 aid to help productivity;
3 aid to help cure regional problems resulting from the decline.

Over the last few years the level of aid given to the Member States has been rising as they had to meet the redundancy costs of the rationalization of the their coal industry. However, under all this the EC policy towards this sector remains as stated in article 4(c) of the Treaty, that 'the primary purpose of any coal industry . . . must be economic profitability'[2].

In 2002 the Treaty of Paris expires and the sector will come under the Rome Treaty which is likely to signal a 'get-tough' attitude on Member States' policy towards this industry. In terms of its policy towards this sector, any victories that the EC has had in seeking to achieve its objective have been pyrrhic as Member States have, in effect, done exactly what they wanted. Since aid was first allowed in 1965 Member States have given some ECU 75 billion to the industry and, on current trends, this will continue to rise even further. Hence the major problem continues to be over the lack of transparency of aid which inhibits the detection of all forms of assistance.The heart of the problem, in terms of state aid policy, is '(the) Commission has adjusted to the industry not vice versa'[3].

The EC has had to adjust rules due to the reluctance of Member States to accept them. This is a problem that the EC has to seek to overcome with its new proposal. The new proposal which is the basis for the new regulation, once the old one expires in 1993, seeks to increase transparency and clarity of existing aid schemes. In addition it should step up restructuring of the sector. It has to be seen if the EC is going to be more steadfast in promoting change or if it is to continue to make conciliatory noises. Perhaps when Member States become fully aware of the inevitability of decline in this sector then, for political reasons if nothing else, they will start to impose the EC's rules with more alacrity. Clearly another forum where the EC can seek to spark change is in its aims for the internal energy market.

The internal energy market

A second area of challenge and change for the sector is in the desire of the EC to create an internal energy market (IEM). The aim of this is to integrate the energy markets within the EC by introducing a greater degree of competition so lowering costs while maintaining Member States' security of supply considerations.

In addition, it aims to provide a wider element of economic and social cohesion, which is necessary if the longer-term ambitions of the EC are to be achieved. Moreover, it is about shifting the emphasis in terms of energy use from planners to the sphere of the market. Thus energy, and by implication coal, will be like any other commodity whose use is determined, to a great extent, by the free interplay of market forces.

Technically the EC should already have a common market in this sector. However this is a sector that tends to be tightly regulated and, therefore, a number of obstacles exist to the attainment of a true single market. These barriers tend to limit intra-EC trade (presently just some 3 per cent of EC coal production is traded in such a fashion), promote vertical restraints within various sectors of the market and restrict the level of imports from third countries.

Important elements in distorting the EC market for coal, as noted above, are the vertical arrangements between EC producers and consumers which tend to exist in most, if not all, EC coal producing Member States. These take the form of long-term market guarantees between the domestic producers and consumers thus limiting any competition from third parties. In short, these agreements take the form of a contract where the consumers of coal, in the main the big electricity and steel producers, agree to take an agreed quantity of coal at a specified price. Strictly speaking these agreements do not rule out the use of coal produced elsewhere in the EC, thus do not technically represent a barrier to trade. However, they do restrict competition from other fuels and imports.

As regards imports this is an area of trade that is not governed by the Common Commercial Policy. Hence Member States are allowed to set their own limits upon how much coal they choose to import from third countries. To prevent trade deflection there is very limited circulation of imported coal within the EC. This combined with biased public procurement policies in this sector, as well as the state aid problems noted earlier, combine to form strict restrictions on trade within the EC. But coal imports are becoming harder to resist as the price becomes increasingly competitive. Indeed it is expected that there will be a 78 per cent rise in imported coal in the decade up to the year 2000. With the liberalization of energy markets the coal sector is going to be hit by competition from other fuels which will almost inevitably hit the level of coal consumed in the EC. The fundamental change in the EC's policy is that it has shifted its goal and is thus seeking to manage policy rather than let policy be shaped by industry. The desire for liberalization, and increased competition will have profound effects upon those areas which produce coal creating social and economic change. These changes will have an important bearing upon the development of coal policy.

Regional problems and the decline of coal

Inevitable consequences of the move towards a more open market for energy, and thus the likely decline of coal, are the regional problems that will accompany it. As these coal producing regions are areas of prolonged decline any increase in unemployment will tend to make their problems even more acute. The move towards a more efficient coal industry is likely to exacerbate these problems. Indeed its decline will tend to foster a knock on effect on supply industries thus the decline will have a strong local multiplier effect. These regional problems will not be helped by the fact that these areas tend to be:

1 dominated by a single industry;
2 divided into a large number of relatively small and dispersed communities;
3 geographically isolated, suffering from an inadequate infrastructure;
4 environmentally challenged; and that
5 ex-mining skills are not easily transferred to other industries.

Hence 'the effect of all of these factors is to make coal dominated areas particularly vulnerable to economic changes and unattractive as a location of new industries and investment'[4].

As a result they are able to get regional aid under the 1985 refinement of regional aid – classified under group two objective areas, that is areas of industrial decline.

Bearing in mind these problems, the coal sector gets specific help and assistance. The benefit it gets helps to off set the social and regional costs of decline. In addition, the state aid regulation states that help given to the coal industry must 'solve' the social and regional problems related to 'developments' in the coal industry. A good proportion of this aid is given to finance the social security payments related to structural change.

The EC has also offered re-adaptation aids which aim to cushion the decline in this sector. For those workers facing redundancy, aid is given to encourage retraining, to facilitate mobility, etc. These are believed to have produced a very significant easing of the restructuring process (see Rees and Thomas 1992) but need to do more to seek the proper re-allocation of labour.

Another policy put forward is RECHAR, which is an EC initiative to strengthen support for the coal face. Its aim is to promote feasible economic initiatives likely to increase employment prospects for ex-miners, as well as improving the social and physical environment. It will offer regeneration to these; the main beneficiaries of this scheme will be the UK and Germany.

The environment

One of the problems of coal, as suggested above, is its poor image and record as a environmentally friendly fuel. This is a significant handicap when the political arena is increasingly stressing the importance of `green' issues. This creates an increasing anti-coal sentiment in certain spheres. Environmental legislation, aimed at reducing the emission of coal's polluting by-products at both EC and national levels, is restricting the ability of the fuel to compete in an increasingly competitive energy market. The main EC legislation is the 1988 Large Combustion Plants Directive which set ceilings for the output of these pollutants into the next century and has thus put pressure on the sector. It is anticipated that when the directive is reviewed next year the emission level will be reduced thus putting greater pressure upon the industry. In addition the cost of 'cleaning' the coal-fired power stations is often prohibitive and deters coal consumption even further.

The coal producing countries of the EC

The purpose of this section is to look in more detail at the EC coal industry by examining the industry within the main coal producing countries. Within the EC there are four coal producing Member States of note (UK, Spain, Germany and France); though there are other coal producers, such as Greece and Ireland, their coal sectors are so small as to be insignificant alongside the major producers (see Figure C1.2).

France

France's policy towards coal and the energy sector in general is very much geared around meeting the problems posed by its own lack of natural resources. In France there is a virtual monopoly over coal production by the state-owned producer Charbonnages de France (CdF). However, there are a limited amount of other producers some owned by the major electricity producer (EdF), and some very small private concerns.

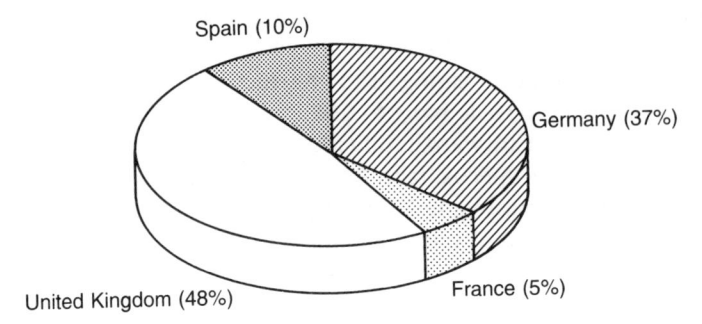

Figure C.1.2 EC coal production by country, 1993 (source: Eurostat)

Within France there are three major coalfields (1991), two of which (Nord Pas de Calais and the Centre Midi) are due to cease production in the near future. This will leave a single major coalfield (Lorraine) which has already been drastically scaled down. The future of the coal industry, as in other EC Member States, is bleak as the CdF is cutting production drastically. It is estimated that, by 2010, coal production in France will be 0.04 mtoe[5], down from 8.83 mtoe in 1987. A decline of over 99 per cent in under three decades.

Traditionally, energy policy in France has been dictated by planners rather than the market. A result has been that, for many years, high cost pits have been kept open for purely strategic reasons due to France's lack of a plentiful indigenous energy source. For this reason, France, more so than any other member state, has embraced nuclear power. Indeed its use in electricity generation increased by some 437 per cent between the years 1973 and 1988. This has created a surplus in energy production which EdF is exporting to other Member States. The importance that the French have attached to this source has hit other forms of energy hard and can be seen as a direct contributor to the decline in the use and production of coal.

As a result of this decline, employment has fallen markedly (Table C1.1).

Table C1.1 *Employment in the French mining industry*

Year	Employment
1975	80,000
1980	55,000
1985	48,000
1990	20,000
1993(est)	>10,000

Source: Eurostat

The EC coal industry: into the twenty-first century

To be more specific about these figures, the personnel employed underground, it is estimated, will have fallen from 30 000 in 1980 to around 6000 in 1993. The production figures (Table C1.2) suggest this decline will continue.

Table C1.2 *French coal production*

Year	Level of Production (mtoe)
1987	8.83
1990	6.5
1995	5.25
2000	4
2010	0.04

Source: Eurostat

The consumption of coal has remained stable in France over the last decade or so. Indeed, over the period 1990–2005, there is expected to be a rise of 4.6 per cent in coal consumption. However this rise is likely to be met by increases in imports, which over the same period are estimated to rise by 32 per cent. This rise will increase the French dependency upon imported coal to 82 per cent by 2005. To cushion the effects of these changes France has been generous in giving assistance to its coal sector (Table C1.3).

Table C1.3 *State assistance to the French coal industry*

Year	Total intervention (M ECU)	Intervention per tonne (ECU)
1990	166.2	15.4
1991	165.3	16.3
1992	186.9	19.9

Source: Eurostat

The French coal industry has, like other coal producing Member States in the EC, a rather parlous financial situation. In the period 1990–91, there was a 5 per cent reduction in production costs and a 0.6 per cent fall in revenue. This has helped turn losses per tonne of ECU 36 (1990) to ECU 31 in 1991. In addition there was an increase in productivity as output per man hour rose from 534kg in 1988 to 800kg in 1992.

To help the coal industry there exist vertical arrangements between the EdF and the CdF. The current agreement covers the period 1989–93. Under this agreement there is a guaranteed market for coal but it is taken on a declining scale; from the most recent figures available, they will take 2.3

million tonnes in 1990 which will fall to 1.8 million tonnes in 1991. In turn, the minimum price at which coal is delivered to the EdF is set some 10 per cent above the cost of imports. This has the aim of covering the aid and the social costs of the decline in coal production.

It is clear that the French, like other EC states, are moving away from an explicit energy policy towards the market. As a result there is the increasing tendency for coal to be substituted by other fuels, most notably gas, as well as by imports from foreign companies.

Table C1.4 *Coal by source used in EdF stations*

Year	France	EC	Other
1987	49	1	50
1988	46	0	54
1989	34	4	62
1990	24	6	70
1991	20	2	78

Source: Eurostat

Germany

Germany has eight coal producing companies, the biggest of which is Ruhrkohle. It is a private sector concern and dominates coal production in, what is by far and away, Germany's largest coal field, the Ruhr. The company is owned by a variety of companies of which Veba (a large private sector industrial group) is dominant. The company controls a number of other mining companies in this area. The second biggest company is Saarbegwerke which is, by and large, state owned. There are other companies, but these are small and completely privately owned. Hence within this sector there is a mixture of state and private ownership. Much of Germany's coal is, as was noted earlier, produced in the Ruhr (approximately 80 per cent); hence the dominance of Ruhrkohle over the German coal industry.

Like the industry in other Member States the German coal industry does not seem to have a bright future. Up to the year 2005 it is expected that the consumption of coal will rise by 1.1 per cent (1990–2005). However, over the same period, domestic coal production is expected to fall by 38.5 per cent. Hence there is expected to be a sharp rise in the level of imports by over 1000 per cent. As a result of this massive rise solid fuel import dependency will increase from –1.8 per cent to nearly 42 per cent by the end of the period.

On the whole, in terms of changes in production, the German coal industry has fared better than other Member States. This has been helped by the long-term vertical arrangements between coal and electricity producers as well as the high level of subsidy that the industry receives. The figures for coal production over the period 1988-92 fell by just 8 per cent compared with an EC average decline of 42 per cent. In terms of staff employed underground, in Germany, there has been a fall of 17 per cent compared to an average decline of 36 per cent across the rest of the EC over the same period (1988–92). Over the period 1989–91 production costs rose by 4.3 per cent and revenues by 4.8 per cent, the rise in the latter figure being due to an increase in price. But despite this there was still a loss per tonne of coal mined equal to ECU 12 (1991).

Table C1.5 *German coal production and consumption 1987–93 (millions of tonnes)*

Year	Production	Consumption
1987	82.4	n/a
1988	79.3	81.1
1989	77.5	78.4
1990	76.6	80.3
1991	72.7	82.6
1992	72.2#	80.1#
1993	63.8*	79.3*

#estimate *forecast
Source: Eurostat

As a result, at the moment, there are rapid production cuts in all coalfields and further consolidation is likely. One of the major reasons for the fact that the industry has remained relatively protected has been various market distortion mechanisms, most notably state aids and vertical arrangements.

In terms of state aid, in absolute terms, Germany is the largest donor, giving some 86 per cent of all coal aid for current production in the EC (1992).

Table C1.6 *German state aid for current production*

Year	Total intervention (MECU)	Intervention per tonne (ECU)
1990	4204.8	54.9
1991	4502.7	61.9
1992	4334.6	60

Source: Eurostat

Much of this aid is to cover losses and to help the sale of coal to the troubled steel sector. However, with Germany's current economic troubles, it is unlikely that the generosity of the government will persist. In the desire to cut the budget deficit the large subsidies to the coal sector are a prime target for reduction. The implications of this for the speed of change and rationalization within this sector cannot be understated.

Also, vertical arrangements help guarantee a market for coal to the electricity producers; this is the so called 'jahrhundertvartrag', which amounts to a restrictive agreement and thus a vertical restraint upon competition in the energy market. The EC has allowed some DM 5 billion worth of aid to sustain this contract. The agreement lasts up to 1995 when it is due to be renegotiated. The sales of coal to the electricity generators are aided by a coal levy placed upon electricity power users. This enables the power industry to cover the additional costs of using indigenous coal.

But the market for energy is changing as demand and social regulations alter the environment in which these firms operate. Indeed there has been a 40 per cent rise in the use of gas in the electricity sector. In turn, it is predicted, that there will be a reduction in the use of coal for electricity generation of some 5 million tonnes by 1998. But the decline of coal may be protected by its close political allies. As was noted: 'We have practically no oil and very little gas. Coal is the only resource we have. There is a strong security of supply argument'[6].

But in some instances it may not only be the market that forces change upon the Germans. It may also be the EC with its plans to get tougher on state aid and on the environment. However, the Germans are likely to resist. The closure of the fields would have a strong regional impact and erode the associated manufacturing base, especially in the Ruhr. Indeed it is estimated that procurement to the coal sector accounts for some 14.5 per cent of the manufacturing base so the decline will inevitably have a drastic effect.

Ruhrkohle is responsible for some 80 per cent of German production of hard coal and is thus being greatly affected by the changes going on within the industry. The combined effects of recession, dwindling state coffers, a decline in sales to the steel sector and a fall in the rate of increase in electricity consumption (both recession induced effects) mean that 12,000 jobs will go in the company's coal operations by 1995. The problems of the steel sector could yet double this. The response of the company to these challenges is to diversify into other sectors. Indeed some 39 per cent of its turnover is now derived from environmental technology, trading, power engineering and construction. Twenty years ago some 98 per cent of the company's turnover was reliant upon coal. However this is rather small compensation for the big changes in the coal sector which is still at the core of the company's activities. The problems of Ruhrkohle have also been hit by the desire of the steel companies to break a long term contract for the supply of coal. The decline of Ruhrkohle and of the coalfield in general is reflected starkly in the way that employment in the sector has been cut. It has fallen from 191 000 in 1970 to an expected level of 65 000 by 1995.

Spain

Coal production in Spain is dispersed widely among a large number of companies, approximately 200. The biggest company is Hunosa, which is state owned. The bulk of the rest of the firms are controlled by the private sector. These companies combined form Carbunion, which is an association of coal producers, who collectively negotiate contracts with the main consumers of coal. As such, the nature of the coal industry is different from that in other Member States with there being a large number of companies as well as there being a broad mix of public and private sector firms. The main coal producing area is in the Oviedo region of northern Spain.

The trend for overall production, like other Member States, is one of decline. It is estimated that over the period 1987–2010 it will have declined by some 22 per cent. Though steep, this is less than the anticipated decline in the rest of the EC, which is expected to show an average decline of 46 per cent.

Table C1.7 *Spanish coal production and consumption*

Year	Production	Consumption
1987	19.3	n/a
1988	19	27.8
1989	19.3	30.2
1990	19.6	30.2
1991	17.9	30.8
1992	18.6#	32.8#
1993	18.5*	32.5*

#estimate *forecast
Source: Eurostat

In terms of consumption, it is clear that, with the help of the state, this has not fallen greatly. Indeed, over the period 1990–2005, there is expected to be a 32 per cent increase in consumption. From this it can be seen that there will be a sharp rise in imports over the period, a rise somewhere in the region of 130 per cent. This increases the import dependency of Spain for coal from 26.6 per cent in 1985 to nearly 70 per cent by 2005. Coal faces a big challenge from the use of natural gas in energy production. The use of gas is expected to rise fifteen fold over the 1990–2005 period.

Hence, throughout Spain, there is a restructuring of the coal industry, as underground pits are closed and others are rationalized. However, over the period 1988–92, coal production in Spain has barely changed; it seems to have bucked the trend that has hit most other EC coal producers. Indeed in the 1991–92 period there has been a rise in coal production of 4 per cent. In turn the losses in terms of employment have also been lower than the rest of the EC with, over the period, there being just an 8 per cent decline. However, by the end of 1993, it is estimated that the public sector coal pits would have shed a quarter of their capacity and a third of their employment. Thus the bucking of the trend appears to be only a temporary phenomenon.

The financial situation of the industry again is not as bad as other Member States with, in 1991, the deficit per tonne of coal being ECU 37. This has been helped by a strong domestic rise in the price of coal. However this outcome is due to special factors or abilities and the resistance to change rather than a strong performance.

The situation of the underground pits is helped by market distortions of which a vertical arrangement between the coal producers and the electricity companies (UNESA) is an example. On the whole, the price and quantity of open cast mining is left largely to the market. However prices given to the coal producers are kept in line with prices charged elsewhere to electricity companies by producers of other rival fuels so as to encourage the adjustment of the coal sector.

In the past, change in the sector has been resuscitated by the level of aid given to the sector; in the EC it is the second highest donor to this industry. (Table C1.8).

Table C1.8 *Spanish state assistance to the coal sector*

Year	Total intervention (MECU)	Intervention per tonne (ECU)
1990	499.2	26.4
1991	667.4	37.3
1992	483.3	26

Source: Eurostat

Much of this aid is to cover the losses of companies, some PTAs 50 million in 1991. The desire of the Spanish government to modernize their economy along the lines of the EC core, and the necessity to reduce the budget deficit means that if change doesn't happen 'naturally' then change will be promoted.

United Kingdom

British Coal, the old National Coal Board (renamed to help the moves to privatize the firm), is the dominant producer of coal in the UK. Indeed 95 per cent of all coal mines are owned by British Coal; however a few small producers do operate under licence from the company. Open cast mining is, by and large, a private affair with the firms again operating under licence from British Coal.

The persistent decline of coal over recent decades has affected all coalfields in the UK. Over the past decade the process seems to have speeded up as the UK government has moved away from an energy policy towards a market in this sector. Some fields, for example South Wales, have been severely rationalized, and some have ceased production all together.

Table C1.9 *United Kingdom coal production (millions of tonnes)*

Year	Production	Consumption
1988	101.4	113.3
1989	98.3	108
1990	89.3	108
1991	91.5	111
1992	83	102.8
1993	83*	102.8*

*estimate
Source: Eurostat

Over recent decades the major consumers of coal were the electricity producers, taking some 75 per cent of domestic production in 1990. The future of coal consumption will, in the future, be hit by the re-negotiation of the vertical arrangement between the coal producers and the electricity generators; by the year 2000, electricity generated from coal will fall to 40–50 per cent. In explicit moves towards an energy market the decline in demand for coal will necessitate reductions in capacity rather than forcing coal upon producers. Hence the recent pit closure plan. The emphasis will be upon British coal to find new markets rather than relying upon the government for favours.

Production will continue to fall as a result of increased competition especially in the light of recent events. There is the possibility of temporary assistance from the government. Eventually the future of production will depend upon the marketing strategy of the newly commercially based and soon to be privatized British Coal.

This restructuring process is likely to continue in the future as coal production, up to the year 2005, is expected to fall further. Over the period

1990–2005 coal production is expected to fall by 46.7 per cent, while consumption, over the period, is anticipated to fall by 13.8 per cent, with a rise in imports of somewhere on the region of 190 per cent. The main market for coal, power generation, expects to see a decline in the use of coal of 14 per cent, while there will an expected vast rise in use of gas, estimated to be in the region of 1110 per cent, underlining the so-called `Dash for Gas`. As result of these changes the import dependency in terms of coal will rise from 10.5 per cent to 48 per cent over this period.

The coal sector has been hit hard by the government's desire to put the entire energy sector on a commercial basis. Indeed the privatization of electricity has helped removed the traditional distortions in favour of coal in the production of energy. In turn the government has sought to operate coal on a commercial footing with the intention of making it compete directly with other fuels which threaten to remove it from its main markets. It is estimated that once privatization is complete, British coal will be half its current size with the use of subsidies, albeit temporary, to cushion the blow.

In these terms coal not only faces a competitive disadvantage but also a rather negative image as the dirty man of energy production. The environmental consequences of coal are important considerations in its use. The cost of cleaning coal-fired power stations is huge; thus the electricity sector is wary of leaning too heavily on the coal. Hence because of this the so-called 'Dash for Gas' occurred. The scale of the decline can be seen in that in 1943 there were 958 pits and by the end of the century there will probably be just 15.

In line with this decline in the number of pits there has also been a big decline in the number of miners. Staff employment has fallen by 42 per cent between 1988 and 1991 and it is estimated to fall by another 30 000 by the middle of the 1990s.

Compared to other Member States British Coal is on a relatively sound financial footing. It had, in 1989, a deficit of ECU 13 per tonne; by 1991 this had turned into a surplus. The pit closure plan announced in 1992/3 is likely to push British Coal back into deficit due to the large redundancy costs. However, this must not distract from the big gains in productivity and costs that have occurred over the last few years. With the imminent privatization of British Coal, the UK will be unique in the EC as having the only fully privately owned coal sector. Indeed it is the UK which has moved furthest towards a market for energy than any other Member Sstate. However, if coal is to compete on a level playing field with other fuels, other competitive distortions need to be removed, for example the support given to nuclear power (see Robinson 1993).

Another feature that differentiates the UK coal industry from the sector in other Member States is the reluctance of the government to give assistance to the industry. In fact the UK government offers no state assistance to cover costs of current production, the only aid offered is to cushion the blows of redundancy. Under an EC state aid regulation a Member State is only allowed to subsidize up to 20 per cent of its energy production. Thus, because the government subsidizes nuclear power, it is not allowed to offer any assistance to the coal sector. There are limited forms of market distortions in the form of vertical arrangements between the coal and electricity producers; these agreements end in 1993 and the electricity producers have signalled that they will be demanding a lot less coal. This has been a key factor in the recent problems of British Coal. In the light of this crisis there have been cries that the UK government, for strategic reasons, should not let the sector decline. However, actions by the government would be more about offering a temporary respite in the face of the inevitable decline of the sector. In the face of this, emotions should be detached from the hard commercial realities of the sector.

Conclusion

Overall the picture for the coal industry in the EC is bleak. The EC has sought to manage the decline of the industry but Member States, with the relatively high degree of discretion in this area, have cushioned these effects. For this reason it is unlikely that a true market for coal will emerge. It appears to be politically costly for Member States to allow it to decline naturally. But the EC is importing more of its coal as the economics of the issue become more apparent. The decline is inevitable over the long term and many Member States will see their level of coal production fall over the next few decades. These states should recognize that over the longer term the favours given to the coal sector do more harm than good and they must move to a more liberal trade in all forms of energy. Doing this would offer more favours to EC industry than a biased energy policy. We have yet to see if governments will respond.

Bibliography

Comité d'Etude des producteurs de charbon d'Europe occidentale (1993) Situation générale de l'industrie charbonne de la Communauté Européenne, Brussels.

Commission of the European Communities (1993), *Draft Commission Decision Establishing Community Rules for State aid to the Coal Industry*, Brussels.

Commission of the European Communities (1993) *Market for solid fuels in the Community in 1992 and Outlook for 1993*, SEC(93)441 final, Brussels.

Commission of the European Communities (1993) *Commission Report on the Application of the Community's Rules for State Aid to the Coal Industry in 1991*, COM(93) 116 final, Brussels.

Commission of the European Communities/DG XVII (1992) *Energy in Europe: A View to the Future*, Special edition, September 1992.

Commission of the European Communities/Rees, W. and Thomas, R. (1991) *Study of the European Communities Readaption Aids to the Coal and Steel Industries*, Durham University Industrial Group.

Commission of the European Communities (1993) *Panorama of EC Industry*, Brussels.

Commission of the European Communities (1993) *The Internal Energy Market*, COM(88)238, Brussels.

European Parliament (1988) *Report on European Coal Policy*, A2-0147/88.

European Parliament (1991) *Coal and the Internal Energy Market EP*, Director General for Research no.17.

Financial Times (1993) Power For Europe 22/6/93, pp.15–19.

Macgowan, F., (1989) *A Single Market for Energy*, RIIA/SPRU.

Robinson, C.(1992) *Making a Market in Energy*, Institute of Economic Affairs.

References

1 Note: All statistics within this case study regarding past aid, the future level of coal production and consumption, state aids, reserves, financial data, etc. were gathered from the European Commission.
2 As quoted in the Commission of the European Communities report in the market for solid fuels.
3 As quoted in Macgowan. *A Single Market for Energy.*
4 See The European Parliament *The Internal Energy Market.*
5 Million tonnes of oil equivalent.
6 Quoted in the *Financial Times*, 22 June 1993, p.18.

Questions

1 Identify the major forces promoting change in the coal sector.
2 To what extent do you believe a free market is achievable within the coal industry?
3 How important has the EC, as an institution, been in promoting change within the coal sector ?
4 What do you believe the major effects of the decline of coal to be? What should the appropriate policy response to these problems be ?

Case 2   The European Community's Environmental Management and Audit Scheme

Pamela M Barnes

Introduction

The subject of the following case study is the operation and application of the European Community's (EC) Environmental Policy. The topic chosen to illustrate the problems which industry may face when EC environmental legislation is adopted, is Council Regulation EEC No. 1863/93. This regulation established a voluntary Environmental Management and Audit Scheme (EMAS) to be used by companies in the industrial sector across the Community.

The EMAS is the beginning of a new approach by the European Community, which it is hoped will encourage more commitment from companies to environmental protection. Many companies are sceptical of the benefits for them of adopting environmental protection measures. The new scheme does go some way towards helping to overcome this scepticism. While the framework of the scheme is set for the whole Community in the regulation, registration for the scheme is voluntary.

The purpose of this case study is to pose a series of questions concerning the EMAS regulation.

1   What are the implications for businesses as they adapt their business management plans to include the provisions of the EC legislation?
2   Will a company find sufficient benefits from registering for the scheme to outweigh the financial implications?
3   Will the pressures on companies who register for the scheme be the same for the small and medium sized enterprises (SMEs) as for the large multinationals?
4   How effective an environmental protection measure will voluntary registration be?

The material in this case study is also used to illustrate points made in Chapter 2.

The main components of the scheme

1. Companies are to be encouraged to develop an environmental strategy.
2. Companies are to set their own objectives for environmental performance and develop management systems which will achieve those objectives.
3. Companies are to initiate a pattern of eco-auditing to assess their environmental performance and to provide the information needed to develop their environmental management systems.
4. Companies have to show commitment to externally validated assessment of their progress in meeting these objectives.
5. Companies also have to make information about their environmental performance available to the public in a 'concise, comprehensible form' [1]. This statement has to be externally verified. Although the verifiers do have to consult with the company on the detail which is to be made public.

The regulation is site specific and not company specific. A company may register any site where industrial activity is carried out. This includes mining, quarrying, manufacturing industry, some energy generating activity – electricity, gas, steam and hot water production and some waste management activities. Companies which comply with the eco-auditing requirement and the public statement will be able to use the appropriate EC eco-audit logo at the registered site.

The decision about the commercial value of participation in the scheme remains in the hands of the individual companies. As participation in the scheme is on a voluntary basis the success of the legislation will depend on the extent to which companies are persuaded that the potential costs are outweighed by the possible benefits.

There are a number of issues which remain for a company to consider.

1. The short-term compliance costs of registering for the scheme. The financial implications include:
    (a) the registration fee for the scheme;
    (b) administrative costs;
    (c) disruption to the plant operation during the audit;
    (d) the cost of the staff or consultants to carry out the audit;
    (e) the cost of the external verification;
    (f) the cost of the publication of the environmental statement.

2. The longer-term investment implications of participating in the scheme.
3. The requirement to publish an environmental statement.

The environmental policy of the European Community

The development of the policy

The European Community (EC) did not include in the Treaty of Rome, signed in 1957, any mention of policy to protect the environment. Instead the policy was launched in the first of a series of action programmes in 1972. It was given a place in the Treaty when a chapter on the environment was included in the Single European Act of 1986 (SEA). The Community accepted that it had a clearly defined responsibility to protect the environment.

Until the SEA, some of the environmental legislation had been open to challenge by some of the EC states because it had been based on an interpretation of three articles of the Treaty of Rome, and not an explicitly stated article of the Treaty. However, the chapter in the SEA, amending the Treaty of Rome, gave EC-wide environmental action a firm legal basis. This has been strengthened in the Treaty on European Union (TEU), which uses the term 'Policy' for Community Environmental actions for the first time.

Since 1972 more than 200 pieces of legislation have been produced by the European Community, covering all aspects of environmental concern. Much of the legislation in the past has been addressed at remedying problems which were the result of industrial practices. But the SEA established three principles on which action was to be based in the future.

1 the principle that prevention was better than cure;
2 that damage should be rectified at source;
3 that the polluter should pay for the clean up.

Underpinning these principles for action was the commitment by the Community to ensure that environmental protection became part of the considerations of all the EC policies. This means that in the future in preparing industrial, social, agricultural and regional policy the environmental consequences have to be taken into account.

In the Treaty on European Union the profile of environmental policy was raised. The commitment to include environmental concerns in all aspects of EC policy making was emphasized. The European Parliament (EP) (see Chapter 2, Making the Community work: The European Parliament) was given a larger role in environmental policy making. The EP is considered to be the most environmentally conscious of the institutions, so this move has been welcomed by the environmentalists.

Principle of subsidiarity

Greater use can be made of the Article 130s of the Treaty, so that the individual Member States may introduce more stringent environmental legislation than the EC. This is very much in keeping with the commitment in the Treaty to greater application of the principle of subsidiarity. The idea being that action should only be taken by the European Community if it affects the whole of the Community. If a problem is specific to one country then it is the responsibility of that country to take the necessary action.

A new environmental policy – the Fifth Environmental Action Programme

The framework of environmental policy has been set since 1972 in a series of action programmes produced at five yearly intervals by the Commission. The EC adopted its Fifth Environmental Action Programme (EAP) in 1992. This programme, like its predecessors was not a definitive list of legislation, but a statement of the areas where the Community felt that action was needed in order to protect the environment. Unlike the earlier programmes, however, the Fifth EAP set out longer term objectives, which it wanted to achieve by the end of the decade. These objectives will also provide the basis of environmental protection for the Community into the twenty-first century.

In the Fifth EAP the Commission identified a number of key problems, such as climate change and acid rain, which needed urgent action. The proposals the EAP contained are to form the basis of a strategy which is aiming to achieve the goals of sustainable development within the EC and to help to overcome these problems of global concern. The Programme was in fact entitled 'Towards Sustainability'[2].

In order to overcome the problems which were identified in the Fifth EAP, various sectors of economic activity have been targeted where environmental protection had to be given a firmer place – manufacturing industry, agriculture, transport, energy, tourism. In targeting these areas a new approach was accepted. The Commission of the EC recognized that proposals which merely increased the number of pieces of legislation were not the most effective routes to take. So, in addition to legislation, the Commission had proposed in the Fifth EAP the use of a number of approaches, to support the legislation.

The nature of future legislation which a company may face

What will the Treaty changes and the proposals of the Fifth Action Programme mean for the type of legislation which companies will be required to implement?

The centralized command and regulatory approach used since 1972 in the framing of EC environmental policy will not be abandoned, but the number of pieces of legislation of this type will fall. Standards will still be set in legislation which has a health implication for example, but different

The European Community's Environmental Management and Audit Scheme

approaches will also be used. These will include:

1 greater use of more market based instruments;
2 improvements to the way in which information is collected and passed on to both industry and the consumer;
3 new institutions and funding measures will be introduced.

Industry – a targeted sector

The view expressed in the Fifth EAP was that industry itself had a clear responsibility to change its practices in order to protect the environment. Following the publication and adoption of the EAP, two pieces of Community legislation were introduced which embodied this new approach. They were the EC's Eco-labelling scheme[3], launched in June 1993 and the EC's Environmental Management and Audit Scheme launched in July 1993[4].

Both schemes are based on:

1 voluntary registration;
2 allowing market forces to operate;
3 a requirement to inform the public;
4 the objective of long-term improvement of the environment.

The underlying rationale for both the schemes is to provide the consumer with sufficient information to be able to choose between products. As their preferences will be for the more environmentally friendly products the company which demonstrates its green credentials will have gained a competitive edge. The 'consumer' may be anyone requiring information about a company's environmental practices.

In the case of the eco-label, the information is for the consumer, buying the product directly. By means of the EC eco-label the customer is informed that the product being purchased is less damaging to the environment than its competitors' products. It is a relative measure, not an absolute.

In the case of EMAS, the use of the public environmental statement and eco-audit logo, indicates that the company is carrying out regular eco-audits at the specified site. The audited information is then being used in the company's business management plan to improve its environmental protection measures. In this case the 'consumer' may be investors, banks, or other companies which they supply with components. These logos provide proof for the public of the green credentials of the company

Environmental Management and Audit Scheme (EMAS)

The EMAS regulation is not intended to be a measure of management performance with regard to environmental protection. It is establishing a standard which states that effective systems for managing the environment are in place. It is a measure of commitment by a company to introduce procedures to improve its environmental performance.

The key element of the scheme is the use of eco-auditing to identify if the environmental protection objectives which the company sets for itself are met. Initially an eco-audit is 'a regular and systematic examination of the environmental conditions in a company in order to identify the key environmental issues facing that company'[5]. This then becomes what Dr Robin Bidwell described in his evidence to the House of Lords as 'a management system for ensuring that the environmental performance of a company is adequate'[6].

The results of the eco-audits are used to adapt the business management plan of the company to incorporate the audit findings. Once begun, a pattern of eco-auditing has to be continued, to provide the information to monitor and update the company's practices to ensure that they are in line with the strategy set to meet those objectives. This is the optimum; in reality many companies have only carried out a single audit to check if they comply with environmental regulations. The EMAS regulation is designed to encourage companies to use the techniques as the basis of a long-term strategy which demonstrates their commitment to environmental protection.

Origins of eco-auditing

There are many different types of audit which can be conducted and for different purposes. British Petroleum carry out five different audits apart from compliance and new investment audits, all of which have an impact on management practices.

1 Site audits on individual facilities
2 Activity audits on cross-business operations such as transport
3 Corporate audits on individual businesses such as chemicals.
4 Associate audits of companies which act as BP agents overseas
5 Audits which monitor BP's record on issues such as the protection of the tropical rain forests.

As with many multinationals, BP carry out varying levels of audit on different parts of the organization.

1970s developments

The large US multinational corporations were the first to adopt environmental audits in the 1970s. Pressure came from the introduction of domestic liability laws in the US. It then became part of standard practice for the US multinationals to use the same systems in their European locations. These audits were limited in their objectives. Their primary purpose was to act as a means of checking that the business was complying with environmental legislation and regulations. They were checks, and not intended to change or develop new approaches to management.

1980s developments

During the late 1980s and early 1990s, European companies began to conduct systematic examinations of their environmental performance. These environmental audits were broader in their objectives than mere compliance audits used in the US in the 1970s. They were seen as an important tool for tackling eco-problems in European companies. Shell Oil in 1981 began the first of their series of more proactive audits which went beyond mere regulation compliance checks.

The requirements of eco-auditing do vary within the Shell Group but the general principles have been established and published. Health, safety and environmental audits are conducted within the group worldwide in the agrochemical plants. Audits of oil and gas explorations are carried out every three years. An annual internal plant audit is carried out and then a more extensive audit, with external verification every three to five years.

Advantages of an eco-audit

There are a number of advantages which a company can gain from an environmental audit, which fall into six main categories.

1 Awareness of legislation

Given the rise in the number of pieces of environmental legislation, it is important for a company to be aware of any areas of activity which may have to be altered.

2 Cost of dumping waste

The cost of dumping waste is growing at such a rapid rate that significant savings can be achieved by finding ways to recycle the waste. Pilkingtons, the glass manufacturers, found a number of savings could be made following one of the eco-audits which they carried out in 1991. Pilkington glass manufacturers found that when they rejected a batch of glass on quality grounds, the cost to the company of the lost product was £40 per ton. But each rejected batch cost more to dispose of as it provided five tonnes of waste for a landfill site! By taking greater care during the production process and cutting down on the instances of poor quality production they were able to make substantial savings.

The Pilkington audit was based on a one page check list with six main headings.

(a) Materials and energy used in the process.
(b) Public perception of the site.
(c) Impact on the locality.
(d) Disposal of the waste product by the factory.
(e) The working environment.
(f) New investments and processes.

Many companies use a similar checklist as the guidelines for an eco-audit.

3   The cost of insurance

Insurance companies are becoming more nervous of insuring, following a number of very costly environmental disasters during recent years. They are therefore making an eco-audit a prerequisite of providing insurance cover.

4   The cost of fines

Companies are facing the prospect of legislation which will result in mandatory environmental liability cover. Legislation is under discussion for Europe which will introduce the type of penalties which already exist in the United States of America. Already European legislation exists which can levy fines of an unlimited amount to pay for the cost of a pollution incident. As discussions progress about the use of criminal as well as civil courts, then company personnel are faced by the possibility of jail sentences. Eco-audits are one way of ensuring that the management of a company knows what the possible problems could be.

5   Green credentials

A company's pollution record is part of its public 'face'. Companies who were seen to be taking a responsible attitude to environmental issues and thereby gaining a green reputation have found that their competitiveness has been enhanced. The Body Shop must be regarded as the 'classic' example of this. Other wholesale and retail chains have found a similar experience, e.g. the DIY chain B & Q.

6   Savings on administrative costs

Company costs were cut down because they were able to save time in planning applications by as much as six months – they knew the problems in advance at particular sites and were able to plan their applications accordingly.

Reasons for EC legislation

The European Community's voluntary scheme for eco-audits is an initiative designed to provide a common framework for environmental audits. As the interest in eco-auditing and its advantages has grown, a number of issues have emerged which EC legislation attempts to provide solutions for.

1 Consistency of approach

The EC is not attempting to dictate which procedures are adopted in each Member State, but to provide a recognized framework for action across the Community. This is important as it is possible that companies, by carrying out an eco-audit may gain a competitive edge over the others, and this would lead to a distortion of the level playing of the EC's Single Market.

2 Frequency of auditing

Despite the growth of the interest in eco-auditing most sites have only had one eco-audit. It has been difficult therefore to decide if more are needed, or how often they are required. The EC regulation provides a framework timetable for the audits.

3 Public interest

In response to public pressure some companies, who eco-audit, do release the information. The Norwegian industrial group, Norsk Hydra, were pioneers in the use of independent consultants to verify its internal audit and then publish the results. This was an attempt to silence a vociferous and prolonged campaign by environmental groups in Norway. A number of sites of the company were actually picketed by the interest groups in the early 1980s and the benefits of being able to issue a public environmental statement were clear!

The EMAS provides the means by which public interest in the environmental practices of companies may be dealt with. The EC regulation gives clear instructions about the contents and release of a public environmental statement, which has to be externally verified. If public statements are to be released, clearly they are of more value if they can be compared.

Progress on EMAS

The Regulation was adopted by the European Community Ministers of the Environment (see chapter 2 Making the Community Work: The Council-the Decision Makers) on 29 June 1993. It was published in the Official Journal of the European Communities on 10 July 1993 and each Member State had to introduce it three days later. The Member States are responsible for administering the scheme, but have to follow the guidelines set in the regulation. This means that each state has to appoint the competent bodies to administer the scheme by July 1994 and the accreditation boards by April 1995.

EMAS is the result of more than three years of discussions between the Commission (see Chapter 2 Making the Community Work: The Commission) with industry and the national governments. Many criticisms have been made of the distance and lack of communication between the EC policy makers and those responsible for implementing the policy in the past. The EMAS is an example of where the EC have tried to widen the consultation process and enable those who would be responsible for the implementation of the legislation to have their views included in the legislation.

A number of changes were made to the legislation during the consultation process, probably the most important being the switch from a mandatory registration scheme for all companies to a voluntary-based scheme. The regulation in its final form is designed to enable companies to show a high level of commitment to improving their environmental performance, without being subject to excessively stringent external control.

There is no 'starting point' set for environmental protection measures in the legislation. The intention is to enable those companies who have not undertaken an eco-audit previously or adapted their business plans to take account of the results of an eco-audit to take part. This is in addition to encouraging the participation in the scheme of those companies which have been following various forms of eco-auditing since the early 1980s.

The response of chemical industry to ECO auditing

In Italy, Germany and the UK the chemical companies are increasingly seeing independent audits of environmental compliance as a feature of corporate environmental management. This is not the case in the rest of the states of the EC. Few companies apply the same standard across borders unless this is required of them by legislation at Community level, or there is a specific corporate strategy adopted which is designed to address a problem which is global in nature, e.g. reducing CFCs. Few companies whose operation is cross-border impose comprehensive environmental standards throughout their global operations.

Those chemical companies where the use of eco-auditing procedures have been used since the early 1980s have found a number of benefits.

1 Environmental legislation

This is an industrial sector which is faced by a large body of environmental legislation. As the body of legislation is growing so to is the attitude of governments to those industries which contravene the legislation. More civil actions are being brought by individuals against companies who pollute the environment. By conducting an eco-audit and through this identifying measures which can be put into operation to protect the environment, a company has ready a viable defence against such actions.

2 Public pressure

There have been a number of very high profile incidents of pollution from the chemical industry (e.g. the escape of toxic emissions from the Union Carbide plant in Bhopal, and incidents related to chemical plant safety, e.g. at the Sandoz plant in Basle) which have resulted in a great deal of public pressure being brought to bear on the companies to take remedial action. An audit of practices is the necessary prerequisite to identify the nature and the scale of the problems.

The impact of 1 and 2 will vary with the position of the company in the supply chain. Companies who are active downstream are more likely to respond to the pressure of the public and introduce changes to their corporate strategy as a result of the consumers' perception of them than companies who are upstream. Companies such as the suppliers of feedstock or chemical intermediate suppliers who are more removed from the consumer will react more to actions from the regulatory bodies. The Commission of the EC is seen in Europe as a major regulatory body which could put pressure on a company to adapt its corporate strategy.

3 Capital intensive

It is a capital intensive sector of industry. If an eco-audit identifies savings from the recycling of waste or more efficient use of materials then there are clear advantages to be gained.

4 Energy Intensive

It is an energy intensive sector. An eco-audit can identify ways in which energy may be saved.

5 Long investment cycles

It is a sector in which there is a long investment cycle, a sector which is working with long term strategies in place already. Eco-auditing and the introduction of changes to business management plans with long term effects are therefore more acceptable in the chemical industry than in many other sectors of industrial activity.

6 Dialogue

It is also seen as a valuable means by which the sector can become involved in the dialogue with the EC and national government bodies about future legislation and measures to curb emissions. Information is at hand as the result of these audits so that senior management involved in such discussions are thoroughly briefed and prepared.

7 Internationally competitive

This is an internationally competitive sector of economic activity. European companies are competing in global markets with Japanese and American companies who are leaders in the use of eco-auditing. If the European companies are to compete globally then they need to be able to show to potential customers that they too are using the same techniques to improve their environmental protection measures. The European companies have to be able to prove that they are global players; they are sourced from worldwide markets as well as exporting products to the Japanese and the Americans.

The Responsible Care Initiative

The chemical industry has adopted a programme known as the Responsible Care Initiative which had a number of parallels with the EMAS. This was originally begun in Canada and then adopted in eight states of the EC, the United States of America, Japan, Argentina, Mexico, Brazil with other countries also showing interest in the states of Central and Eastern Europe.

The Responsible Care Initiative is a declaration of commitment to continuous improvement in all aspects of health, safety and the environment. Six codes are measured in each company.

1. Employee safety.
2. Pollution prevention.
3. Process safety.
4. Product stewardship (life cycle analysis of the product).
5. Distribution of the products.
6. Company awareness and emergency response.

In the United Kingdom this required the companies to have their management systems, including their environmental management systems certified to British Standard BS 5750 (IS 09000 series). This is not a measure of environmental performance, but can be applied to any management function which is concerned with improving quality. Since 1992 BS 7750 has been developed based on the pattern established in BS 5750, but focusing on the environmental management systems of a company.

The British Standard BS 7750 was introduced on 16 March 1992. It was designed to be compatible with the EMAS regulation which was being discussed at the same time. Again, like BS 5750, and EMAS, BS 7750 does not lay down specific environmental performance criteria. It is a standard which is designed to establish the procedures by which environmental objectives may be set and worked towards within the company. It is a voluntary regime designed, as is EMAS, to improve management performance and as a consequence the competitiveness of a company. As voluntary codes, both require significant commitment in terms of cost and resources.

But while compatible with EMAS, BS 7750 differs from the EMAS regulation in a number of aspects.

1   BS 7750 is company and not site specific.
2   The additional requirement under EMAS for an externally verified public statement. (The public statement has in fact led to very active criticism in the UK from the UK Petroleum Industry Association.)

The advantage of EMAS over the Responsible Care Initiative

The Responsible Care Initiative has not been adopted in all EC states, Danish and Greek companies do not subscribe to the scheme. The British Standard has not been adopted by all companies. The EC legislation as a regulation is applicable within each of the Member States of the European Community. Therefore there is consistency of approach achieved for all the chemical companies operating within the EC who register sites for EMAS. The presence of the EC legislation is important to remove some of the uncertainty which could exist and undermine competitiveness within the Single Market.

The benefits of EMAS

The initial response to the EMAS regulation from the chemical sector was a cautious one. In the United Kingdom the Chemical Industries Association (CIA) welcomed the regulation, as the objectives were ones which companies in the sector were already working towards. They were uncertain if EMAS would be of practical significance in the United Kingdom. In the view of the CIA the benefits from EMAS would come from:

1   increased public credibility;
2   the development of environmental management systems;
3   increased openness about activities affecting the environment;
4   the voluntary nature of the scheme was desirable.

But the potential for costs would be high.

1   if the scheme was not kept simple and bureaucracy free;
2   as a result of management costs and fees for auditing and verification. The costs implications in the preparation of the public statement could be seen as a sizeable concern;
3   if the fees for registration for the scheme were too high.

The reservations of the UK chemical industry are clearly related to the costs and bureaucracy of the scheme. The CIA are of the opinion that if the EC scheme is to have any effectiveness then it has to be seen to be influencing both the consumers and the government, and that a very proactive campaign aimed at the wide adoption of the scheme has to be introduced.

The CIA would not like to see the voluntary aspect to the scheme removed, but that makes it more important for the scheme to be widely adopted if it is to have any effect. This clearly is an aspect of the scheme which the EC has not taken into account in its deliberations about the regulation.

Even in the chemical sector, which has been pushed in recent years to be environmentally concerned for the reasons outlined above there is increasing scepticism about the benefits from environmental protection. It is obvious that both the new approach to environmental protection and the acceptance of this particular piece of EC legislation require the Commission to undertake an early review and consultation procedure to evaluate the effectiveness of the operation of the policy.

The response of small companies

The scheme is new. The means to implement the scheme have to be in place in each of the states of the EC by summer 1994. Following from this the regulation contains a requirement for a review of its progress after five years. This is when most larger companies feel that the change to a mandatory registration may come.

It is difficult to evaluate the problems for companies because the regulation is so new and the different countries of the EC are still in the process of introducing the necessary measures. Some criticisms of the schemes and evaluation of its likely impact on small companies is possible by looking at other quality management systems based on similar procedures which have been introduced.

The Danish experience, based on eco-auditing

In 1988 eco-auditing was launched in Denmark as a new and potent method for companies to use to improve their environmental performance. Much of the information which the Danish Government and Danish Environmental Protection Agency were relying on came from the United States of America and the use of the technique in the Netherlands.

The companies in the US and the Dutch companies using the eco-audit procedures were large-scale enterprises. The Danish industrial sector is dominated by small and medium enterprises. They are not large enough to support their own environmental departments who can manage the eco-audit and then plan the new company strategy based on its findings. The administrative burden is great in SMEs which are likely to have a very loosely structured organization and limited knowledge of environmental conditions.

The objectives of EMAS are not merely to see the establishment of a single eco-audit, but to ensure that this becomes part of a recognized pattern leading to change in the company so that environmental protection is progressively improved. The Danish experience among the SMEs would suggest that these firms will need a great deal of government support in terms of subsidies to fund the audits, technical assistance, and simple and easy to apply national legislation, otherwise EMAS will remain a large-scale enterprise scheme only.

The British small firms experience – BS 5750

BS 5750 was introduced in the late 1970s to act as a readily recognized guarantee of a company's quality assurance standards. This is now being replaced by BS 7750 which is compatible with EMAS. The intention of BS 5750 was:

1 to provide the customer with information so that they did not find it necessary to carry out their own assessments;
2 to ensure that suppliers were not subject to numerous inspection visits. More than 22 000 British companies are registered for the standard.

While being designed for other purposes, BS 5750 does provide some lessons for EMAS as it requires registration procedures including the payment of a fee, evaluation of a company's practices, the alteration of a company's strategy based on the information collected, and the use of a logo.

The following criticisms have been made by SMEs companies of what BS 5750 means for them in practice.

1 It involves a great deal of paperwork.
2 It is costly. Consultants' fees may range from £400–£500 per day and there may be a need for 15–20 days work. There is also the cost of the registration fee.

For example Franklins, a London based company supplying air fresheners to a supermarket, was told that they had to register for BS 5750 or lose the contract. The cost of registration for that company was £4 000. The firm had a workforce of seven and an annual turnover of £750 000. The additional burden of this fee would have been too great[7]. In their case Franklins were able to negotiate with their customer and did not have to register for BS 5750. For some small suppliers to large concerns this may not be an option.

3 The meaning of the standard may be misunderstood; it is NOT a product standard, but the logo may be incorrectly used to suggest that it is.

The EMAS regulation carries with it a great deal of uncertainty. Much of the uncertainty is in exactly those areas which the Danish companies and the UK BS 5750 registered companies have found problems.

There is provision made in the regulation for assistance to be provided to small and medium sized companies so that they can meet with the requirements of the regulation. But the extent to which that assistance will be provided and its nature is not clarified.

Implementing EMAS in the United Kingdom

The period following the publication of the regulation in the Official Journal of the European Communities was a period of intense consultation in the UK with various interested parties. The UK government issued a series of proposals in a consultation document[8] and called for comments. This consultation period drew to a close at the end of September 1993.

The results were then processed so that the necessary measures for implementation of the EC legislation will be fully operational by April 1995 (see Chapter 2 Making the Community Work: The European Court of Justice). This consultation at the national government level was in keeping with the pattern of consultation on the legislation which had been built up throughout the three years of negotiation at Community level. It was also part of the greater openness and consultation which the Commission had advocated in the Fifth EAP.

A number of conditions are set out in the regulation for a company which wishes to register a site for the EMAS. The conditions are listed in Appendix C2.1. Simplified List of Requirements for EMAS Registration.

Once registered the company has to show that it is committed to a cycle of improvement by ensuring that the environmental review process is a continuous one. The Eco-audit cycle is demonstrated in Appendix C2.2.

The site may be deleted from the register if the company fails to submit its validated environmental statement and pay the fee within three months of the given deadline.

The frequency of audit is left to the individual company to decide upon, but must not occur less than every three years. The list of registered companies will be published annually in the Official Journal of the European Community. It is not clear from the regulation if a black list of companies who are no longer registered, having appeared in the past will be published, or if it will merely be a question of a name no longer appearing.

The EC regulation echoes closely the British standard on environmental management. The EC regulation includes verbatim much of the technical content of the British standard BS 7750 as the EMAS requirement. Despite this it is not the intention of the EC scheme to require compliance with any one single national environmental standard. Instead the intention is to make the scheme sufficiently flexible to allow its requirements to be met either by following a standard or some other means which best suits the company concerned. Taking this into account, and also the restriction at the moment of EMAS to industrial sites, there are more than 100 000 to 150 000 sites within the UK alone to whom the legislation is applicable.

For companies in the UK this is an area which remains unclear. BS 7750 and BS 5750 are company specific and the EMAS regulation refers to specific sites of industrial activity. Both the British Standards and the EMAS have fees for registration purposes. At the end of 1993 the pricing policy for BS 7750 and EMAS had not been fixed by the UK Government.

It was not clear if the same levels of fees would apply as had done to BS 5750. In that case the fee for registration was based on the size of the company. It could vary from a few thousand pounds for a small company to £30 000 for large companies.

What was also slow to be clarified was if there were to be two registration fees. Some companies may not wish to register for EMAS because of the requirement to make the public statement but may wish to register for BS7750. Some may wish to register for both, some may wish to register in the UK for BS 7750 and in the rest of the EC some specified sites for EMAS. There are a number of unresolved financial implications.

The regulation states that companies certified to accepted British standards by accredited bodies will meet the requirements of the EC legislation. There has been a lot of interest in the UK in adopting the British standard. BS 5750 was adopted by a number of small and medium sized firms in the UK because of pressure from the government purchasing agencies which made it a requirement of contracts. BS 7750 was adopted because of pressure in the international marketplace. Japanese inward investment was the driving force for the introduction of wider quality standards and therefore the use of eco-audits in the polymer industry in the UK. The Ford Motor Company increased its standard requirements for component suppliers above the BS 5750 standards and thereby added to the pressure.

The environmental statement
Giving the green credibility?

The publication of the verified environmental statement has been greeted by the environmentalists as a major step forward. It has had a much more mixed reception from the companies themselves.

The environmental benefit to be gained from the publication of the environmental statement is clear. It provides an opportunity for monitoring of a company's environmental protection measures by a number of different groups. It gives the 'consumer' the information which is required in order to make choices about the companies from whom they purchase their goods.

More information would be provided by the statement to environmental interest groups so that they could become more involved in the process of policing the implementation of environmental legislation. The environmental interest groups have made repeated calls in the past for information such as data on emissions to sewers to be released to them by companies to enable them to more closely monitor pollution incidents. The statement would provide a great deal of this type of information.

The contents of the environmental statement are listed very thoroughly in Article 5 of the EMAS regulation. The statement must include:

1. A description of the company's activities at the site being registered.
2. An assessment of all the significant environmental issues of relevance to the activities concerned.
3. A summary of the figures on pollutant emissions, waste generation, consumption of raw materials, energy and water, noise and other significant appropriate environmental aspects.
4. Other factors regarding environmental performance.
5. A presentation of the company's environmental policy and the management system implemented at the site involved.
6. The deadline for the next public statement to be issued.
7. The name of the accredited verifier.
8. Details of significant changes at the site since the last statement.

Green credentials?

This would seem to fulfil the requirements of the interested groups. Some environmentalists remain concerned about a number of aspects relating to the public statement.

1. The scheme is voluntary not mandatory.
2. Will it be concise and comprehensible?
3. Will companies be able to find loopholes in the legislation because of inadequate explanation of terms such as 'significant environmental issues'?

Company opposition to the statement.

For the companies the public statement presents a different set of problems.

The environmental audit may produce results with far-reaching consequences for a company's strategy. The benefits for the companies would lie in the release of information which would satisfy the pressure from

The European Community's Environmental Management and Audit Scheme

the customers and the suppliers, which has been the determining factor in the adoption of other quality management systems. The independently verified public statement would provide information for investors, bankers, customers, and the company itself to ensure that environmental issues are being dealt with.

The public statement, however, requires more than a mere acknowledgement of the fact that an eco-audit has been held. The companies have to demonstrate over a period of time that they have used the information to alter their company's approach to environmental protection. It may be that this will result in the closure of a particular facility. It may have implications for the company's purchasing, production, marketing or sales policy. The decision making process and implementation of these changes may not be the type of information which a company would want its competitors to have access to.

The procedures in the EMAS for the eco-audit are very complex and almost unlimited in their extent. They presuppose that both the auditors and the verifiers have a high level of technical expertise. A company considering registration for the scheme will not do so if there are any doubts at all about the expertise of the auditors and the verifiers of the audit. The release of incorrect information would be too damaging to the company concerned.

This may be less of a problem in the UK where there is already a well developed structure of accreditation arrangements for the two quality management standards, BS 5750 and the developing BS 7750. The United Kingdom Government proposed that the National Accreditation Council for Certification Bodies (NACCB) should monitor the developments for EMAS. This was so that EMAS could be introduced quickly into the UK. A company which was applying for certification to act as the independent verifiers for BS 7750 would be able to apply for additional certification to act for the EMAS.

In the public statement a company is opening itself to the possibility of additional pressure from environmental groups. The public statement is designed to give information. It is not intended to give the environmental groups a role in the decision making process within a company. The public statement does however give the environmental groups the information to challenge more often the environmental protection measures which a company has in place.

The eco-audit logo and its use

Attached in an annex to the legislation are examples of the eco-audit logo and the statement which it is intended will accompany the use of the logo at the registered sites. These are shown in Figure C2.1.

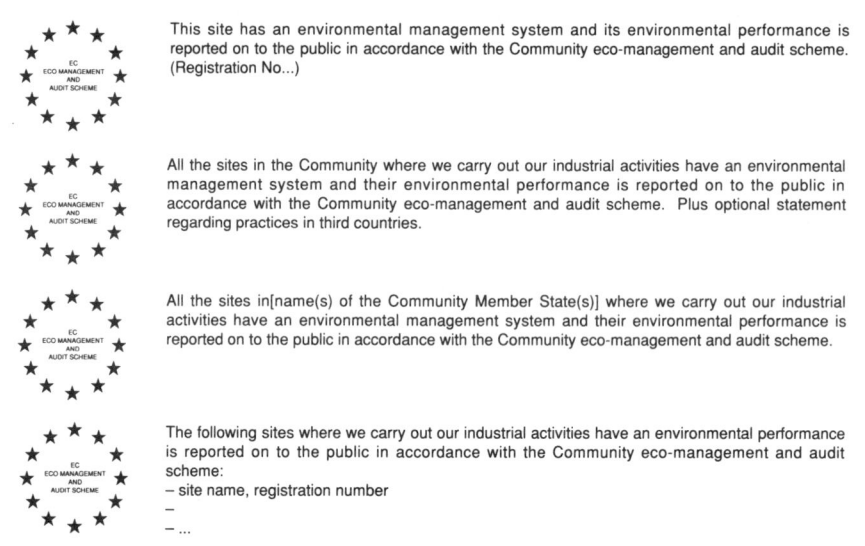

★★★ ★ EC ★ ★ ECO MANAGEMENT ★ ★ AND ★ ★ AUDIT SCHEME ★ ★★★	This site has an environmental management system and its environmental performance is reported on to the public in accordance with the Community eco-management and audit scheme. (Registration No...)
★★★ ★ EC ★ ★ ECO MANAGEMENT ★ ★ AND ★ ★ AUDIT SCHEME ★ ★★★	All the sites in the Community where we carry out our industrial activities have an environmental management system and their environmental performance is reported on to the public in accordance with the Community eco-management and audit scheme. Plus optional statement regarding practices in third countries.
★★★ ★ EC ★ ★ ECO MANAGEMENT ★ ★ AND ★ ★ AUDIT SCHEME ★ ★★★	All the sites in[name(s) of the Community Member State(s)] where we carry out our industrial activities have an environmental management system and their environmental performance is reported on to the public in accordance with the Community eco-management and audit scheme.
★★★ ★ EC ★ ★ ECO MANAGEMENT ★ ★ AND ★ ★ AUDIT SCHEME ★ ★★★	The following sites where we carry out our industrial activities have an environmental performance is reported on to the public in accordance with the Community eco-management and audit scheme: – site name, registration number – – ...

Figure C2.1 The eco-audit logo

The regulation states that the use of the eco-audit logo will not be allowed for sites which fail to comply with the requirements of Community and national environmental regulations. It does not state if the use of the logo could be withdrawn if the independent verifier refused to confirm the details of the public statement. This would lead to a lot of adverse publicity for a company. The credentials of the independent verifiers are therefore very important. The regulation contains a detailed annex which sets out criteria which the verifiers have to meet.

It will be important to ensure that the public is made aware of the meaning of the logo. It is *not* a product quality mark in the way that the eco-label is. It *is* a mark to show that a company is carrying out certain procedures to improve its environmental protection measures.

Effectiveness of legislation?

Voluntary versus mandatory

Although the current framework is based on voluntary registration of the company's sites, a number of the larger companies are preparing for the possibility that it may become mandatory for them in the future.

This is a controversial issue. Industry itself is divided about the approach. In some sectors the voluntary approach has been welcomed. However other sectors of European industry point to the US example.

Industry in the United States of America, with its more extensive body of environmental legislation, and its longer history of the use of eco-auditing to avoid the worst consequences of that legislation, is opposed to any audit regulation. This is on the grounds that the purpose of the audit is for a company to identify problems and improve its environmental performance. Given this, the last thing any company would want is for the information to be made public!

In a report of a poll of UK company directors[9] the findings were that only one in seven companies had taken initial steps in eco-auditing. About 25 per cent of companies reported that they had then instituted a formal environmental policy. When the figure was broken down the findings showed that this was based on size. Of the 25 per cent taking action more than half were large companies. This overall meant that very few small companies were taking action.

The single cause which was most often cited by any company in the study was pressure from legislation. This would appear to reinforce the arguments for mandatory legislative action.

There is no bar in the EC regulation on an individual Member State adopting a mandatory scheme for all or merely certain industrial processes. The regulation currently covers only businesses in the industrial sector. Amendments have been tabled to the regulation which have permitted the Member States to extend the regulation, on an experimental basis to other sectors. This would bring the distributive trade and the public service sector within the scope of the regulation as well.

Conclusions

Pressure is mounting on companies to alter their business management plans to give environmental protection measures a greater priority. This comes as a result of the growing body of environmental legislation. The pressure is also continuing despite the increasing scepticism being voiced by both industry and the consumers about environmental issues. In Europe in recent years the more pressing economic problems from increased levels of unemployment have begun to take a higher place on agendas for industrialists, policy makers and consumers.

The European Commission, in recognition of the emerging trends, has turned to other means than merely imposing rigid environmental standards through legislation. The EMAS is the embodiment of a great deal of new thinking within the Community. The scheme is voluntary, but in order to ensure that distortion to the operation of the market does not occur, it has been produced in the form of a regulation, which has to be applied throughout the EC.

EMAS is the Community's attempt to rationalize practices which are in place in some companies under a broad umbrella of acceptable action across the whole of the EC. It is also designed to progressively improve the environmental performance of the EC as a whole and thereby help in the progress towards sustainable development within Europe. The legislation has twin objectives.

1. First, to encourage a company to improve progressively its environmental performance.
2. Second, to provide information about the measures which a company introduces to its business management plan to ensure that the objective is met. This information can then be made available to the public by the use of the eco-audit logo and the publication of the verified environmental statement.

The key element for both objectives is the use of eco-auditing procedures. An environmental audit is required in order to give details about the environmental operations of a given organization. It is not intended to be a static procedure, but to be the linchpin in an active strategy adopted by a business to improve its environmental protection measures and procedures. As with any audit it involves the systematic investigation by independent experts of the standard working routines and procedures within an organization.

The number of companies within Europe using an environmental audit as the preparation for changes to their businesses strategy plan is still small and tends to be concentrated within the largest companies. In the UK the Institute of Directors estimate that only one in seven companies actually use the tool of an eco-audit. However, the use of eco-auditing is likely to rise throughout Europe. The scope of the EC's regulation could encompass as many as 100 000 to 150 000 sites in the UK alone where eco-audits will be required.

The EC's Environmental Management and Audit Scheme has been developed in response to a call for a consistent and clear framework, so that action taken in one Member State of the EC or by one company does not inhibit the operation of the level playing field of the Community' Single Market. In creating this self-regulatory voluntary approach to the legislation the Community is focusing on the problems of protecting the environment. Industry is being targeted very clearly as responsible for altering its practices so that the objective of progressive and sustainable development can be achieved within Europe.

The take-up rate for EMAS is not clear. Concerns remain for all companies, no matter what the size. EMAS will receive widespread use if the companies can be persuaded that they will benefit. The Commission of the European Community view is that the market will persuade the companies and in order to do so the publication of information is crucial. However, it is this and the concerns about cost which will make the companies very reluctant

The European Community's Environmental Management and Audit Scheme

to be the first to adopt the legislation. They will have to be persuaded that there are little or no commercial risks and many companies may wait until they see if others register and benefit first.

References

1 Official Journal of the European Communities (1993) Series L.L 168 10 July 1993. Council Regulation EEC No. 1863/93 of 29 June 1993 allowing voluntary participation by companies in the industrial sector in a Community eco-management and audit scheme. Article 5.
2 Commission of the EC (1992) *Towards Sustainability. A Community Programme of Policy and Action in relation to the Environment and Sustainable Development.* COM (92) 23 Final. Brussels March.
3 Official Journal of the EC (1992) Series L.L 99 11 April 1992. Council Regulation EEC No. 880/92 of 23 March 1992 on a Community award scheme for an eco-label.
4 Council Regulation EEC No. 1863/93 of 29 June 1993.
5 Christensen, P. and Nielsen, E. H. (1993) Environmental Audits, Clean Technologies and Environmental Protection in Denmark. *European Environment.* Vol.2, Part 3, June 1993. p.18.
6 House of Lords (1992) Select Committee on the European Communities. Session 1992/1993. 12th Report. *A Community Eco-audit Scheme.*HL. 42. 8 December, 1992, p.53.
7 Batchelor, C. (1993) A victim of its own success, *Financial Times.* 21 July, p. 13.
8 Department of Trade and Industry/Department of the Environment. (1993) Implementation of the EC Eco-management and Audit Regulation and accreditation arrangements for certification to BS 7750. Joint Consultative Document. DTI/DoE. July.
9 Cowe, R. (1993) *Guardian.* 21 June p.10.

Appendix C2.1 Simplified list of requirements for EMAS registration

The company, must for the sites it wishes to register:
1 Define its environmental policy. (This must be a written statement which includes an assessment of the management system already in place.)
2 Set the targets which it wishes to achieve, giving the time scale.
3 Put into place the plans and procedures to meet the internally set objectives.
4 Put into operation the audit procedures, according to the time scale in the regulation.

5 Publish the results of the audit, once it has been externally verified.
6 Set new targets in the light of the findings and begin again.

Source: Based on the Official Journal of the EC No. L 168/12. 10 July 1993. Annex II of the Regulation.

Appendix C2.2 The ECO audit cycle

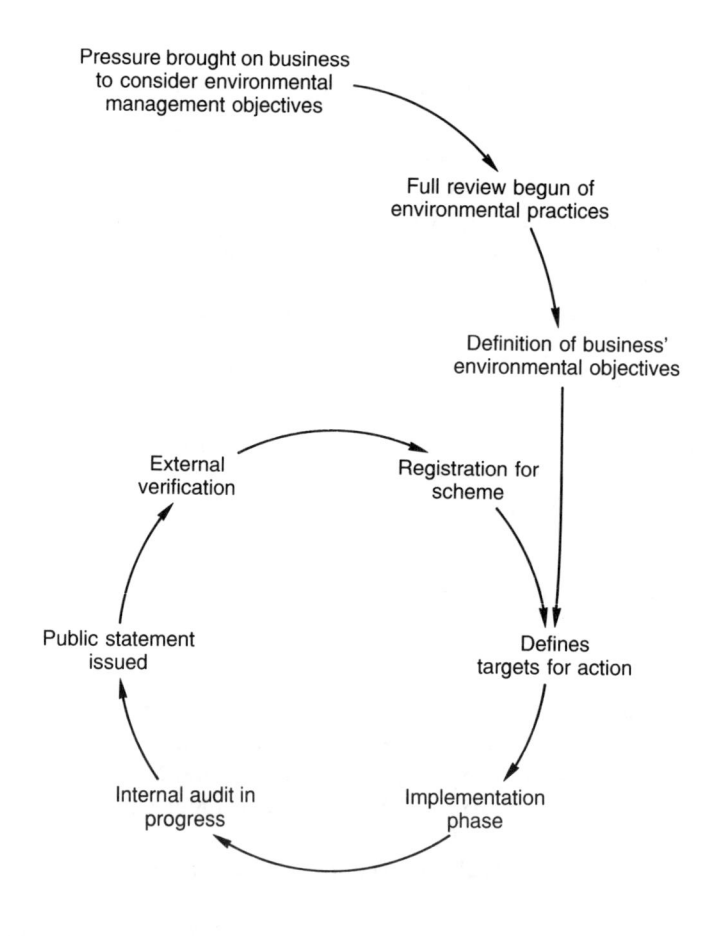

```
Pressure brought on business
to consider environmental
management objectives
          ↓
    Full review begun of
    environmental practices
          ↓
    Definition of business'
    environmental objectives
          ↓
External         Registration for
verification     scheme
                    ↓
Public statement     Defines
issued               targets for action
    ↑                ↓
Internal audit in    Implementation
progress             phase
```

The European Community's Environmental Management and Audit Scheme

Questions

1. Discuss the possible costs and benefits to a company of issuing the public environmental statement required by the EMAS regulation.
2. In what ways do the problems of registering for EMAS differ for the SMEs and the large industrial complexes?
3. Discuss the arguments for and against the EC providing assistance for the SMEs rather than the individual states of the EC.
4. In the past many environmental problems have occurred as a result of the market failing to operate to protect the environment. Evaluate the likely environmental impact of EMAS based as it is, on allowing the market to operate more freely.
5. Anita Roddick of the Body Shop has declared that she 'cannot understand why this legislation is based on voluntary action and not mandatory action'. Outline the arguments for and against keeping the voluntary basis of the regulation.
6. The conclusion reached by the UK's Chemical Industries Association is that EMAS will not be of great practical importance. Outline the reasons why this conclusion was reached. What changes should be made to the regulation to ensure that the chemical companies do register?

Case 3 The 'myth' of the level playing field: the case of contested takeovers within the EC

Leigh Davison

Introduction

Chapter 4 describes the establishment of an EC-wide merger control regulation, but this cannot, as this case clearly demonstrates, be taken to mean that a 'level playing field' for contested takeovers exists across the EC. That is, guaranteeing equal opportunities for taking control of quoted companies in every Member State, and, therefore, being subject to a common framework of rules governing the behaviour of the various parties involved. At present equal opportunities do not exist as evidenced by the fact that the bulk of hostile takeovers arise in one EC Member State: the UK. In Germany and Holland, for example, such activity represents an alien tradition and, accordingly, rarely occurs. The case seeks to explore why the UK corporate sector is so 'open' to hostile bids and why the opposite is true of Germany.

At the heart of the matter are what have been termed structural and technical barriers to contested takeovers. If sufficiently strong, they can make a company effectively bid proof. Structural barriers result from the business culture that prevails in each Member State. For example, it is common practice in Italy, France and Spain for the ownership of quoted shares to be limited to a small group of trusted friends/family, thereby considerably reducing the possibility of a takeover attempt. In Germany the close interrelationship the major banks have with the industrial sector, as well as the ties between companies themselves, likewise act as an effective barrier against contested takeovers. Only in the UK and Holland are the structural barriers relatively weak.

Unlike the UK, technical barriers to takeovers are very strong in both Holland and Germany. Technical barriers predominantly concern the extent to which a company, in its articles of association, can establish restrictions that either reduce the likelihood of a contested takeover being successful, or arising in the first place. The articles of association of a Dutch quoted company, for example, can allow the issue of priority shares which afford the holder a considerable degree of control over the company, such as the authority to make a binding proposal at a meeting of the shareholders on the appointment or dismissal of management. In addition their approval may also be required on the following matters: the issuing of new shares; the amendment of the company's articles of association and various other important decisions. By concentrating these powers in a few 'friendly' hands, the company reduces its attractiveness to a potential raider.

Contested takeovers and the German business environment

The German equivalent of the UK public limited company is termed *'Aktiengesellschaft'* (AG). The technical and structural barriers operating within, and seen as a natural part of, the German business environment ensure that AGs are for the most part secure from predatory takeovers. The recent failure of Pirelli, an Italian tyre manufacturer, to take control of its arch rival, Continental AG, the Hanover-based tyre producer, bears witness to this fact. This is examined in detail later. As in Holland, hostile bids are very rare. It would not be wrong to suggest that hostile takeover attempts can be viewed as alien to the German national corporate culture; this is not to say, however, that 'friendly' mergers are frowned upon, nor does it mean that AGs are loath to going abroad to purchase a foreign based company. A well known example of this is Deutsche Bank taking control of Morgan Grenfell, a UK merchant bank.

Structural barriers

Structural barriers to contested takeovers are particularly strong in Germany, giving quoted companies considerable protection. The reverse is true regarding the UK corporate environment.

1   Debt finance

It is well established that debt finance has played a far more prominent role than equity in providing for the needs of German industry. Stock markets have not been seen as the provider of long-term capital; companies have traditionally relied upon loans from their 'Hausbank'. Consequently market capitalization is relatively low when compared with the UK position. The net outcome of this reliance on debt finance is that only a small market for quoted shares exists, which, in turn, means that the possibilities for corporate raiders are very restricted. *The Economist* (3–9 July 1993) points out that only 425 German companies have publicly quoted shares while the UK figure, despite its smaller economy, stands at 1950.

2 Share ownership

Table C.3.1 provides a breakdown of ownership of German Aktiengesellschaften in 1990. It reveals that banks, in addition to providing loans, have considerable equity holdings – this is particularly true of Deutsche, Dresdner and Commerzbank, who, together, hold around half of the said equity holdings – which must reinforce the bond between 'Hausbank' and company, thereby making a successful takeover of a company less likely. The relationship between the two often goes a stage further with a representative of the bank being a member of the company's supervisory board.

Table C.3.1 *Owners of Aktiengesellschaften (%; 1990)*

Banks	8.7
Insurance companies	3.2
Investment funds	3.3
Industry	41.7
Private households	18.7
Government	6
Foreign investors	18.7

(Source: Deutsche Bundesbank)

Table C3.1 reveals that the largest owner of quoted equity is industry itself. Moreover this link between corporations is strengthened by the practice of a company having management representatives from other industries on its supervisory board. Members of Continental's supervisory board, in 1990, for example, held managerial positions at the following corporations: Daimler-Benz AG, IBM Deutschland Gmbh, Preussag AG, Veba AG and Siemens AG. These near-incestuous relationships can act as a formidable barrier to an attempted takeover. On these matters David Goodhart, writing in the *Financial Times* (12 August 1988), has stated:

> Tracing the obstacles to hostile bids in Germany has to start from the fact that there are only about 500 publicly traded companies. A large number of those public companies, probably more than a third, are protected by one very large minority, or even majority shareholder – a family trust, or a financial institution. Many others have a handful of shareholders, including other companies, each with a sizeable stake.

Technical barriers

Not quite on a par with Dutch quoted companies, German AGs none the less are able to put in place a set of technical barriers which enable them effectively to defend themselves against any predator. The important barriers are now detailed.

The 'myth' of the level playing field

1 Shareholders

AGs, such as Continental, Deutsche Bank, Mannesmann, BASF and Bayer, have sought to limit the power of any individual shareholder by adopting what is termed the 5 per cent or 10 per cent rule. The management of an AG ensure that the company's Articles of Association contain a clause which restricts a shareholder, irrespective of the number of voting shares held by that individual, to 5 or 10 per cent of the voting rights. For example, article 20 of Continental's articles of association stipulate: 'If a shareholder owns shares with a total par value which exceeds 5 per cent of the capital stock, such shareholder's voting rights shall be limited to the number of votes granted by shares with a total par value of 5 per cent of the capital stock.' Thus no one shareholder can amass sufficient voting power to threaten the incumbent management. A national pressure group, the Deutsche Schutzvereinigung Fur Wertpapierbesitz, DSW, is, however, actively seeking the implementation of the principle of 'one share, one vote'.

One way for a predator to circumvent the above-mentioned restriction is by the formation of what is called a 'concert party': the predator and a group of trusted allies each buy 5 per cent of the victim's voting equity in order to get control. Of course, the AG under attack may seek to establish a 'defence pool' whereby 'friends' of the current management of the AG hold voting equity in order to frustrate the predator's hostile intentions. A formal defence pool, however, is illegal under German law.

To reduce the likelihood of a takeover attempt being successful, an AG can issue non-voting shares up to an amount equal to 50 per cent of its total equity. This practice, it has been claimed, ensures control of the company is maintained within a chosen group of equity holders. Some companies engage in the practice of cross-shareholdings as a way of reducing the threat of takeover. Having a 'friendly' company take an equity stake in your business, at the same time as your company takes a minority interest in it, means that for both companies the exposure in terms of the amount of their shares available to a potential predator is reduced. Such defensive cross-shareholdings are more frequent in France, however.

In Germany it is common for shareholders to deposit shares with their bank. If a shareholder does not wish to exert his/her voting right, he/she can give permission for the depositary institution to act as a proxy. Concerning these shares, the depositary bank must inform the owners how it intends to vote on the motions to be decided at, say, the company's annual general meeting of shareholders. Of course the shareholder, if he/she disagrees with the depository bank's line on voting, is free to instruct the bank on how to cast his/her votes. For an AG such as Continental, the fact that its 'hausbank' (as well as owning an equity stake in it and, of course, having a representative on the company's supervisory board) has also this power of proxy only serves to make the bank of even greater importance to the company, especially if management have to fight off a predator.

2 The supervisory board and the management board

An AG, such as Continental, has both a supervisory board and a management board, or executive board, unlike in the UK where a public limited company has a single board of directors. A two-tier structure exists and this obviously has implications for a predator who is seeking to remove the existing management team and thereby gain control of the AG.

The management board, which is concerned with the day-to-day running of the AG, is appointed by the supervisory board. In particular, the former reports to the latter about such matters as business strategy and any other major developments concerning the AG. In addition, the supervisory board also receives reports about the AG's profitability position and any other 'important incidents' that have surfaced. The overriding function of the supervisory board of an AG is to keep a watchful eye on management to ensure the continued successful performance of the company.

To fulfil this task, the supervisory board members have the following powers: access to the AG's books; to call an extraordinary shareholders' meeting, if they deem it necessary for the AG's continued wellbeing; reach a decision on business issues that the management board cannot by itself determine, such as, the closure of a plant and/or the sale of a subsidiary. Finally, the supervisory board can dismiss one or all members of the management board 'if there is just cause'.

Clearly, then, for a predator to succeed in taking over an AG it must have a majority on the supervisory board so as to be in a position whereby it can attempt to control the management board, and thus the daily running of the company. If an AG employs more than 2000 people on a regular basis then half the members of its supervisory board are chosen by its employees; the other half are elected by shareholders. If a stalemate arises, the chairperson of the board, usually a shareholder's representative, has the casting vote. The removal of the members of the supervisory board normally requires a 75 per cent majority of the votes cast. Hence, the management only require just over 25 per cent of the votes cast to 'block' a predator.

3 Identification of share ownership

A major problem for a potential predator is that share ownership in the company it is interested in buying is very often difficult to ascertain. This is because bearer shares are the most common type of share in Germany and are not registered. This, however, can be a double-edged sword: it will suit an AG that a predator has difficulty identifying the owners of bearer shares issued by the company; however, this lack of information about ownership means that an AG may not be aware that a predator is quietly increasing its share holdings in the company, especially as German law allows the predator to purchase up to 25 per cent of the AG's equity without having to disclose this fact. The comparable figure for the UK being any acquisition by a predator which exceeds 2 per cent, as required by the Companies Act 1989.

Continental AG experienced a version of this in late 1989. Rumour had it that a predator was accumulating the company's shares but Continental's management, on account of the above law, were not in a position to confirm or refute this speculation. Its management, therefore, ordered the matter to be thoroughly looked into. The ensuing investigation, which included a survey of banks in Germany and abroad regarding 'the structure of Continental share deposits' held by them, did not reveal 'any concrete information regarding any potential raiders'. This finding led Horst W. Urban, the then Chairperson of Continental's management board, to claim that

> There was no concrete substantiation for the fleeting rumours of a takeover. (Continental AG's Annual Report, 1989.)

Nonetheless both the company's supervisory and management boards thought it prudent at the next annual general meeting of shareholders to pass a resolution reinforcing the current restriction on voting rights.

Pirelli versus Continental: an illustrative example

Both Pirelli and Continental AG are middle-ranking tyre manufacturers, with the former being based in Milan, Italy, and the latter having its headquarters located in Hanover, Germany. Concerning the volume of world tyre sales in 1990, Pirelli's market share stood at 6 per cent whilst Continental did slightly better at 7 per cent. The global tyre industry is dominated by 'the big three', namely Michelin, Goodyear and Bridgestone. A merger between Pirelli and Continental would, in terms of sales, place the resultant company nearly alongside the big three and it would be seen as a truly global player.

Pirelli's first attempt to enhance its global presence was when it tried to take over Firestone, the ailing giant US tyre concern. Bridgestone, a Japanese owned tyre group, seized control of Firestone, leaving Pirelli to look elsewhere for a suitable candidate to take over. Likewise, Continental remains equally intent on establishing itself as a global player; the company's annual report for 1989 openly asserts that it is committed to globalization. Like Pirelli, Continental has sought to achieve this goal by adopting a policy of strategic acquisition. A route to joining the big league of tyre producers was for Pirelli to acquire Continental, or vice versa if Continental so decided.

In September 1990 Pirelli's hostile intentions towards Continental became public knowledge, with the German company rejecting Pirelli's unwanted overtures. By the end of the said month, the Pirelli concert party was boasting that it controlled over 50 per cent of Continental's voting equity. The management of Continental did not have the information to refute or substantiate this claim. As noted earlier, Continental had a clause in its articles of association limiting a shareholder to a maximum of 5 per cent of the votes cast at a shareholders' meeting. However, and Pirelli must have been aware of this development, at Continental's annual general meeting in 1989 supporters of the DSW just failed in their attempt to eliminate the voting rights restriction.

Matters came to a head at the extraordinary meeting of Continental's shareholders held on 13 March 1991, as four crucial motions were voted upon.

1. Henceforth, revision of the voting rights restriction will require a majority of at least 75 per cent of votes cast at a shareholders' meeting.
2. The abolition of the voting rights restriction.
3. The dismissal of shareholder appointees to the supervisory board will no longer be based on a simple majority vote but will require a majority of at least 75 per cent of the votes cast.
4. The management should take the necessary steps so as to enable shareholders at the next annual general meeting to adopt a motion giving the go ahead for the merger.

The Pirelli concert party, on the grounds that their intentions towards Continental were purely 'friendly', made it known that they would abstain when motion number 4 was voted upon. The motion was massively rejected, with abstentions equalling 36 per cent of the equity present at the meeting. In other words Pirelli and its allies did not have sufficient voting power to take control of Continental. Pirelli later disclosed that it held shares and options totalling approximately 39 per cent of Continental's equity. It is known that the following Italian concerns were, at one time or another during the takeover attempt, part of the Pirelli concert party: Mediobanca, Sopaf SpA, Intalmobilare, Fiat and Riunione Adriatic di Sicurta.

Given that at Continental's last annual general meeting supporters of DSW had come close to removing the company's voting rights limitation, it is not at all surprising that the Pirelli camp voted in favour of motion 2 at the extraordinary shareholders' meeting. In fact 66 per cent of the equity present voted for its abolition; to be passed the motion required a simple majority in its favour. The Pirelli camp scented victory, however, this was not to be. In May 1992 a court in Hanover annulled the motion on the grounds that in

The 'myth' of the level playing field

March 1991 Pirelli failed to declare that it controlled in excess of 25 per cent of Continental's voting equity. Pirelli at first continued to stalk its intended prey, but at Continental's next annual general meeting, Ulrich Weiss, chairperson of the supervisory board, ruled that the Pirelli concert party would be limited to a 5 per cent voting right. This effectively undermined Pirelli's ability to again seek the abolition of Continental's voting rights restriction. Eventually, Pirelli, whose financial position had deteriorated markedly, decided to abandon its plan to take over Continental.

Contested takeovers and the UK business environment

As noted earlier, the relative weakness of structural and technical barriers in the UK makes its corporate sector the most 'open' for contested takeovers in the EC.

Structural barriers

1 Corporate culture

The sheer number of contested bids, relative to those occurring in other EC member countries, demonstrates that they are, for the most part, an accepted part of the UK corporate environment. This is not to say, however, that some bids do not meet fierce resistance from the management of the company targeted for acquisition, such as when Nestlé, a company based in Switzerland, sought to take control of Rowntree. Critics have advocated that the UK'S openness to takeover activity fosters short-termism, by which they mean management seek to maximize short-term profitability – thereby keeping the share price high and providing a good dividend – so as to please the extremely powerful shareholding city institutions, such as banks, insurance companies and pension funds, instead of looking after the longer term interests of companies. The case for hostile takeovers has received support on the grounds that the takeover threat helps keep management on their toes. In addition, it has been claimed that an under performing company, an indicator of which could be a low share price, can be brought back to efficiency as a direct consequence of a successful bid.

2 Financial institutions and the role of management

These institutions, operating on behalf of their respective clients, have enormous financial muscle, the use of which keeps management's eyes focused upon maximizing shareholder value. It clearly is in the interest of these institutions, given the above goal, to keep structural barriers low, for a hostile bid causes a sharp rise in the target company's share price, generating them a possible financial gain. In Germany, as has already been noted, the position is very different. The stated barriers, such as the voting rights restriction, tilt the balance of power between shareholders and management, saved from any real likelihood of having to face a contested bid, so that it firmly lies with the latter and its allies.

This puts into perspective why the goal of German management is focused on the long-term wellbeing of their respective company and not orientated towards maximizing shareholders' value. In the UK, however, directors of a company have a greater degree of responsibility to its shareholders. Within the context of a takeover, the City Code on Takeovers and Mergers applies and, as its name indicates, the Code comprises of a non-statutory set of regulations governing the conduct of the various parties involved in a bid. The Code requires both the offeror (predator) and the offeree (target) companies to act in the best interest of their respective shareholders. In the case of the target company, this means that its board of directors should seek appropriate independent advice upon receiving an offer and must not resort to any form of action which could frustrate the offer without first gaining shareholders' approval. Moreover, shareholders must be kept informed of all the relevant facts in a timely manner, so as to enable them to form a judgement on the offer. Finally, all shareholders must be treated equally. The Code clearly seeks to put shareholders of the offeree into a position where they can decide the outcome of the bid. The primacy of shareholders has resulted in a recent study asserting:

> Thus, contrary to their counterparts in many European countries, directors of UK public companies are required in practice to place shareholder interests ahead of their own. This provides a significant legal and cultural force which mitigates against the frustration of a contested bid on primarily self interest grounds (a study by Coopers & Lybrand Management Consultants. UK section, 1990, p.8).

By statute – section 303 of the Companies Act 1985 – shareholders of a listed company require only a simple majority of votes cast to remove its board of directors, irrespective of what is stated in a its articles of association. Directors having usually to be re-elected every three years.

Technical barriers

1 Shareholders

With regard to voting equity, the principle of 'one vote per share' is predominant. Nevertheless, there are some exceptions. Differential voting rights attached to ordinary shares is one example. A company's equity could be split between ordinary shares, carrying voting rights, and ordinary 'A' shares, which had no or only a restricted voting right. This has been used to protect and maintain family control of a concern, but such a share structure is comparatively rare when dealing with those companies listed on the stock exchange.

The 'myth' of the level playing field

A second exception is that in theory it is possible for a UK company to include in its articles of association provisions which restrict the voting rights of an individual shareholder, irrespective of the size of the equity stake held, and secondly to place a limit on the number of shares a shareholder may acquire. Companies with such provisions are very rare. One reason for this is that in order to put in place the above restrictions, an appropriate motion would require the support of a 75 per cent majority of shareholders. This is very unlikely as major private and institutional shareholders would rightly view this as a dilution of their power and a strengthening of management's, especially as the restrictions could act as a significant barrier to a contested bid, thereby having the potential to undermine shareholder value.

2 Identification of share ownership

The use of bearer shares in the UK is extremely rare. Furthermore, a company when filing its annual return must include a register of shareholders and provide certain information about its directors. This is available for public inspection. So are documents from listed companies which have to be filed in order to satisfy the City Code and the rules of the Stock Exchange, and these will provide information concerning acquisitions/disposals and any changes in share capital. In addition the company must keep a separate register which will contain details of those parties and their nominees who hold a substantial interest in the company's share capital. At present, the Companies Act 1989 defines substantial as 3 per cent of the company's nominal capital.

Nestlé versus Rowntree: an illustrative example

Interest focused upon the future fate of Rowntree, the York-based sweet producer, when early on the morning of the 13 April 1988 Jacob Suchard, a chocolate manufacturer, snapped up around 15 per cent of Rowntrees' equity, paying 629 pence per share – a premium of 34 per cent above the price (468 pence) the shares were trading at on the previous day. This Swiss-based dawn raider claimed that if no other predator sought to gain control of Rowntree, it would desist from mounting a full scale bid for the company. Nevertheless, it further increased its equity stake in Rowntree to 29.9 per cent, the maximum permitted under the City Code before a full blown takeover has to be mounted. Accordingly the price of Rowntree's shares soared.

On 26 April a second cash-rich Swiss concern, Nestlé, entered the scene intent on taking control of Rowntree. Nestlé, a multinational food giant, had, given its small domestic market and a desire to enhance its global presence, already implemented a strategy of growth through acquisition. In

1985, for example, it acquired a major US foods concern, Carnation Foods. Ironically, being Swiss-based meant that Nestlé itself was highly unlikely to fall prey to another predator. Nestlé's interest in Rowntree went beyond just preventing a rival (Suchard) from taking it over. It was motivated by the probable synergies that could accrue from the takeover.

Nestlé, known for its 'block' chocolate bars (the 'milky bar' in the UK) by acquiring Rowntree, for example, would gain a company whose well-known brands (Rolo, KitKat, Smarties, Polo, Aero) were firmly established in the countline segment of the sweet market, especially in the UK, thereby broadening and balancing its product portfolio. Synergistic benefits were also claimed in the area of distribution, and, at the time, it was further argued that Nestlé had the financial clout to fund the costly promotions Rowntree's strategy of establishing its stated brands in continental Europe required – which so far had only achieved limited success. Of course the fact that Rowntree had created these brands and was actively seeking to improve its market share in continental Europe does not suggest a staid, out of touch management; although the policy of diversification which led it into the restaurant business and snack foods, among other things, was questioned. Given also that Rowntree was making satisfactory profits and had made efficiency gains from reducing the size of its workforce, it cannot be asserted with any degree of truth that Rowntree's was an ailing company and therefore ripe for takeover.

Nestlé in launching a full-scale bid for Rowntree offered 890 pence per share, thus paying a premium of 90 per cent and thereby valuing the company at around £2.1 billion. The management of Rowntree, not surprisingly, argued against accepting the bid and a defence campaign was duly launched. It pointed out that, given Rowntree's history of success in creating and establishing brands, especially when compared with Nestlé`s record, Rowntree did not need Nestlé. The Rowntree campaign sought the 'blocking' of the takeover by having it referred by the Director-General of Fair Trading, with the approval of the then Secretary of State for Industry, Lord Young, to the Monopolies and Mergers Commission (MMC). This would place the takeover on hold for at least three months while the MMC investigated whether or not it was in the public interest for the takeover to go ahead. Referral of the takeover to the MMC, however, was unlikely given that the 'Tebbitt' guidelines, named after the Industry Secretary who generated them in 1984, stated that the issue of referral was to be decided primarily on competition grounds. Nestlé had only a small presence in the UK, and, therefore, its taking control of Rowntree would not significantly reduce effective competition in the UK sweet market. On 25 May the Secretary of State announced that the takeover would not be investigated by the MMC.

The 'myth' of the level playing field

On the following day, Suchard mounted a full-scale bid for Rowntree and offered 950 pence per share, a considerable improvement upon Nestlé's first bid. Nestlé countered by improving its offer to 1075 pence per share, a massive premium of 130 per cent and which put Rowntree`s value at just over £2.5 billion – remembering that before a predator started seriously acquiring shares Rowntree was valued at around £1 billion. After secret negotiations between Rowntree and Nestlé, which started after the Conservative Government refused to refer the takeover to the MMC, the management of the former in late June came out in favour of Nestlé`s improved bid, advising shareholders to sell. Rowntree`s independence was at an end.

The Bangemann proposals

The EC Commission is not blind to the various forms of structural and technical barriers which, to a varying degree, exist in individual Member States. Obviously a single European market requires an EC-wide framework of rules governing the conduct of the various parties involved in a hostile bid for a quoted company. In May 1990, in an attempt to move the EC towards meeting this goal, Martin Bangemann, the then EC Commissioner for Industry, tabled a number of proposals; as yet not implemented. A summary of these is given below.

1 Maintenance of equity

Concerning the takeover bid period of time, the target company, or offeree, can acquire a maximum of 10 per cent of its own equity, subject to this being sanctioned by shareholders. Included within this 10 per cent rule are shares in the offeree held by its own subsidiaries.

2 Managerial change

The removal of members from a supervisory board or a board of directors, appointed by shareholders, will only require a simple majority of the votes cast at a shareholders' meeting. The existing position, where in some Member States it is possible for a company to require a figure greater than a simple majority of the votes cast, will be prohibited. It will outlaw the practice whereby the ownership of a certain type of share entitles the holder to an exclusive power to make proposals regarding the appointment of management.

3 Voting right

Concerning voting equity, the principle of 'one vote per share', irrespective of the scale of an individual share holding in a company, is proposed. Non-voting equity is to be limited to 50 per cent of total equity issued.

On the issue of regulating the conduct of a depositary institution, in relation to proxy voting, Bangemann accepts the safeguards contained in the proposed 5th company law directive as being sufficient. In particular, it directs that a proxy institution must inform shareholders who have deposited their shares with it, as to how the institution intends to use these votes, at say, the next annual general meeting. This provides these shareholders, if they disagree with the proxy's voting intentions, with an opportunity to instruct the proxy how to vote.

The problem of bearer shares and nominee shareholdings is not dealt with by the Bangemann proposals, so it will remain difficult for a predator to ascertain the ownership of these shares. In general, the proposals focus upon the technical barriers to takeovers but have very little to say concerning the various structural barriers which, to a varying degree, still exist in Member States.

Questions

1 Using illustrative examples explain the difference between structural and technical barriers to contested takeovers which to a varying degree, exist in EC Member States.

2 'In the light of the attempted takeover of Continental by Pirelli and Nestlé's acquisition of Rowntree, it is clear that an EC-wide level playing field for contested takeovers does not exist.'

Examine this assertion.

3 Assess the claim that the Bangemann proposals are not in themselves sufficient to tackle the variety of barriers to contested takeovers that currently flourish within the EC.

Case 4 Restructuring the steel industry in the European Community

Alan Jones

Introduction

Despite the long history and earthy reputation of steel production, steel is a very modern product. It is not one product but serves hundreds if not thousands of functions. In Europe steel production is very advanced; steel technology in Europe is among the best in the world; 70–80 per cent of its products have been developed in the last ten years. It is a sophisticated industry that has responded well to competition in all of its traditional markets. It has adjusted to the changing pattern of demand with new high value added products. In addition the most cost effective production is to be found in Europe (see Table C4.1).

Table C4.1 *Comparative steelmaking costs*

UK	413
France	493
Germany	558
Japan	572
USA	513
S. Korea	511
Taiwan	511

Source : House of Lords European Community Committee

However, in the 1990s the industry finds itself in difficulty, with the same low cost, high technology producers finding it impossible to make profits and complaining of unfair competition from producers in central and eastern Europe, who take less than 3 per cent of their market.

Profits and prices have fallen from record high levels in 1989 to life-threatening losses or hand-to-mouth profits in 1993. Though the nature of the problem is not exclusively European it has many facets that reflect the peculiarities of the European industry. The first of these is its relationship to the European Community; this relationship has undergone a period of uncertainty as the EC adapts its views on competition to an industry that has always operated in a structured environment. The second is the stubbornly national character of the companies that make up the industry and their inability to break free of national politics to create a truly European industry. A corollary of this is the problem of an inappropriate structure and the need for re-structuring to meet current and future market needs. Externally there is the perceived problem of competition from Central and Eastern Europe but also the aggressive use of anti-dumping claims in the USA that puts pressure on the EC Commission to adjust internal policy on subsidies and state aids and have helped, recently, to force the pace on steel re-structuring.

The steel industry and the EC

The steel industry enjoys a special status in the European Community; covered by its own treaty (the Treaty of Paris) it has always been the subject of guidance and intervention. The special characteristics of the industry have given it a central place in industrial policy concerns. The strategic significance of the industry, that led to the creation of the European Coal and Steel Community (ECSC), has receded as a factor, but other features; the sensitivity of the industry to changes in the level of aggregate demand, the high proportion of employment supported by the industry, the regional concentration and specialization of the industry, the high level of direct state ownership in the industry (45 per cent of the industry is nationalized in the EC), and not least of all the existence of the Treaty of Paris itself, have contributed to the perpetuation of this special status. A central question for the industry in the EC is whether this special status should remain or whether steel should be regarded in the same way as other industrial sectors subject to the new freedom of the internal market.

Many commentators feel that there is little justification for the special status of the industry. Within the EC Commission itself this status has been in question for some time. However, the directives emerging from Single European Act (SEA) have no direct influence upon this sector; the regulations of the Treaty of Paris with a tighter application of the 'State Aids Code' have been accepted, under pressure from the industry, to be sufficient until the Treaty expires in 2002[1].

The 'General Objectives For Steel-1995' (GOS-95), which sets out the European Commission's steel strategy under the Treaty of Paris for the period 1990–1995, expects the industry's costs to benefit indirectly through the impact of the SEA upon energy industries and through the liberalization of the capital and transport markets. In addition, it was agreed in GOS-95 that further integration and cross-border rationalization of the industry were to be encouraged. It was equally clear that in the build up to the Single European Market (SEM), cartel arrangements that had been formalized under the D'Avignon plan would not be acceptable as informal arrangements after its demise.

Restructuring the steel industry in the European Community

The GOS 95 report was written in the background of high demand with an industry that was flourishing, having recovered from the severe test of the 1980s with the aid of the 'D'Avignon' plan (1980–88). It was also written with a new free market spirit deriving from the anticipation of the realization of the SEM. The EC Commission was, on the whole, glad to be relieved of the quota system imposed under D'Avignon and there was a feeling that the Treaty of Paris was an anomaly that could also be dispensed with, preferably before its expiry date. Although it accepted the special status of the industry, GOS 95 represented a clear statement of the free market principles which the Commission had accepted as necessary. The report emphasized the Commission's limited information-gathering role under the Treaty of Paris and focused upon its function of creating a free market in Europe by challenging covert state aids difficulties.

However, the restructuring process experienced between 1980 and 1988 did not represent a permanent solution to the problems of the EC steel industry. Profits and prices peaked in 1989 (see Figure C.4.1) at the beginning of a run down driven by falling industrial production particularly in the metal using industries (see Figure C4.2) which has turned out to be a Europe wide recession.

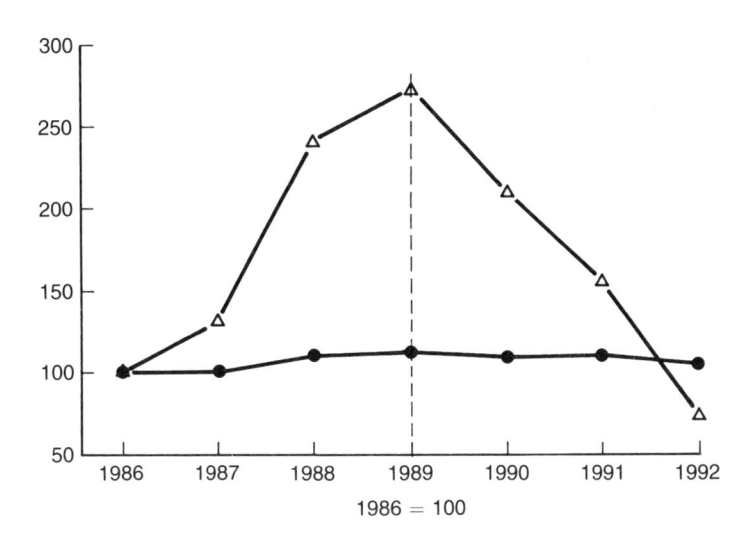

Figure C4.1 Indices of steel production (-●-) and profit (-△-): 1986 = 100 (source: OECD 1993)

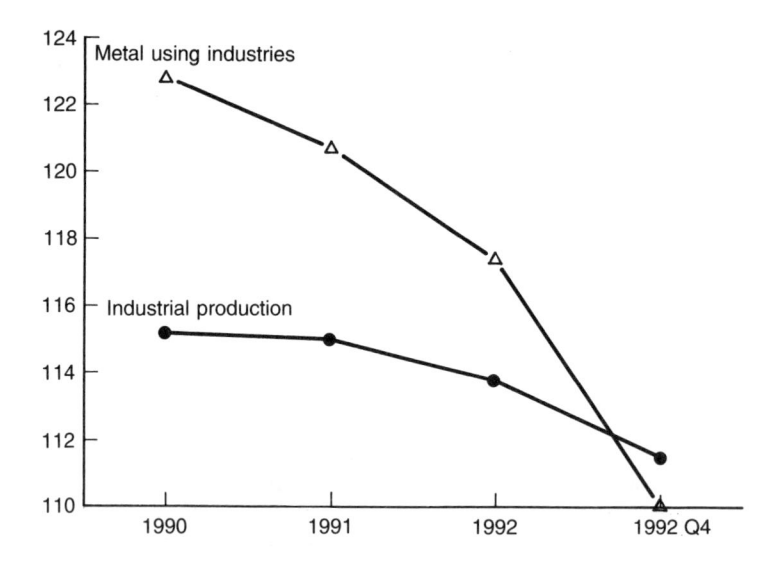

Figure C4.2 EC(12) production indices: 1985 = 100

The industry, left undefended after the expiry of the D'Avignon plan quickly found itself in operating conditions that exposed its remaining weaknesses. The EC industry, as represented by Eurofer, anticipated the downturn at its earliest stage but attributed the problem to short-term difficulties finding their markets vulnerable to new foreign competition, particularly from Central and Eastern Europe but also from China and Turkey[2]. They were anxious also about the future direction of prices as stockholders built up stocks. In addition there were uncertainties in export markets in particular the US market where Voluntary Export Restraints (VERs) were about to expire, but were expected to be replaced with similar, possibly tighter arrangements.

Nevertheless in 1989, Eurofer with the strongest support coming from German, French, Italian and Belgian producers, were already discussing a 'voluntary emergency code' to be prepared by the Commission for the eventuality of a downturn. This seemed to be a request for the creation of an informal quota system exploiting the requirement of the Commission to give advanced information upon the size and structure of steel markets under the Treaty of Paris. A similar system is already operated among producers in Japan who operate voluntary quotas to maintain prices and profit[3].

This ambiguity in the industry's attitude to the free market was not well attuned to the new free market commitment of a Commission that was concerned with creating a free market for steel and was beginning its campaign against subsidies and other anti-market practices in the steel industry and elsewhere[4]. It is, however, a feature of the companies in the industry whether they operate in the private or nationalized sector of the industry. In times of trouble the industry has little hesitation in calling upon its special status as a basis for special pleading.

As profits declined down to 1992 it became clear that the re-structuring that had taken place under the D'Avignon plan had not resolved a fundamental problem of the industry in the EC; the problem of overcapacity.

In October 1992 Eurofer wrote to the European Commission with proposals for what it called 'restructurization' offering to accomplish the change itself if the Commission would give specific kinds of help. The problem was characterized as arising from the recession in the EC, the difficult monetary circumstances caused by the collapse of the ERM, 'worldwide existing overcapacities' including those in the EC, an increase of imports due to 'unfair competition' from 'middle and Eastern Europe,' the problems of anti-dumping cases pending in the USA, and the failure to achieve a multilateral steel agreement within the GATT[5]. It laid down a specific set of solutions.

1   It called for a plan for re-structuring in which it offered to contribute to the incentives to reduce capacity from its own resources.
2   It requested that the resources of the ECSC be used to assist with the process and further requested the use of the reserve funds of ECSC for the purpose.
3   It called upon the Commission to resist the use of subsidies in the industry and to permit them only in circumstances where subsidies are exchanged for reductions in capacity.
4   It advocated a co-ordinated policy during the period of restructuring to be followed by the industry. It claimed that the existing arrangements of the Treaty of Paris enabled the Commission to comply.
5   It requested that there be more effective protection against imports from central and eastern Europe in the form of quotas with automatic duties when quotas were exceeded.

It was clear that this call from the industry would test the free market resolve of the Community. The Commission accepted the view that the industry was in difficulty but was reluctant to involve itself in what it saw to be the regulation of the industry and did not wish to participate actively in the decisions relating to cuts in capacity. Point 4 above was interpreted as a request to invoke article 58 of the Treaty of Paris declaring a 'manifest crisis' in the industry, which would enable the kind of market regulation that operated under the D'Avignon plan. As a compromise the Commission agreed to engage an 'independent personality' – Mr Fernand Braun – to undertake an appraisal of the situation. The results of Braun's appraisal and the report of the recommendations of the Commission were heard by the Industry Council on 26 February 1993. As a result of that the Industry Council made formal proposals for the re-structuring of the EC steel industry:

1. It rejected the request to consider the difficulties to be a 'manifest crisis' under article 58 of the Treaty of Paris.
2. It supported the 'industry's' efforts to reduce capacity and asked for 'the formulation by the industry, before 30 September 1993, of a precise and sufficiently extensive programme of definitive capacity reductions phased through, in principle, to the end of 1994 or if warranted to the end of 1995'[6].
3. It approved support measures from the EC (within the strict state aids' guidelines) adding contributions to existing social aids under Art. 53(a) of the Treaty of Paris, allowing states to contribute a supplement to social costs under the State Aid code, promising further funds under the EC structural funds. This package as well as increasing the available funds for restructuring from EC sources also enables states to augment this process with their own funds as long as these payments enable reductions in capacity. The payments will be to offset social costs either through redundancy payments or pensions or through development of alternatives to steel production. (See the Spanish case below.) Also the Commission would consider proposals for joint financing of capacity reduction programmes from groups of companies covering a particular sector or region.
4. It committed the Commission to the quick assessment and examination of proposals for joint ventures and rationalization plans that ensured a lasting re-organization within the sector. (In the context of existing competition law.)
5. It agreed to transmit to firms advance information about market price trends, production and deliveries by product type in the industry on a quarterly basis besides its existing six monthly 'forward programmes information' under Art. 46 of the Treaty of Paris. These would include a request for an indication of how firms were to respond to them.

The Council also agreed a range of measures to deal with the 'external' problem. These included more frequent surveillance and review of imports and import prices. They were aimed substantially at reviewing and strengthening existing quotas and arrangements on imports from central and eastern Europe, but included a commitment to achieve agreement of a Multilateral Steel Agreement (MSA) and a commitment to avoid the permanent adoption of 'excessive and unjustified trade measures' by the USA.

All of these measures were subject to the successful presentation of a 'credible programme' for capacity reductions by 30 September 1993. Failing that compliance the external and internal measures would lapse. In addition it rejected the level of capacity reductions offered by the first Braun Report as inadequate and the Commission re-appointed Braun to continue the effort at further capacity reductions up to the September deadline.

A peculiarity of the solution is that companies that lose capacity will be compensated by those that do not; the funding for this compensation will be covered in the first instance by loans from the ECSC repayable by the year 2002.

Clearly the Community has embarked upon a more wary attempt to restructure the steel industry than its previous efforts. The philosophical context has changed since 1980, but so also has the fiscal position of the Member States. On the face of it the agenda may be seen to have been set by Eurofer but the Council proposals are not a new D'Avignon plan. The EC has avoided taking responsibility for the process of capacity reductions and sought to maintain and confirm its commitment to the free market. The proposals for re-organization are still subject to competition law and the Commission has avoided all reference to the market structure proposals that might have emerged if the crisis was accepted as a 'manifest crisis'.

In the period up to the deadline a number of issues have to be resolved by the industry and by the Commission. The industry is not necessarily a unified industry; there is, as has been indicated by one BSC chairman, a great deal of mistrust among the European companies. The industry is split between state owned and private sector companies, it is further split between state owned companies that have moved into profit and efficiency (like Usinor-Sacilor in France) and those like ILVA in Italy whom the Commission regards as beneficiaries of (illegal) state aid. The central difficulty of the Commission arises out of the need to resolve the issue of the use of state aids, particularly in Italy, Spain, and east Germany since this represents the greatest objection brought by the private sector. It is also important from the point of view of the Commission that the arrangements do not contribute to further difficulties in trade talks with the USA. The question still remains whether these particular proposals will have the necessary impact and generate the re-structuring necessary to ensure the future of the industry outside the direct intervention of the state.

Restructuring

The problem of overcapacity

Pedro Ortun Director General of the Directorate of Basic Industries (DG III) of the EC Commission believes that there is now excess capacity in the steel industry of between 20 and 30 tonnes of finished products and 30 and 40m tonnes of crude steel. It is clear that the problems of re-structuring which the industry had thought had been met by D'Avignon have re-emerged as the central difficulty of the industry. Capacity calculations are not uncontroversial, the extent of the potential market is not always clear in recession. However, in 1989 when profits, prices and production were at their highest, it was still apparent that there was overcapacity because even at this high level of output it had been estimated that output was running 3-4 per cent ahead of consumption.

At the moment the 'maximum production potential' is 192.6 m tonnes but it is accepted by experts that this includes at least 30m tonnes of ineffective capacity; a more realistic figure being between 155 and 160m tonnes of effective capacity[7].

The overcapacity is located in almost every area of production, in crude steel production and in hot rolling mills and in all the main product areas in both flat products and long products[8]. Ironically the largest overcapacity is in coated steels, an area that was predicted by GOS 95 to be ripe for further investment.

Effects of overcapacity

Overcapacity and the crisis of profitability in the industry reflect the character of the industry in the EC and the market framework in which it is accustomed to operate. Under the D'Avignon quotas steelmakers could be allocated output in such a way that guaranteed prices and profit. The nostalgia for D'Avignon-type solutions even on the voluntary basis offered by Eurofer, is explained by this. The industry remains capital intensive and the costs of withdrawing from the industry are substantial, thus given the fluctuating fortunes of the market many producers prefer to weather out the downturns with excess capacity and low or no profit, rather than be faced with the enormous cost of withdrawal. This situation is complicated by the heavy presence of nationalized producers in the EC industry. The D'Avignon plan was moderately successful in reducing capacity and re-structuring, but it failed to eliminate the problem of subsidies to industries and the impact of state funded investment. The impact of subsidy upon the industry is felt mostly through prices; subsidized losses enabled state enterprises to maintain their level of output in a period of falling demand by lowering prices to levels that are not commercially viable. In the European case this puts pressure upon those private producers that compete in the same market, so that the British Steel Corporation and the private German producers, for example, have found profit-making harder. Profit has been falling faster than output reflecting the need by the industry to operate close to capacity because of high fixed costs, see Figure C4.3. (In integrated steel production 70 per cent of costs are fixed costs.)

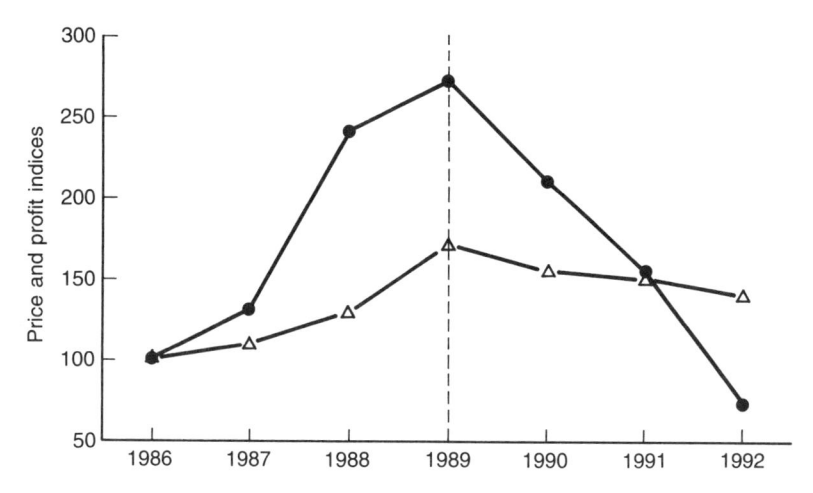

Figure C4.3 EC steel profit (●) and price index (△) trends: 1986 = 100 (source: OECD 1993)

In addition, though quality and technology in production have been sustained by high levels of investment, this investment has not always been consistent with commercial norms. According to one consultant there has been overinvestment in downstream production activities, leading to a movement of overcapacity from upstream activities to later stages of production[9]. Investment by seeking to 'modernize' production in nationalized industries has been mostly responsible for this. The EC Commission itself is partially responsible, however, for encouraging investment from large profits in 1989 and 1990[10]. The cost of losses to overinvestment has been felt in the creation of overcapacity in some high technology products and in medium-sized private operations. (See the case of Kloeckner Stahl below.) Nationalized industries in Italy have supported this investment by a growing burden of debt, creating a situation where it has some of the biggest and most modern plant and therefore some of the most difficult capacity to reduce.

Overcapacity and national industries

The overcapacity is not spread uniformly across the EC; countries that have already responded to the need to restructure after the D'Avignon plan, especially France and the UK, are victims rather than creators of overcapacity. The main centres of overcapacity are in Germany, Belgium, Spain and Italy; each of them has national characteristics in their production or in their markets that perpetuate the problem.

Germany

The German steel industry has undergone considerable difficulties recently, the filing for protection from creditors by Kloeckner Stahl and Saarstahl, and a painful takeover of Hoesch by Fried. Krupp have sapped confidence in the industry. Thyssen, the biggest and most successful of the German companies, has threatened to abandon steel production altogether. German producers are bitter that their firms are under pressure while Italian and Spanish producers enjoy subsidies that maintain less-efficient productive capacity. Germany is expected to be asked to lose 9 million tonnes of capacity in the Braun plan and some of the Thyssen threat rhetoric has to been seen in this context; the real situation is more complex.

It may be expected that Kloeckner is a more efficient plant than subsidized competitors elsewhere, but, like many German companies, it has felt pressure as prices fall because of the higher cost structure of German companies (see Table C4.2).

Table C4.2 *Distribution of steelmaking costs*

	UK	France	Germany
US $ per ton CRC shipped			
Materials			
Coking coal	41	41	44
Iron ore	62	61	69
Scrap	39	39	38
All other materials	153	160	179
Total materials	295	301	330
Labour			
Costs per hour	18	27.5	33
Costs per ton	5.4	5.2	5.3
Total labour	97	143	175
Financial Costs			
Depreciation	20	36	42
Interest	1	13	11
Total financial	21	49	53
Total pre-tax cost	413	493	558

Source: House of Lords EC Committee 1993

Restructuring the steel industry in the European Community

High labour costs and the burden of higher fuel costs because of the German legal requirements to use higher priced, poorer quality German coal is problematic for all German producers. Combined this with this, Kloeckner have been a victim of developments in new technology; the company invested heavily in the production of coated steels, usually used in the car industry, but firms that size cannot supply the range required by the car industry. They are caught because they supply a product that requires the economies of scale in steel production in a market that has experienced rapid innovation. If they lose orders to larger producers that can supply the range required, they also lose the benefits of economies of scale from their upstream steel making plant. In the end, of course, Kloeckner was bailed out in a deal with its German bankers and the EC Commission, which in return for a 20 per cent reduction in capacity and a share in profit from its non-steel subsidiaries over the next few years, wrote off part of an DM175m debt.

Saarstahl, which was owned by the French company Usinor Sacilor, was less fortunate, losing DM30m per month and having received DM3.7bn in subsidies and soft loans since 1978, it was allowed to go down; a victim of the new sense of rigour in the regional government's fiscal policy. Interestingly in both the cases of Kloeckner and Saarstahl, Thyssen and other German steel makers added to the general pressure to allow the companies to go bankrupt, presumably hoping that the loss of capacity would reduce their own capacity losses in the EC restructuring exercise.

Krupp-Hoesch, the product of (for Germany) an unusually aggressive take-over by Krupp in 1992, is now about to close one of its two steel plants. Hoesch is a successful specialist in coated steels with its own upstream plant. The parent company Krupp Stahl also announced the probable closure of its Hagen and Siegen steel plants. Clearly the benefits of merger and the closure of hot steel plants are to be derived from the economies of scale of operating one steel plant. These manoeuvrings, which have been accompanied by a considerable amount of rhetoric from Krupp management about EC steel policy, must be seen as a late blooming of re-structuring in defence of the German national industry. The German industry claims to have felt the pressure of competition from central and Eastern Europe more forcefully than its other European partners with more than half of the imports coming into the German market. This is true as can be seen from Table C4.3, but the figures have to be seen in the context of German consumption of 30.5m tonnes, including imports of 17.2 m tonnes (finished products). Central and eastern European imports were just over 7.6 per cent of German consumption in 1992. Ruprecht Vondran, Chairman of the German steel federation, regards Eastern European imports as having a disproportionate de-stabilizing effect in the long products market where much of the German industry weakness lies. Much of the German concern is based on the presumption that these imports are being 'dumped' in EC markets because of artificially low energy and raw materials costs. There is also a concern that markets are being 'spoiled' by these producers selling prices that are lower than they need be.

Table C4.3 Rolled steel imports into (a) EC and (b) Germany (tonnes 000's monthly average)

	1989	1990	1991	1992 (Jan–Nov)
(a)				
Former Soviet Union	44.6	57.0	93.5	112.4
Poland	36.5	48.9	48.8	68.8
Czechoslovakia	53.4	64.5	81.5	120.25
(b)				
Former Soviet Union	5.4	7.8	52.8	61.03
Poland	24.8	23.5	24.8	50.03
Czechoslovakia	21.1	27.0	35.8	60.2

Source: *Financial Times*, 25 February 1993, p.23.

It is a market that is dominated by direct sales to consumer industries and foreign producers, especially the BSC, have found it difficult to gain a foothold despite a cost structure that is much more advantageous[11].

German banks, who are major shareholders and major lenders to the industry, deter foreign entrants and domestic re-structuring; they also seem willing to sustain German steelmakers over a longer period of losses or poor profit than other European shareholders would be willing to do. It is now clear, however, that the re-structuring has begun in earnest, the main victims will be among the labour force with some 35–50 000 job losses expected. The Braun plan would seem to have occurred opportunely and will greatly help to reduce the costs of an exercise that would probably have been necessary anyway. The German industry does not see it that way and Ruprecht Vondran has complained that the burden of capacity losses is falling upon the private sector while state owned companies are making a minimal contribution to capacity reductions. German companies have a 5 million tonne crude steel and 3.8 million tonne rolled steel capacity reduction in hand which will be completed by the end of 1994 with a total loss of 50 000 jobs[12].

Vondran is particularly concerned with his own government's support for the replacement of the obsolescent capacity of the East German EKO-Stahl at Eizenhüttestadt. The new plant will be composed of a new electric arc steel mill, continuous casting and hot rolling mill, and a modernized cold rolling mill. All of this will be achieved with considerable state aid. The problem for the Commission lies in the fact that, though the new arrangement considerably reduces finished steel capacity and closes pig iron capacity entirely, it increases the hot steel capacity of the plant overall. In the restructuring under the Braun plan the Commission has set a principle that state aid support should only be allowed in circumstances where it is compensated by proportionate capacity reductions. Thus far the Commission has put up some resistance to the German proposal despite some modifications. The German government has formally linked its acceptance of the Commission's final plans for the Spanish and Italian industry to its own proposals for EKO-Stahl. Since the Commission's proposals for these other state aided industries depend upon a unanimous vote in the Council, it seems likely that the German government will have its way[13].

Belgium

The overcapacity in Belgium centres on its poor melting capacity. Cockerill Sambre, Belgium's ECSC producer, has a formidable reputation in marketing its products but is encumbered by its melting capacity. Belgium and Luxembourg together have an excess capacity of 10 m tonnes, which could be reduced by co-operation between Cockerill Sambre and Arbed the Luxembourg producer. Up to now rationalization of this kind, though proposed, has been prevented by political interference in Belgium where the melting capacity would be expected to close.

Italy

The Italian industry has presented the EC with its most difficult challenge. ILVA the country's biggest producer has been the focus of concern about state aids and their impact upon the industries of other Member States. The Commission has called for capacity reductions of 3m tonnes from the industry but has been met with considerable resistance from ILVA and the Italian state authorities. ILVA, like other Italian producers, has enjoyed considerable support from the state and in many forms but mostly in the form of preferential purchases and written off loans. This latter problem is at the centre of a dispute between the Commission and the Italian government. ILVA wanted to be allowed to pass a £3billion debt on the state holding company IRI. IRI is a joint stock company operated under Italian company law, but it is wholly owned by the Italian treasury. The Commission claimed that this transfer of debt constituted a state aid outside the State Aid code. In return for permitting such a large state aid the Commission would expect a capacity reduction of at least 3 million tonnes. ILVA lost 2.3 trillion lire (£1billion) in 1992 and is currently losing 100 billion lire per month (£42m) and has run down its capital from 600 to 120 billion lire; it has, in addition, debts amounting to 9 trillion lire. The position of the Commission has been that Italian re-structuring should not be at the expense of private competition. In May 1993 ILVA's chairman Hiyao Nakamura threatened to prevent EC advisers from entering his works; there was a feeling in ILVA and in the Italian government that the Commission was too partisan for the Northern producers and was not sensitive to the specific problems of the Italian industry.

In particular it was felt that cutting capacity at the new Taranto works (the most modern and largest integrated plant in Europe) seemed particularly hard. The Taranto plant has an unfortunate problem of location, set in the Mezzogiorno it was meant to supply a new FIAT plant in the region; the steelworks was built but the car plant was not. This has caused particular difficulties, with Northern Italy increasingly a target in the French Usinor-Sacilor's Mediterranean market strategy. Italy already imports 35 per cent of its requirements, and French and German producers feel that ILVA can only compete through the support of the Italian state.

On 14 July, the Commission lost patience and issued an injunction against the contents of the ILVA plan and insisted upon a new plan being delivered by 14 August[14]. Later in July the Italian government rejected the ILVA plan and promised to present a new plan from an independent consultant, in time for the September meeting of the Industry Council. Mr Andreatta, the Italian foreign minister, presented the main aspects of the report in a letter to Karel Van Miert, the Vice President of D.G.IV, the Commission Directorate in charge of competition policy on 17 August. At the Industry Council meeting on 20 September 1993, decisions on state aid issues were postponed to 18 November to allow for further discussion. At the time of writing the Italian proposals have been broadly accepted by the Commission. In these proposals it is reported that the plant at Bagnoli near Naples, which is currently mothballed, will close definitively, and two Taranto pre-heating furnaces will be closed. As a result of this, 1.7 million tonnes of capacity will be closed and the Commission will be able to authorize aid of 4 500 billion Lira. As part of the re-structuring it is expected that ILVA will sell some installations in Terni and Taranto. It is expected that 11 200 jobs will be lost. In the end it is the Council that will decide upon the acceptability of this and other proposals relating to state aid and ownership in November and with it the future of the Steel re-structuring.

Spain

Most steel subsidies were ended by the D'Avignon re-structuring but the Spanish steel industry has had a different background to the other EC countries, derogations from the state aid code on its entry into the community, allowed it to subsidize production and investment up to 1990. The main ECSC producer, the state-owned Corporación de la Siderúrgica

Restructuring the steel industry in the European Community

Integral (CSI), was formed from an amalgamation of the two producers Ensidesa (in Asturias) and Altos Hornos (in the Basque country) in 1992; the merger represented the first step in restructuring the industry.

The Spanish government proposals for re-structuring which were presented to the Council in November 1992 were rejected as inadequate; it was felt that the capacity reductions did not adequately balance the amount of state funding going into the plan. The proposal was to cut the Basque steel-making capacity by 1.3 million tonnes and to lose 45 per cent of the labour force (9700 jobs) over a period of one and a half years. Controversially, a new high technology electric arc plant with a 1 million tonne capacity was to be built in Sestao in the Basque country. Initially this was to be funded by the Spanish government and shareholdings were then to be offered to private investors. The Spanish government were concerned at the time with the interpretation of state aid in the plan which the Commission estimated at 600 billion pesetas (£3billion). The 600 billion estimate includes 276 billion pesetas which represent the value of the Altos Hornos and Ensidesa assets and 236 billion in social costs of the redundancies.

A revised proposal was put to the Industry Council on 30 September 1993, which was conditionally accepted. Clearly, account had been taken of the Spanish submissions on the nature of state aids; these were now assessed at 2.8 billion ECU (£2.1 billion). The conditions are:

1 the closure of the Basque plant must be undertaken and must be irreversible;
2 the hot-rolled plant at Ansio be closed by 30 June 1995;
3 the majority of the Sestao investment must really come from the private sector;
4 the implementation of the plan can be controlled by the Community authorities[15].

Final approval was based on the acceptance of these conditions by the Spanish government. It was important to resolve the issue of state supported industry because the private companies were not willing to make firm commitments to their own contributions to the Braun plan proposals until these issues were resolved. The Spanish have received some sympathy because of the particular difficulties of reducing capacity in regions where the average unemployment level is in excess of 30 per cent. The Industry Council passed the proposals in the event with little comment when they were finally approved in December 1993.

European Business

Restructuring and reorganization

It remains to be seen whether the Braun plan will provide an effective basis for the re-structuring of the industry or whether it will fall short of the radical re-alignment felt to be required by many commentators. A successful conclusion to the preparations for re-structuring, which the Braun plan and the associated 'global agreement' would represent, would only be the beginning of a longer process. Its success would depend upon the extent to which the capacity reductions of the private sector create arrangements which match the need for efficient production to the needs of the EC steel market. It will depend also upon the extent to which the conclusion of the capacity reduction exercise marks the beginning of a more flexible and dynamic market. The return of steel to the status of a normal product in a normal market under the existing arrangements will also depend upon the extent to which state owned producers are allowed to take the commercial consequences of their decisions about production and investment.

The problem goes beyond broad questions of capacity; it relates to organizational structure as well; the Japanese industry has seven producers of strip steel with an average capacity of 8.5m tonnes each, the EC has 16 producers with an average of 4.7 m tonnes each. Up to now the post-D'Avignon industry has shown only tentative signs of re-structuring on a commercially effective basis under its own steam. The expectation in the late 1980s was that the D'Avignon plan would accelerate the process of integration across borders; similarly it was expected that the turn down after 1989 would put pressure on the private sector to rationalize their production and this would imply some cross border re-structuring.

In practice there has been little change in the core of integrated producers and a number of failures in attempts to re-structure at that level. Usinor Sacilor (SOLLAC) took over Saarstahl, but Saarstahl ended up in receivership after Usinor Sacilor refused to continue its support (see above). Usinor Sacilor (SOLLAC) pooled some merchant bar and electrical sheet operations with the Belgian company Cockerill-Sambre. Usinor-Sacilor in particular has been more active than most in the market, positioning itself in a number of EC partners' markets with joint ventures and the purchase of distribution companies[16]. In all it has spent in the region of £800m on foreign acquisitions (including US acquisitions), mostly in areas that improve distribution rather than production. BSC bought a small producer in Germany – Troisdorf, but failed in its bid to buy the distribution division of Kloeckner Stahl, beaten to it by the German company VIAG.

Apart from the Saarstahl purchase, changes in the German market have mostly been made by German firms, Preussag (a non-steel company) bought the state-owned Salzgitter and, as indicated above, Krupp bought Hoesch. There are new cross-border arrangements in early stages of development among speciality producers between Vallourec (France), Mannesmann (Germany) and Dalmine (Italy) but the overall picture until the Braun plan has not been one of major re-structuring but of market positioning. The best hope for restructuring, seems now to lie with the Braun proposals, though some would argue that the best solution would be to allow the market mechanism to work[17]. The underlying cost efficiency (see Table C4.2.) of some producers in the market, BSC and Usinor Sacilor for example, show the potential for a dynamic and effective industry. The proposed privatization of Usinor Sacilor has also given the hope that its occasional surreptitious recourse to state support will end[18]. Given the probability that ILVA will also be privatized then there is some hope that processes of interpenetration that characterize the best expectations of the Internal Market will finally be experienced in the steel industry. The EC re-structuring represents a formalized move in the direction of a free market for steel. Given the political context, it probably also represents a more realistic option than simple reliance on the market mechanism creating an orderly retreat in the industry and leaving effective capacity to compete. Those who argue the free operation of the market mechanism ignore the record of the industry to date and fail to indicate how this freedom may be achieved in the current political circumstances. The Braun plan is important because it creates the possibility of the establishment of a free market and a long term resolution of the problem of state aids.

Table C4.4 *EC integrated steelmakers by size (1990)*

Company	Country	Output (tonnes m)	Ranking in world industry
Usinor-Sacilor[1]	France	23.0	2
BSC	UK	14.2	4
Thyssen	Germany	11.6	7
ILVA[1]	Italy	11.4	8
Hoogovens	Dutch	5.4	18

[1]Indicates nationalized company
Source: International Iron & Steel Institute

Restructuring and the Braun Proposals

The re-structuring of the industry still depends on the response of the industry to the decisions made in the Industry Council meeting in December 1993. The financial arrangements for assisting the re-structuring have been finalized by the Commission and authorized by the Council. These arrangements include 'co-financing' of capacity reductions of some companies by companies that continue to produce with full capacity. This will be achieved using loans from the ECSC as a pre-financing mechanism[19]. The private companies have made proposals for re-structuring in three groups; hot rolled wide strips and bands, heavy plates, and heavy structural sections. In terms of 1991 production figures the groups represent: 93 per cent of Hot Rolled Strip capacity, 81.2 per cent of heavy plates capacity, and 70.8 per cent of heavy structural sections capacity. The proposal implies the closure of 6m tonnes of hot strip capacity, 2m tonnes of heavy plate capacity, and 2.55m tonnes of heavy structural capacity.

Groups
Hot rolled wide strips and bands: BSC(UK), Preussag Stahl AG (Germany), AFL Falck SpA.(Italy), Thyssen AG (Germany), ARBED S.A. (Luxembourg), Cockerill Sambre S.A. (Belgium), Hoesch Hohenlimburg GmbH (Germany), Hoogovens NV (Netherlands), Kloeckner Stahl AG, Krupp Hoesch Stahl AG (Germany), Eizen u. Stahlwerk Roetzel GmbH (Germany) and Sollac S.A. (France).

Heavy plates
BSC(UK), Preussag Stahl AG (Germany), AFL Falck SpA.(Italy) Thyssen AG (Germany), Det Danske Staalvalsverk (Denmark), Dillinger Huettenwerke (Germany) GTS Industries (UK) and Walzwerk Ilsenburg GmbH.

Heavy structural sections
BSC(UK), Preussag Stahl AG (Germany), ARBED (Luxembourg) and Aristrain S.A.(Spain)[20].

This restructuring is, however, conditional upon the successful solution of the problem of state aided industries mentioned above. Though there is widespread dissatisfaction among the private producers of a solution which allows for state aid in East Germany, Spain and Italy, this is to some extent a rhetorical knee jerk reaction which will not place too big an obstacle in the way of the Braun proposals. For its part the Commission has re-emphasized its determination to create a free market by insisting that the re-structuring arrangements do not include any market sharing arrangements. Some of the companies in the industry have indicated that they felt that by paying for the reduction of the capacity of others they should be automatically entitled to the residual market share that those companies will have left behind. The Commission is against this and any other cartel arrangements that might emerge from the cooperation on re-structuring[21]. Whatever the view in the industry, the Commission clearly intends that this should be the last restructuring that will be necessary before the expiry of the Treaty of Paris.

If the proposals are accepted then there will be a new basis for the operation of a free market for steel.

References

1   The ECSC has a strict code for the operation of state aids under article 95 of the Treaty of Paris. This allows state aid for three categories: research and development; environmental protection; and the closure of facilities of firms leaving the industry.
2   Eurofer is the body that represents the large integrated producers in Europe. As early as the middle of 1989 it was apparent to them that the turn-down in demand was likely to test the re-structured industry. See Dawkins, W., Steel producers sense a draught, *Financial Times*, 31 May 1989.
    Eurofer membership: Alto Hornos, ENSIDESA-Spain ARBED-Luxembourg, British Steel PLC-UK, Cockerill Sambre–Belgium, Hoesch-Stahl AG–Germany, Hoogovens–Netherlands, Falck, ILVA SpA.–Italy, Kloeckner Stahl, Krupp Stahl AG, Prettsing Stahl AG, Thyssen Stahl AG-Germany, USINOR-SACILOR–France, Allied Steel & Wire, United Engineering Steels–UK.
3   See *Economist*, 11 July 1992, Vol. 324, Leaner and meaner – Japanese firms sharpen up.
4   The cartel approach has been used on a number of occasions even by the private producers that mostly readily revert to the rhetoric of the free market. See Kellaway, L., Brussels imposes token fine upon stainless steel cartel, *Financial Times*, 19 July 1990 and Leadbetter, C. and Hill, A. Inquiry signals change in Commission's steel policy, *Financial Times*, 15 April 1991 and Giles, M., What us compete? – European companies still prefer collusion, *Economist*, Vol. 319, 8 June 1991.
5   See Memorandum for the attention of the Commission, p. 41 in House of Lords Select Committee on the European Communities: *Restructuring the EC Steel Industry*, Session 1992 – 1993, 24th Report, HMSO, London, July 1993.
6   See EC Bulletin 1/2–1993 p. 29 and *Europe*, 24 February 1993, p. 5 and *Europe*, 27 February 1993 p. 7.
7   See Baxter, A., Questions of history and health for steel, *Financial Times*, 25 January 1993.
8   Flat products include: hot rolled coil for use in pipes and construction; hot rolled plates for ship building; cold rolled sheets for domestic appliances and cars; coated sheets for constructional cladding, domestic appliances and cars. Long products include: heavy sections for steel

frames for buildings and bridges; wire rod for fencing and mesh for the construction industry; reinforcing bars for reinforced concrete; merchant bars for use by the engineering industry.

9 See Beddows, R., How to cure an industry's ills, *Financial Times*, 25 January 1993.
10 See Commission of The European Communities, *General Objectives for Steel – 1995*, COM (90) 201, Brussels, 7 May 1990 pp. VI–1 & 2.
11 See Lorenz, A., forging steel's future, *Sunday Times*, 14 October 1990.
12 See *Europe*, 26 September 1993.
13 See *Europe*, No. 6005 21/22 June 1993, p. 16 and No. 6081 7 October 1993, p. 10. In October 1993 Gunther Rexrodt the German Economics Minister survived an emergency debate in the Bundestag in which his proposal for EKO-Stahl was attacked by Ruprecht Vondran. He then made the German acceptance of the Commission proposals for the restructuring of CSI, the Spanish state owned producer, and ILVA, the Italian state owned producer.
14 If the Italian Government did not comply with the Injunction then the Council could impose a number of sanctions under Art. 88 of the Treaty of Paris. On a majority of two-thirds on a proposal from the Commission, quotas or tariffs on Italian steel products could be imposed by the Council.
15 See *Europe*, No. 6075, 30 September 1993, p. 15.
16 Along with joint ventures with Arbed Luxembourg and Riva in Italy, Usinor-Sacilor has taken 49 per cent in the Italian producer Lutrix, has taken over Ancofer Reinstahl (a German distributor) and has a 59 per cent interest in the large British distributor ASD. It also bought J&L steel products in the USA and Edgcomb (a large US steel merchant).
17 See the evidence of Jonathan Aylen in House of Lords Select Committee on the European Communities: *Restructuring the EC Steel Industry*. Session 1992–1993, 24th Report, HMSO, London, July 1993, pp. 6–16.
18 In July 1991 the state owned Credit Lyonnais Bank bought a Ffr 2.5 bn (£250m) stake in the company. The money for the purchase was raised by a rights issue by Credit Lyonnais which the French Government then took up. See *Economist,* Vol. 320, 14 September 1991, Crying foul: Europe's steel industry.
19 It is worth noting that the loans coming from the ECSC are, of course, based on funds raised from the industry by the ECSC levy. The firms maintaining capacity will receive loans that are repayable by 2002, i.e. by the expiry date of the Treaty of Paris. With these loans they will compensate closures by firms that are losing capacity. As indicated earlier the EC will then contribute to the social costs of the restructuring through Art. 53a of the ECSC treaty, through the structural

funds and by allowing the member states to give assistance under the existing State Aids Code.
20 See *Europe*, No. 6099, 3 November 1993
21 *Ibid.*

Appendices

Steel production (millions of tonnes)

Country	1991	1992	1993
Belgium/ Luxembourg	12.9	11.7	11.6
France	16.5	16.1	15.8
Germany	37.5	35.5	33.8
Italy	22.5	22.2	21.8
Netherlands	4.6	4.9	4.7
Spain	11.6	11.1	11.1
UK	14.6	14.2	14.1
Rest	2.2	2.3	2.3

Effective Capacity for the production of crude steel (tonnes 000's)

Country	1990	1991	1992	1993	change
Germany*	43	54.9	55.2	55.2	12.2
Belgium	14.186	14.05	14.405	14.405	0.219
Denmark	0.611	0.85	0.85	0.85	0.239
Spain	19.578	19.578	19.578	20.2	0.622
France	25.5	25.37	25.6	25.7	0.2
Greece	4.2	4.2	4.2	4.2	0
Ireland	0.33	0.345	0.465	0.465	0.135
Italy	36.89	38.6	39	39.5	2.61
Luxembourg	5.15	5.15	5.15	5.15	0
Holland	7.6	7.6	6.49	6.5	-1.1
Portugal	0.772	0.79	0.89	0.89	0.118
UK	23.7	23.291	23.069	23.2	-0.5
Totals	181.517	194.724	194.897		

*Note that after 1991 another 10m tonnes have been added for E.German capacity.
Source OECD.

EC steel production, imports and apparent consumption

Year	Production	Imports	Exports	Apparent consumption
1983	108.5	10.1	21.9	96.7
1984	120.1	9.3	26.1	103.3
1985	120.6	10	28.8	115.71299
1986	125.6	10.6	26.1	110.1
1987	126.1	9.8	27.2	108.7
1988	137.6	10.3	24.2	123.7
1989	140.2	11.2	22.4	129
1990	136.9	12.4	21.9	127.4
1991	137.6	11.5	22.5	126.6
1992	132.1	11	22.8	123.3

EC(12)   Production Indices, 1985=100 per cent change

	1990	1991	1992	1992 Q4
Industrial production	115.2	115	113.8	111.5 −1
Metal using industries	122.8	120.7	117.4	110 −

Source: OECD

Profitability of EC steel producers (operating profit before interest and depreciation as percentage of sales)

Year	EC	BSC	Year	EC	BSC
1974	21.1	10	1984	4.9	1.1
1975	−0.9	−1.5	1985	7.3	5.4
1976	3.4	5.4	1986	6.1	9.1
1977	−1.7	−6	1987	8	14.2
1978	3.7	−0.9	1988	14.7	17.4
1979	6.9	−9.2	1989	16.6	17
1980	6.3	−13.8	1990	12.8	10.8
1981	0.8	−3.7	1991	9.5	5.6
1982	2.3	−4.1	1992	4.5	3.5
1983	1	−1.2			

Source: House of Lords EC Committee 1993

Restructuring the steel industry in the European Community

Average numbers employed

Country	1974	1984	1989	1990	1991	1992
Belgium/Luxembourg	86.6	51.4	38.2	36.9	35.6	34
Denmark/Ireland	3.5	2.3	2.2	2.2	2.2	1.9
France	155.7	87.1	51.4	48.1	45.3	44
Germany	230.6	156.5	130.5	127	150.5	137.4
Greece	8.7	4.2	3.4	3.4	3.2	3.1
Italy	93.8	81.7	59.3	57	55.6	52.6
Netherlands	23.8	18.7	17.9	17.4	16.9	16.3
UK	197.7	62.3	54.4	52.6	47	42.6
EC(10)	800.4	464.2	357.3	344.6	356.3	331.9
Spain	89.4	69.2	39.8	37.1	36.1	35
Portugal	5	6.7	4.8	4.2	3.6	3.3
EC(12)	894.8	540.1	401.9	385.9	372.5	370.2

Questions

1. Do the proposals for state-aided companies in Spain and Italy support the contention that the EC Commission is determined to create a free market for steel?
2. In other industries re–structuring has been achieved without the aid of the EC; what special features of the industry justify current plans to re-structure the steel industry?
3. What features of the industry explain the failure of the industry to re-structure since the late 1980s?
4. What explanation may be given for the willingness of the EC to co–operate in the re-structuring of the steel industry?
5. What explanation may be given for the insistence by the Commission that the re-structuring of the private sector should be undertaken by the companies themselves?

Case 5 EC tourism: the case of Euro Disneyland

Sue Stacey

Introduction: The importance of tourism to the Community

In economic terms tourism is one of the most important industries of the European Community, with Europe accounting for approximately 60 per cent of international tourism. The sector generates more than 5 per cent of Community GDP and employs approximately 6 per cent of the Community's workforce. Tourism is also important due to its propensity to develop in areas devoid of alternative industry. Thus it provides an income in regions where otherwise there would be economic hardship and deprivation.

The completion of the Single Market in 1992 has meant that there are now increased opportunities for people to travel more freely, both for business and recreational purposes. The Single Market measures that effect tourism can be seen as follows:

1. tax rates on tourist services (transport, travel allowances, hotel and catering charges);
2. the air liberalization and competition package (reduce air fares and encourage development of regional airports);
3. rail and coach travel liberalization (encourage competition among the various types of land transport);
4. wider availability of lead free petrol will encourage more personal travel;
5. the freeing-up of capital markets and financing services will have a profound effect on investment in tourism projects;
6. personal finance will benefit from new credit networks, development of the private use of the ecu and open insurance market;
7. Introduction of consumer measures such as the Package Tours Directive, product liability and unfair contract terms.

By the year 2000 it is thought that tourism could be the Community's largest single industry, with an annual growth rate of between 3 and 5 per cent as forecast by HOTREC.

With increased income levels there has been a subsequent increase in the demand for high quality holidays. Thus the last decade has witnessed a

EC tourism: the case of Euro Disneyland

dramatic expansion in the development of holiday complexes. These have been designed with the intention of providing a complete holiday environment for the discerning tourist. One such development, hoping to take advantage of the enormous European tourism market, has been Euro Disneyland situated to the east of Paris. Encouraged by the size of the potential tourist catchment area and by the forecasts of growth expected with the completion of the single market, Disney decided to expand into Europe.

Euro Disney: the grand plan

The contract for Euro Disneyland was signed on 24 March 1987 and construction for phase 1A of the giant theme park started shortly after. Set 23 miles east of Paris the first phase of Euro Disneyland opened its gates to the general public on 12 April 1992 with all the press euphoria of a royal wedding. The Euro-project in its entirety is set to span thirty years, due for completion in the year 2017, if all goes according to plan. By the time it is completed it should cover an area of land approximately one fifth the size of Paris and be sixty times larger than Disneyland, California.

The initial phase consists of the Magic Kingdom theme park and six themed hotels with a total of 5200 hotel rooms. The second phase scheduled is the construction of a second theme park, – Disney MGM Studios – Europe – a convention centre, a water park and 13 000 more hotel rooms. The finished complex will also include hundreds of apartments and office/retail space. No expense has been spared on the FFr 14.9 billion [£1.4 billion] theme park with minute attention paid to every detail.

Shortly before the grand opening Disney began a tour of Europe with a half-size version of Sleeping Beauty's Castle, announcing to everyone the hours and minutes left before the big day. The topic of Euro Disney was rarely out of the newspapers with predictions of huge profits boosting the initial share price of FFr72 [707p] to FFr 164 [1693p] as the opening date loomed. Again no expense was spared for the actual opening with stars such as Cher, Tina Turner, Michael J. Fox, Bob Geldof and Eddie Murphy being booked to complement the high glamour, high quality image of the resort. It was estimated that the resort would attract 11 million visitors in its first year and by 1996 Euro Disney hope to be attracting 24 million visitors per annum.

Profits were expected as soon as the giant theme park opened its gates to the European market. Euro Disney was to be the 'jewel' in Disney's crown – nothing, it was thought, was overlooked. The problems encountered in parks in California, Japan and Orlando were recognized and no such problems were to occur in this park. Disneyland, California, suffered from having too little land to develop on and thus lost potential profit as its popularity soared. Disney World in Orlando had plenty of land at its disposal, however, very few hotels were developed by Disney, so once again potential profits were being lost – this time to other accommodation providers. In Tokyo the problem was the lack of equity held by Walt Disney. Euro Disney was designed and constructed bearing all these problems in mind and the park should have been set to produce maximum profits for the parent company.

Not including hotel accommodation the expected spending per day for a family of four was estimated to be between FFr 1300 [£130] and FFr 1960 [£200] depending on visitors' propensity to shop. If the, then thought conservative, estimate of 11 million visitors in the first year of operation materialized then the revenue implications for the company were enormous.

In the run up to the opening date everyone was optimistic about the future of Europe's newest, largest and most spectacular theme park. The only problem forseen was that of having to turn away visitors at the gate, as Europe rushed to see Mickey Mouse. As the optimistic Daniel Coccoli, vice president of resort hotel operations, boasted:

> we have to make sure we are ready, because on April 12, something will occur that will happen only one time in our history – all of Europe will check in at once![1]

Site selection

Marne-la-Vallée was chosen as the site for the Euro Disney project from a selection of approximately 200 sites throughout Europe. The location offered vast tracks of flat land ideal for development and its proximity to Paris, Europe's tourist mecca, promised sure success.

Easy accessibility was one of the key factors attracting Disney to their final location. The Euro Disney resort lies on the A4 expressway between Strasbourg and Paris giving easy access for those travelling by car. It was calculated that 17 million Western Europeans would be able to reach the Euro Disney resort by car within two hours. For those travelling by air the resort lies equally conveniently between two international airports, Roissy–Charles de Gaulle and Orly. Both airports offer shuttle services directly to the resort hotels. Visitors from Paris are able to reach the new resort station in just twenty-three minutes by boarding a regional train at the Arc de Triomphe. By June 1994 there will also be a station for the high speed 'Train à Grande Vitesse' (TGV) at the entrance to the park. This will mean that a trip to the resort from Brussels will take only ninety minutes and when the Channel Tunnel opens (scheduled for early 1994) the trip from London will take just 3 hours. Thus Marne-la-Vallée seemed the ideal location for the huge scale theme park, with its vast Northern European visitor catchment area.

The ideal location was also enhanced by the fact that it was the French Government and not Euro Disney that financed many of the infrastructure improvements. The French Government allocated approximately FFr 45 billion [£4.4 billion] to extend the suburban metro to Euro Disneyland's front gates and to provide the TGV station.

The infrastructure improvements were not the only temptations offered by the French Government to help clinch the Disney deal. The 4800 acre site was offered to Disney at 1971 agricultural prices, translating into roughly FFr 45 000 [£4500] per acre. This meant that Euro Disney expected vast profits on real estate appreciation alone. If this were not enough the state-owned Caisse des Dépôts et Consignations also offered a FFr 4.4 billion [£620 million] loan two points below the normal bank lending rate and the government have allowed Disney to depreciate over a shorter 10 year period rather than the 20 year norm, thereby enabling Disney to benefit from hefty tax concessions.

In summary Marne-la-Vallée appeared to be the perfect site, offering many financial advantages as well as being ideally positioned to fully exploit the Northern European market. By 1994 the theme park should fully benefit from all the infrastructure improvements and be no more than five hours from any major northern European city.

Back in 1987 both Disney officials and the French authorities believed they had come up with the 'deal of the century'. Disney had images of huge profits adding to their already healthy balance sheet and France saw Euro Disney as part of the answer to their unemployment woes. It was predicted by French officials that by 1995 Euro Disney would be responsible for the creation of approximately 60 000 jobs[2]. So despite derogatory comments from France's environmental lobby and other French academics both sides were equally desperate to clinch the deal. The only obvious drawbacks foreseen were the unreliability and general inclemancy of the weather; however this problem was thought to have been overcome by constructing covered walkways throughout the complex and providing Disney waterproofs for the all too frequent rainy days.

Corporate structure and finance

The corporate structure of Euro Disney is an extremely complex one and is entirely unique in the Disney portfolio. Unlike the Tokyo Disneyland which is held under licence by the Japanese, and the US theme parks, Disneyland and Disney World, which are directly owned by the parent, Walt Disney, Euro Disney was floated on European stock exchanges as a separate company.

European Business

In reality, this new, separate company has been operated and financed via two owner companies. These two owner companies are Euro Disneyland SCA and Euro Disneyland SNC. Euro Disneyland SCA is responsible for the operation and development of the French resort, under licence from Walt Disney who own 49 per cent of the equity. Euro Disneyland SNC, on the other hand, is responsible for the financing of the project, leasing the assets to the SCA. Walt Disney own a 17 per cent stake in this second company with the remainder being held by a small selection of French companies. Any losses made will be taken by this second company and passed on to its owners who can then claim tax losses against their income. The assets will be depreciated over the concessionary accelerated ten year period, and then sold at fully depreciated book value at the end of twenty years to the SCA. At this point it is planned that the SNC will be dissolved.

This complicated structure was designed to enable Euro Disneyland SCA to make profits from day one and to provide shareholders with dividends in the first year of operation. It also meant that the project could benefit from a comparatively cheap source of finance. To further complicate matters there are two more companies that fit into the overall ownership structure. These are EDL Participations SA, which is the 'General Partner' and Euro Disneyland SA, which is the 'management' company. Walt Disney own 100 per cent of both of these companies.

Diagramatically this structure can be represented somewhat simplified as shown in Figure C5.1.

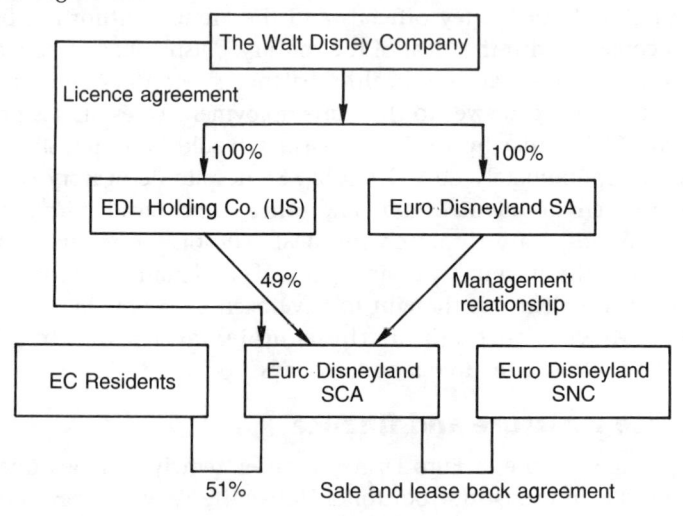

Note: This diagram details the ownership structure of Euro-Disneyland SCA and some of its contractual relationships only.

Figure C5.1 Ownership structure of Euro Disneyland (source: S G Warburg Securities reproduced in *International Financial Law Review*, Weaving the Disney Spell, January 1990)

EC tourism: the case of Euro Disneyland

The somewhat unorthodox structure was carefully conceived in order to maximize benefits to the parent company, Walt Disney. Designing the operating company as an SCA (Sociétés en commandite par actions) means that Walt Disney can achieve maximum control but take relatively few of the risks. Shareholders, or *commanditaires* as they are known, in an SCA take very little or no part in the management of the company. All the control rests in the hands of the *commandites* (the active partners). The *commandites* may elect to be replaced if they wish but unlike most company structures the ordinary shareholders cannot force them to stand down.

To be able to pass a resolution to dissolve the current management of Euro Disneyland SCA, Euro Disney shareholders would have to gain the consent of EDL participations SA (the general partner and holding company). In other words, Walt Disney hold all the trump cards. Even if Walt Disney sold its 49 per cent stake in Euro Disneyland SCA it would still be the controlling company via the management company, receiving a fee for doing so.

Euro Disneyland SCA is the only company of its kind to be floated on the London Stock Exchange, where the attitude has always been one of suspicion if shareholders' voting rights are somehow limited. Yet despite this there was no shortage of customers for the stock when trading commenced on 10 October 1989. Clearly the financing for the Euro Disneyland project has been extremely complex with finance coming from many different sources. The majority of the finance has been provided by the floatation of the stock on European-wide markets, however, the low interest loan offered by the French Government has also provided a large proportion of the necessary capital. Euro Disneyland also persuaded several French and other European companies to sponsor individual attractions on the site, demonstrating the extraordinary marketing powers of Disney. 'Its a small world' has been sponsored by France–Telecom, 'Visionarium' by Renault, 'Videopolis' by Philips and 'Orbitron' by BNP.

The most notable feature of the finance package, however, has been the relatively meagre financial contribution from the parent company. The Disney parent invested less than FFr 1 bn in the park [£98 million] constituting approximately 6 per cent of the overall cost of the development. This statistic is certainly astonishing when one considers the absolute power that Disney exerts over the European park. Walt Disney have managed to achieve an enviable position of creaming off the lion's share of the profits while being exposed to a disproportionately low element of risk. To quote Nick Gilbert writing in the *Independent* on 23 August 1992.

> The American Disney cut a remarkable deal for itself in setting up its first European Park. Euro Disneyland amounts not only to a franchise operation but to one in which the franchise owner calls all the shots.

The following explains how profits accrue to the Walt Disney company. Disney collect royalties on practically everything, not just the rides but also on merchandise and the hotels. This accounts for approximately 7 per cent of Euro Disney's total revenue, and is in addition to the 49 per cent of the park's net income which Disney receives as dividends. However it is the ingenious management fee structure that Disney devised that means Disney will not be subjected to any great losses arising from the park.

Disney charge a base fee of 3 per cent of total revenue for managing the park which is payable for the first five years of operation. After the initial five year period this base fee is set to double. However, if the operating cash flow for the park reaches FFr 1.4 billion [£140 million] then the parents' share will increase to 30 per cent. If the operating cash flow rises above FFr 2.9 billion [£280 million] Disney's share rises once more to 50 per cent.

Table C5.1

Operating cash flow (£ million)	Management fee (% of operating cash flow)	
	Within 5 years	After 5 years
0–140	3	6
>140<280	30	30
>280	50	50

Source: Adapted from figures in 'Le Défi Mickey Mouse', *Financial World* 17 October 1989

If the revenue projections of Euro Disney turn out to be correct and the site achieves pre-tax profits of £176 million in 1995, Walt Disney will be set to receive approximately £194 million from a combination of management fees, dividends and royalties in that year. This is to be contrasted with the somewhat smaller figure of £47 million that outside shareholders would receive in the same year[3].

Site performance since opening

As previously mentioned Euro Disney estimated that they would attract 11 million visitors in their first year of operation. It was estimated that half of these visitors would be from France with the next highest number coming from Germany. See Figure C5.2 for further breakdown of visitors.

EC tourism: the case of Euro Disneyland

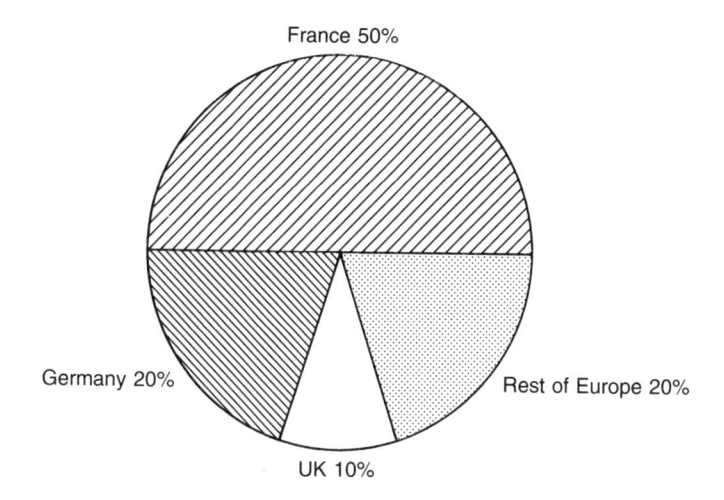

Figure C5.2 Breakdown of expected visitors to Euro Disney (source: adapted from figures in Mickey Mouse is coming to town, *Europe*, 1991)

Things got off to a poor start, however, from day one. The opening day of the park proved to be highly disappointing with numbers being well down on those expected. Euro-Disney officials had fully expected to be turning visitors away as the park filled, but by midday the Euro Disney car park was only half full.

Reasons suggested for the poor turnout were, first, that warnings of 'chaos on roads' around the site put off many potential visitors and secondly, a one–day rail strike cut the direct rail link to Euro Disney from the centre of Paris. Unfortunately for Euro Disney the poor attendance did not prove to be a one-day phenomenon; the opening day was to set the tone for the rest of the year.

Looking back, the giant theme park was beset with difficulties as soon as the contract was signed with the French Government, and construction began. Firstly, the French Government insisted that Euro Disney was to fund and operate an office for tourism in the Magic Kingdom. This was to promote travel to the rest of France. Secondly, the French Government demanded that some of the attractions on the site were to be renamed in French. Euro Disney officials were angered by these demands but did relent and renamed some of the rides. 'The Swiss Family Treehouse' became 'La Cabane des Robinson', 'The Dragons Lair' became 'La Tanière du Dragon' and 'The Enchanted Castle' became 'Le Château de la Belle au Bois Dormant'.

183

Directors of several French museums complained bitterly about Euro Disney as they believed that it would provide a permanent threat to French culture. The resort was proclaimed to be a 'culture of the lowest common denominator'. Euro Disney officials were, however, keen to be accepted in Europe and therefore tried to utilize as many local resources as was possible. This only seemed to add to their problems. Local contractors were hired to construct the resort but whereas Disney were keen to impose their own exacting standards on to the construction companies; the contractors were more than a little reluctant to accept them. The European construction firms wanted nothing to do with American standards and were keen to keep their own traditional working methods. On failing to get their own way sixteen of the construction firms filed lawsuits against Euro Disney for alleged cost overruns just a few weeks before the grand opening.

The problems did not end there. Operating staff became very unhappy with the strict disciplines that Disney imposed. In particular the French workers were angry about the ban on facial hair and on being searched by Disney security on leaving the site. This resulted in the unannounced 'wildcat' strike of Euro Disney's night watchmen.

Perhaps the most unusual complaint came from the Union for French Midgets (the *Association des personnes de petite taille* – APPT). It complained that Euro Disney discriminated against their members by offering them jobs as Mickey and Minnie but not as the more normal role of secretary or gardener for example. Court action was threatened.

A further costly incident occurred in June 1992 when French farmers, blaming the United States for the common agricultural policy reforms, decided to express their anger by blocking the entrances to Euro Disney for nine hours with tractors and burning tyre heaps, forcing 2000 school children arriving in coaches to turn away.

These initial teething problems, numerous as they were, cannot, however, be viewed as the predominant cause of the resort's financial problems. The bottom line being that the resort failed to attract the numbers that were predicted not only on troubled days but every day. It was predicted that the site on average would be receiving 30 000 to 35 000 visitors per day; however, in the first year of operation the average was approximately 25 000 only per day.

Officials were also concerned that these visitors spent comparatively little once they had paid for their accommodation and entrance fee into the park. On average, prices at Euro Disney were 20 per cent higher than those in Orlando in 1992. This resulted in visitors to the French resort cutting back spending on expensive souvenirs, going instead on far more rides than average visitors to the US parks.

The shortfall in visitor numbers was largely due to the relatively low

EC tourism: the case of Euro Disneyland

number of French visitors to the park. It was predicted that over 50 per cent of visitors would be French; however, from April 1992 to December 1992 the French constituted only 30 per cent of the total.

The effect of the low visitor numbers coupled with high French interest rates and the collapse of the real estate market meant that instead of the promised 'profits from day one' Euro Disney reported a loss of FFr 188 million [£23.8 million] for the period to 30 September 1992. It was, however, decided by Euro Disney officials to pay a FFr 1 dividend to shareholders to reflect the long-term confidence in the project. Walt Disney agreed to defer their 3 per cent management fee until the park broke into profit.

The second year of operation has not shown any signs of improvement for the troubled resort with more losses being recorded for each quarter. By the third quarter estimated losses for the 1993 financial year were in the region of FFr 1.8 billion [£209 million]. When the actual losses were finally announced, in November, they were a massive FFr 5.3 billion [£610 million]. This included a FFr 3.6 billion [£417 million] write–off for pre-opening costs and redundancies. See Figure C5.3.

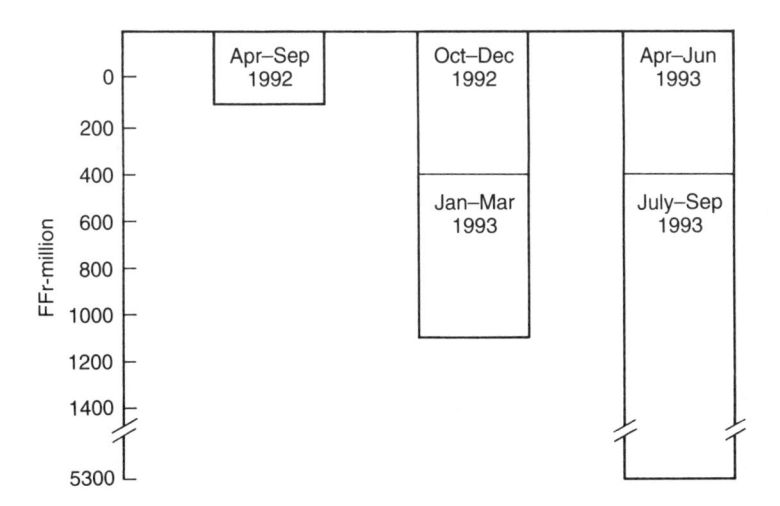

Figure C5.3 Euro Disney losses since opening (source: adapted from the *Financial Times*, 9 July 1993, p. 23)

As early as October 1992 Robert Fitzpatrick, the then chairman of Euro Disney, was discounting his earlier claims of 'profit from day one', instead announcing 'It'll take three years before Euro Disney can be properly judged'.

Many attempts have been made by Euro Disney to boost the number of visitors. In September 1992 the company launched a massive advertising campaign in an attempt to improve the park's flagging image. Winter hotel rates were also dramatically reduced. By early 1993 the resort had introduced special reduced entrance fees for local residents to encourage more French visitors, and October 1993 saw enticing promises of cars to be won every day. Visitor numbers were boosted with an increase in the number of French visitors in particular. Profits, however, were not boosted.

French interest rates remained high for most of the 1993 financial year cutting deeply into the resort's funds. Every one percentage point movement in French base rates affects Euro Disney's profits by approximately FFr 100 million[£9.8 million[4]. Combined with the fall in real estate prices this means that Euro Disney will not be seeing any profits for some time to come.

Quick profits were essential to enable Euro Disney to raise enough capital to finance the second phase of the ambitious theme park. This second phase has now been put on hold. This inevitable decision will further hamper the company's ability to break into profit as more attractions are needed at the site if Euro Disney is to hold on to its visitors for any length of time.

At present visitors are, on average, spending only a day at the resort whereas the average stay at the American theme parks is much longer. A trip to Euro Disney for most families will not constitute their main annual break, meaning that it becomes an extremely costly mini–break. This factor is thought to have put many potential customers off visiting the resort. The development of a second park and additional attractions could have helped to alleviate this problem.

On 19 October 1993 Euro Disney announced major restructuring plans. In an attempt to cut costs at the resort the leisure group decided to merge the management of the theme park and the hotels. These were previously run as separate entities. This corporate restructuring means dramatically reducing the staffing numbers at the resort. 950 planned redundancies were announced by Euro Disney officials which will reduce the total number of workers from 11 100 to 10 150. Peak summer 1992 employment total was 19 000. The latest planned reduction of 950 jobs will seriously reduce the number of full-time workers at the Euro-Disney resort.

The announced restructuring strategy for Euro Disney coupled with the 1993 financial results has done nothing to allay the fears of the company's investors, and the whole credibility of the venture is being questioned.

Share price movements

The poor performance of Euro Disney in the past two years has had a dramatic impact on the share prices for the company. The shares which were

EC tourism: the case of Euro Disneyland

originally floated at a price of FFr 72[707p] peaked to an all time high of FFr 164[1693p] just prior to the park's opening. From then onwards prices fluctuated considerably but moved in a generally downwards direction. The high 1993 year end losses caused the price to plummet to an all time low of 436p on the London Stock Exchange and FFr 38 on the Paris Bourse (see Figure C5.4).

Competition

Contrary to what Euro Disney would have everyone believe there is an alternative to Mickey Mouse. Long before the idea of Euro Disney was even conceived, Europe had developed a thriving industry for theme parks. These include Bobbejaanland in Belgium, Legoland in Denmark, Parc Asterix in France, Phantasialand in Germany, Efteling in the Netherlands, and Alton Towers in the United Kingdom.

None of these parks are on the same scale as Euro Disney; however, neither are their prices. 1992 adult prices for the all-inclusive parks, Phantasialand, Efteling, Parc Asterix, Bobbejaanland and Alton Towers, ranged from £7.50 per day for Phantasialand to £15.75 for Parc Asterix. Reductions for younger children are available at most. At Legoland admission for 1992 was £4.10 for adults and £2.25 for children. All rides are paid for separately. These prices are to be compared with the high 1992 opening price of £23 per adult at Euro Disney.

Figure C5.4 Euro Disney share price (source: *Financial Times*)

Considering the difference in scale, technology and quality of Euro Disney compared with the nearest competition, the relative entrance fees may not seem unreasonable. No expense was spared when constructing the de luxe Magic Kingdom theme park, however it is not only the entrance fee that visitors to Euro Disney have to consider. The whole complex has been designed to encourage as much consumer spending as possible. After the initial entrance fee parents have to negotiate their way around snack bars and restaurants at every turn and expensive souvenir retail outlets on every corner. For most children a memento of their magical voyage to the park is an essential. With Disney sweat shirts retailing at £30 and a small ice cream costing £2 it is hardly surprising that many parents have chosen one of the less expensive alternatives. Parc Asterix has been one such alternative to benefit, announcing a dramatic increase of 26 per cent in visitor numbers in the 1993 summer season. The twenty hectare park lying twenty-five miles north of Paris cannot boast the extravagant attractions of Euro Disney, it does, however, feature the largest roller coaster in Europe, a slash ride and many attractions for younger children. Once inside the park parents are relieved to find that the emphasis is not on yet more consumer spending, but picnicking is positively encouraged and souvenirs are realistically priced.

Parc Asterix has been attracting approximately 1 million visitors annually since its opening in the late 1980s, a mere fraction of the 17 million visitors that the Magic Kingdom received in its first eighteen months of operation. Thus it has never been viewed as a credible threat to the, perhaps, over-confident Disney officials. Euro Disney, on the other hand, was viewed as an enormous threat to Asterix, situated only 50 miles away. Now, however, as Parc Asterix have just announced, a multi-million pound plan for expansion, it appears the fears were ungrounded.

Parc Asterix may well have benefited from the arrival of Euro Disney. High prices charged at Euro Disneyland may well have led parents to seek a cheaper alternative. Faced with children longing to visit the new French theme park, Parc Asterix may well have become a very credible alternative.

Park failure

There are perhaps many contributory factors why Euro Disney has not been the roaring success that was predicted. With the creation of the single market the giant theme park seemed ideally located to benefit from the predicted increase in intra-EC travel, encouraged by easier access, a relaxation of import allowances and a growing community spirit. So what happened to the US/EC dream?

Worldwide recession has been cited as one cause, high prices deterring many potential visitors. Exacerbating this problem was the relatively high

EC tourism: the case of Euro Disneyland

position the franc maintained against other currencies, in particular the pound and the lira. This further increased the already high price to the recession-hit European countries.

The geographic location of the park has also received a proportion of the blame for low visitor numbers. Paris has never been renowned for its good weather and even Disney does not seem quite so magical in a downpour.

All of the above problems may have affected the number of visitors to the theme park; however, potential profits for the complex were also seriously dented by other factors. First, the high interest rates in France, resulting from the country's commitment to the exchange rate mechanism, vastly increased the company's capital costs. Second, the recession-led collapse in the property market severely restricted Euro Disney's ability to achieve its vast estimated profits from property development projects. Thirdly, some of the greatest criticism has been laid at the door of the parent, Walt Disney, for the management fee structure it negotiated for itself.

One final problem faced by the resort is perhaps the one which is most written about and for this reason it will be examined in some depth. It is the problem that all international companies face to a certain extent – the problem of cultural diversity.

Cultural considerations

When assessing the feasibility of a European Disneyland it now seems apparent that Disney officials did not give enough consideration to the possible problems that arise from cultural diversity. Foreign culture divergencies have always been viewed as one of the predominant constraints on global expansion. Successful entry into new countries has occurred only where the culture of the country in question has been both acknowledged, and treated sensitively.

Euro Disney clearly did not give enough regard to the cultural issue, rather arrogantly believing that Disney and its American values could be exported anywhere in the world. Other companies may have cultural and language barriers to overcome but Disney, it was thought, had cartoon characters, loved worldwide, to leap any such barriers. This now appears not to have been the case.

The arrival of Euro Disney in France, despite its promise of jobs, had French nationals in uproar. Jack Lang, the French minister for culture, vehemently declared the theme park to be 'a culture of the lowest common denominator' with others adding insult to injury by calling it a 'cultural Chernobyll'.

Despite the estimated FFr 710 million [£70 million] in taxes to accrue from the complex, along with a 0.3 per cent increase in France's gross domestic product and a welcome boost to the balance of payments, the French still seemed unable to view the coming of Disney as anything but American imperialism. It was notable that President Mitterrand did not attend the opening ceremony, claiming that it was 'not his cup of tea'. This dismissive attitude appeared to infect the entire French population, with the number of French visitors being considerably less than predicted. Those that did attend were not impressed with the catering arrangements, preferring the more sophisticated French cuisine to burgers, hotdogs and steaks. Food features heavily in the French culture, and most other European countries, (perhaps with the exception of the UK) with meal times given almost ritual status in the daily agenda. Consequently consumer spending in the park's many themed restaurants and cafés fell dramatically below expected levels as the French left the park in droves to return home for their evening meal.

One cultural difference that was noted by Disney officials and surprisingly accommodated was the European penchant for alcoholic beverages to be available at all times. Euro Disneyland is the only Disney park to sell alcohol, the others being strictly teetotal. This has made little contribution to the European feel of the park.

It was not only the cultural divergencies of the European customer that were ignored. European work practices were also, justly or unjustly, belittled by Disney officials, with American values and practices being rigidly imposed on the European workforce. Successful applicants to Euro Disney have to undergo intensive staff training at the Disney University, where cultural individuality is frowned upon, corporate homogeneity being the aim.

The strict Disney regime has paid off dividends at all other Disney resorts where the workforce are all polite, smiling, efficient, and, most importantly, indistinguishable from each other. This has not been the experience at Euro Disney, however. The strict rules on appearance, in particular, have rubbed the European workers up the wrong way, the result being Disney officials reluctantly relaxing policies in some areas. Women have been allowed to have more freedom in their choice of undergarment and makeup, for example. These minute concessions, hardly surprisingly, have not managed to appease all of the resorts employees with resulting staff turnover of approximately 50 per cent in the first sixteen months of operation[5]. This has meant increased training costs for the company, reducing still further the probability of breaking into profit. If this is what is to be expected in times of recession, what are the prospects for recruitment in better times?

The replacing of Robert Fitzpatrick in April 1993 with a Frenchman, Phillippe Bourguignon, perhaps shows a change in the attitude of Disney. Maybe we will now see a greater degree of cultural awareness from the company resulting in a more European venture designed with the European visitor in mind.

EC tourism: the case of Euro Disneyland

References

1. Wagner, G. It's a small world after all, *Lodging Hospitality*, April 1992.
2. Michavid, P. R. Wild Kingdom, *World Trade*, October 1992.
3. Gilbert, N. No fun for Europe in dividend Disney World, *Independent*, 22 August 1992.
4. Counsell, G. Euro Disney loses pounds 60m but US parent sets record, *Independent*, January 27 1992.
5. Langley, W. Euro Dismal, *Sunday Times*, August 22 1993.

Bibliography

Carr, J *et al* Weaving the Disney Spell, *International Financial Law Review*, January 1990.
Ferbuson, A. Maximising the Mouse, *Management Today*, September 1989.
Gooding, J. Of Mice and Men, *Across the Board*, March 1992.
Pitt, B. Les Liaisons peu dangereuses, *Director*, May 1990.
Scimone, D. Mickey Mouse is Coming to Town, Europe, May 1991.
Wrubel, R. Le Défi Mickey Mouse, *Financial World*, 17 October 1989.

Questions

1. Outline the factors influencing the decision to locate Euro Disney in France. Do you think that another European location would have improved the project's chance of success?
2. To what extent should Disney adapt its traditional management practices to cater for both the European visitor and worker?
3. Considering the European market for tourism, carry out a SWOT analysis of the Euro Disney resort and hence develop a corporate strategy.

Case 6 European collaboration in aircraft manufacture

Ian Barnes, Derek Chadburn and Rosina Jones

Introduction

There have been dramatic changes in the pattern of competition in the commercial aircraft industry since the mid-1970s. At that time, the American airframe producers Boeing, Lockheed and McDonnell Douglas dominated the global market, but in recent years a consortium of European producers has been created, and now offers a challenge to the US dominance. In 1966, Germany, France, Britain and Spain pooled their resources and formed Airbus Industrie. This was made up of Messerschmitt – Boelkow – Blohm, Aerospatiale, British Aerospace and Construcciones Aeronauticas. By 1993, the European collaborative project had seven models under production or under development. It had increased its share of the world market from 5 percent in the mid 1970s to over 30 per cent.

This success, along with other competitive pressures, led to the departure of Lockheed from the market, and severe pressures being placed upon the remaining US rivals. The American producers attribute the growth of Airbus to the high levels of state help that the partners in the enterprise receive, while Airbus's defenders point to the success of the collaborative process. This collaborative model was to be adopted by the rivals of Airbus, as a way of sharing the risks involved in carrying the enormous development costs of new aircraft.

The objectives of this case study are to:

1 Investigate the usefulness of the collaborative model as a means of organizing the aerospace industry.

2 Examine the strategy of companies facing a cyclical downturn.

The airline industry

The essential element of demand for new civilian aircraft is the state of the air passenger market. Passenger traffic grew consistently from the Second World War on. In the period 1970 to 1990 air travel grew at 7 per cent per

European collaboration in aircraft manufacture

year, however the number of passengers fell by 3 per cent in 1991, as a result of the Gulf War. There was recovery in 1992, with passenger numbers growing by 10.2 per cent compared with the previous year and in 1993 this trend continued.

The International Air Transport Association (Iata) suggested that their 221 members were expected to lose $2.4 to 2.5 billion on international services in 1993, after losing $11.5 over the three previous years. The losses stood at $15.9 billion over the three years, if domestic services were taken into account. They expected to break even 1995 or 1996. Table C6.1 shows the accumulation of losses.

Table C6.1 *Iata corporate results 1988–92*

	1988	*1989*	*1990*	*1991*	*1992*
Net results on international services ($ billion)	1.6	0.3	–2.7	-4.0	–4.8
Net Corporate Results including domestic operations ($ billion)	2.5	0.6	–5.1	–3.3	–7.5

Source: Iata, quoted in the *Financial Times,* 1 November 1993.

The main problem facing the airlines was overcapacity, which led to intense competition on certain routes. This excess capacity had been due to airlines taking an overly optimistic view of future growth trends and even in 1993 carrying capacity grew faster than the number of passengers. While the level of losses should have resulted in airlines leaving the industry, the US company laws make bankruptcy a protracted process, while in Europe many companies were kept afloat by state subsidies.

The consumer appeared to be far more cost conscious, which led to the growth of no frills basic services in the US. Generally air fares have continued to fall in real terms. Merger activity and strategic alliances increased among the larger world airlines. National governments took an active interest in the restructuring process, and the EC proposed that there was an orderly contraction in the industry. States like Belgium would have liked to reintroduce capacity sharing arrangements, but this kind of strategy would have been contrary to the EC's decision to liberalize the industry.

Financially strong airlines like British Airways favoured competition, with uncompetitive carriers going out of business. However, many airlines in Europe are state owned or are state assisted. Air France, Sabena, and Iberia, had substantial state aid. Other states sought EC approval for restructuring airlines, including Ireland for Aer Lingus, Greece for Olympic and Portugal for TAP.

The result of the losses was that airlines:

1 restructured
2 cut expenditure; and
3 deferred or cancelled aircraft orders.

No real improvement was expected in the industry, until the spare capacity had been removed, and the financial position of the airlines was improved. In 1992, one thousand aircraft deliveries were either cancelled or deferred.

Estimating the market for new aircraft

The demand for the industry's products tends to be cyclical depending in part on the pattern of passenger growth. Because the airlines are trying to guess the market in advance, there are times when they overestimate the demand, and this leads to times when there is a surplus of aircraft. Also, new technology can stimulate demand by making older aircraft less profitable for the airlines to use. The choice of one particular kind of aircraft as against another depends upon a variety of factors. It depends on what the airline requires in terms of the aircraft's range, its payload and its suitability to operate out of particular airports. Environmental considerations can be important, particularly with regard to the noise levels at take-off. The general technical merit of the aircraft is of course important, as are factors such as fleet standardization, the availability of spare parts and the training needs of the pilot and crew. Finally, the kind of financial package available to the purchaser is of vital importance.

The main components of demand for new aircraft are:

1 Replacement of older aircraft; and
2 Growth in air travel.

In 1993, it was estimated that 700 aircraft were grounded or for sale. New orders declined significantly, from a peak value of $90 billion in 1989, to $32 billion in 1991 and $20.9 billion in 1992. In 1993, Boeing had 56.9 per cent of the value of the world market for large passenger jets, while Airbus had 33 per cent and McDonnell Douglas had 8.3 per cent.

In the period of rapid expansion of the late 1980s McDonnell Douglas and Boeing had added 10 per cent to their capacity. Airbus planned to increase production from 160 to 220 aircraft per annum, in the period to 1995, in line with their wish to gain an increasing share of the world market. However a capacity reduction of 25 per cent to 30 per cent, was required to bring supply in line with demand This meant a reduction in total output from 800 to 550. Airbus responded to the declining market by cutting output from 157 aircraft in 1992 to 142 aircraft in 1993. Planned output for 1994 and 1995 was 138 aircraft per year.

Some business is guaranteed by the age of the existing fleet. In 1993, 1000 aircraft were 25 years old and very near to the end of their useful life, and this was expected to rise to 2500 in 1995. Aircraft may be replaced early if modern aircraft are significantly more comfortable or efficient to run. Also, there are examples where governments insist that state owned carriers buy from national manufacturers.

In 1993, Airbus estimated that 2100 narrow body jets and 500 wide bodied jets would be retired over the period to 1998, to make way for 3300 new aircraft. Over a longer period Boeing estimate 12005 aircraft to be delivered in the period to 2010, with 25 per cent being replacement orders.

Aerospace and the political system

The civil aerospace industry is still very much tied to the nation state, despite the fact that it competes for its business on a global basis. This is a legacy of the recent past, where it was strongly linked to the military needs of the state. With the decline of the world superpowers, and the risk of military conflict, the balance has changed. Falling military budgets mean that the civilian business is of greater importance.

It is an industry which requires a huge amount of investment and one where the risks are high. Unlike many industries of its size and importance, it is normally conducted by a variety of companies operating within nation states, although frequently linked internationally by licensing, subcontracting and collaboration agreements. It is an industry where the major companies are tied very closely to the national political system. This is because of the strategic importance of the industry, especially as the civil aerospace companies are also producers of military equipment. Added to this it can be a high value added export industry, as is the case with the American Boeing Company.

Governments frequently give financial help to the industry. This can be by financing research projects, or underwriting losses on projects. They can also help indirectly by feeding money into the companies via military programmes. Where military research is being conducted by the company, it is often the case that there is an overspill of technology into civil purposes in terms of materials, fuels, electronics and engines. Civil airliners can of course be used for military purposes, for example for troop transporters or carriers of equipment. For the national governments there is an added bonus, in that support for high technology areas like this, tends to lead to increased investment. (Estimates place the investment multiplier for aerospace as high as 2.2.) In this way the industry helps to promote economic growth. Governments can give indirect help to their aerospace industries by subsidizing export financing or by persuading national-flag-carrying airlines to buy the product.

In return for the assistance the industry receives, governments also expect to be able to interfere in the decision process, in order to further their international relations policy. Heads of state have frequently seen the industry as being a diplomatic tool, to be used to cement relations with other countries. There is frequently a linkage with military projects, and the size of the contracts involved are seen as sufficient to warrant very top level involvement in negotiations over sales, or the nature of collaboration.

The political links between the manufacturers and governments has led to acrimonious squabbles between the US and the EC about the legitimacy of state aid to the industry. This aid comes in two forms:

1 Direct aid, in the form of grants and subsidies, towards the costs of development and manufacture of aircraft. Also help in the form of export subsidies.
2 Indirect aid via defence contracts and research and development initiatives.

The US has constantly sought to reduce the extent of direct aid for the development of a new aircraft, however, the European companies do not have access to indirect help towards development available in the US, said to be worth $1 billion per year. The Europeans have claimed that McDonnell Douglas and Boeing received up to $41.5 billion in state aid over the last 15 years, while the help given to Airbus is estimated to be in excess of $13.5 billion.

In May 1992, an agreement was reached between the US and EC to limit the extent of help that was meant to be given. This agreed that there was to be:

1 no direct subsidies in the manufacture of aircraft;
2 a limit to subsidies towards development of 3 per cent of annual turnover;
3 a timetable for paying back the development costs;
4 a limit on indirect subsidies, fixed at 5 per cent of a manufacturer's civil aviation turnover;

5 transparency about the help given;
6 rules in force concerning inducements.

These rules could be suspended if there were really serious problems facing the industry. There was also a disputes mechanism in place.

In order to maintain the political pressure in favour of the European aerospace industry, the European Aerospace Industry Council (EAIC) was formed, and held its first meeting on 13 July 1993. This organization brought together the very largest civil and military firms in the European aeronautics industry; Aerospatiale, Alenia, British Aerospace, Casa, Dasa. Dassault, Fokker, Rolls-Royce, Snecma, Saab, as well as representatives of the European Association of Aerospace Material Constructors. They called for measures by the EC and the member states to:

1 Maintain competitiveness;
2 Ensure that state aid was maintained, particularly indirect aid;
3 Preserve the competitiveness of the industry, by mechanisms designed to help the industry when the dollar was weak;
4 Make certain that the new GATT round should not weaken the industry;
5 Give help for research and technological development via the Fourth Framework Programme.

Global competition

In the past, Europe's record in the world civil aerospace market was poor. This was in part because the US producers were able to take advantage of a large domestic market and so gain production economies. It meant that the higher labour costs in the USA could be offset by superior productivity. Added to this Boeing in particular had a good reputation for quality, which was combined with skilful marketing, good consumer liaison and imaginative financial packages. Success in the home market meant that it was easier to sell competitively into third markets. The cyclical nature of the market and competition from Airbus, led both the major US producers to cut their output and their labour force in 1992 and 1993.

The American competition

Boeing

Boeing, with a dominant share of the global market throughout the 1980s is by far the major player. With a thriving military aircraft division, its civil sector business is cushioned, cross-subsidized and enhanced by the company's ability to use its dominant US and global position to advantage. The pioneer developer of the jumbo jet, Boeing led the way in the industry in trying to reduce costs and increase productivity by pursuing development of 'families' of aircraft based on one initial research design project. It has enjoyed a virtual monopoly of long haul aircraft sales and, with covert US government/military support, had looked invulnerable to competitive attack until the advent of Airbus Industrie and its range of competing products.

In the 1990s the increasing competition from Airbus caused the company to take an aggressive view of its manufacturing costs. In order to maintain its market share the company aimed to reduce the cost of manufacturing its jets by 25 to 30 per cent, and to halve its aircraft production cycle time by 1998.

The cost of developing new aircraft started to be a serious concern to Boeing, even in the 1980s. The 747 was ultimately a successful aircraft, but its development nearly put the company out of business. Increasingly the company has sought outside participation in its development of new aircraft. The 707 was virtually all-American in content, the 727 had less than 1 per cent foreign content, while the 737 had slightly more. The 767 had Japanese and Italian risk sharing, but the major change in direction came with the 777, a new wide bodied jet. This had a 20 per cent Japanese stake involving Mitsubishi, Kawasaki and Fuji. The need to find new partnerships to share the costs of development led to a series of discussions between Boeing and Airbus about the joint development of a super jumbo with a seating capacity of between 600 and 800 passengers. This is likely to be assembled in Germany. The estimated market for this design could be in the region of 500 aircraft by 2010.

McDonnell Douglas (MDD)

MDD remains the second ranked US player to the giant Boeing, with a history in the 1970s of unprofitable civil projects, growing debt burdens and the albatross of any aircraft producer on the world stage – a flagship with a tendency to crash, the ill-fated DC-10. The early 1980s saw MDD abandon production of the DC-10 and show a growing reluctance to be heavily involved in civil aircraft projects, but improving fortunes in the mid-1980s did see a restart of production of the DC-10, albeit under a new name, the MD11, once public disquiet about the former's safety had sufficiently subsided. McDonnell Douglas failed to clinch a deal with Taiwan Aerospace in 1992, which had the prospect of $2 billion investment in McDonnell Douglas.

Europe's response

The American picture contrasts with European manufacturers who in the past seemed unable to compete effectively. They were selling into relatively small home markets, often with narrow specifications. The costs of development were duplicated as each country sought to promote its own national champion. In many cases the only serious buyers were the national-flag-carrying airline, who had little choice but to make the purchase, or those countries who were encouraged to buy the product as part of an aid package. There were frequent doubts about the technical quality of the product, and generally, they sold badly. This therefore left the US producers in a dominant market position, and in the case of the jumbo jets, there was only one producer in the world, and that meant that Boeing could demand the highest price that the market could stand.

The benefits of collaboration in civil aircraft production in Europe would seem to be considerable. The failure of the 'go-it-alone' national efforts would seem to indicate that a cooperative solution had to be found. In the field of military aircraft, a degree of collaboration made sense, so it seemed a rational move to adopt the concept for civil aircraft projects. Collaboration across national borders meant that the costs of development would be shared and there would be limited duplication of research efforts, along with offering access to existing technological expertise in different states. There would be a wider access to venture capital, and risks would be shared among partners. When the huge costs of developing new aircraft are considered, it is clear that new projects are likely to be beyond the means of individual companies and even national governments. Problems of gaining acceptability of technical standards across Europe would be reduced, as all partners would see it in their interest to ensure that the product was totally acceptable in all markets. Finally, national airlines could be persuaded to purchase the aircraft, so increasing the prospect of sufficient sales to gain the economies of scale required to move down the cost curve and sell the product to third markets. All of this presupposed that the project could be started and financed up to the point where it became viable. The costs of gaining a presence in the world airline market were always likely to be huge.

Instead of a number of national champions all struggling to compete within the narrow confines of the Western European market, collaboration offered the prospect of enhanced market power. From being relatively insignificant national concerns, the right kind of network of collaboration offered the prospect of creating a global power. With the backing of a number of national governments to ensure that access to third markets was made easier, and a production and research capacity to match the larger global players, it is possible to offer a meaningful challenge. In addition, the presence of a major European producer offered an additional benefit – the impact of competition on prices. The Boeing monopoly of the jumbo jet market was broken, which meant that they were no longer able to dictate terms, as airlines had an alternative supplier. Finally, if collaboration offered the prospect of enhancing European integration, then it can expect support from the European Community.

Collaborating with other firms across national boundaries is not easy, indeed many firms have not resolved their communication difficulties of operating within one plant. There needs to be clear definition of the objectives, and an accurate assessment of the financial, technical, and commercial parameters involved. Areas of responsibility have to be made clear, and all those involved in the project must feel a sense of ownership for it. There has to be confidence between partners, and an equitable method of sharing the profits or losses. In order to maximize confidence it is best if collaboration takes place over a long period of time involving a number of projects. At the same time there has to be an awareness and acceptance of differing industrial cultures.

Airbus Industrie – the European player

The four companies which make up the European consortium are:

British Aerospace (BAe)

British Aerospace's 20 per cent share was finally taken up in 1979, some twelve years after the initial launch of the A300 project. This fact and the relatively low percentage share reflects the company's ambivalence about participation and its scepticism about the consortium's likely achievement of anything remotely resembling real commercial success when it eventually becomes a public listed company sometime in the 1990s. BAe produces the wings for Airbus and leans heavily on its history, experience and expertise as a military aircraft producer and its strategic position in the UK economy for both protection and support from the UK government in its dealings with its consortium partners. With the decline in military business, it sought collaborative deals in Taiwan Aerospace to produce regional jets.

Aeerospatiale

Aerospatiale enjoys a 37.9 per cent share and is very much the national champion of France in this sector. Fiercely proud of its share in the project and of the strategic importance of the assembly line of the final aircraft in Toulouse, the Airbus project represents the epitome of French specialist knowledge. In Jean Pierson, the Airbus MD, the French have a powerful influencer over policy. He is a pioneer of the Concorde project and clearly does not subscribe to the (mainly British) lobby now pressing for more accountability, tighter management and increased financial controls.

Deutsche Aerospace (DASA)

(Formerly Messerschmitt–Boelkow–Blohm(MBB) now owned by Daimler-Benz.)

Deutsche Aerospace enjoys an equal 37.9 per cent share in the Airbus project, but due to manifestly different political and cultural heritages did not exercise as dominant an influence as their French counterparts. However, with growing expertise (they started from a base of zero experience in civil aircraft production) they have rapidly descended the learning curve and are now flexing their bargaining muscle. The need to raise general awareness of Germany's role in Airbus, and a wish to acquire further expertise in the industry led to a demand that they enjoy a similar position to their French partners. DASA are responsible for final assembly of only two out of the seven Airbus range (the A319 and A321).

The setting up of Hamburg as an alternative focus to Toulouse was also seen as a way of reducing the dependency on partners, and there was an aspiration to be able to develop alternative sources of supply. This was brought about by a resentment at having to bear the costs of the destructive industrial disputes at BAe in 1989/90 which reduced Airbus output from 12 per month to 1.2.

The influence of DASA grew when in July 1992, they agreed to take a 51 per cent stake in the Dutch manufacturer Fokker. DASA also hopes to be the centre for assembling the new 600–800 seater super-jumbo, which may be built in collaboration with Boeing. The set up costs for this could be as high as $15 billion.

CASA

CASA, the Spanish partner, has only a 4.2 per cent share in the project, and limited influence. Participation has helped to establish the company as a credible and effective partner.

Structure

The Airbus is a project which involves its four partners in a transnational cooperation to build aircraft, with the purpose of creating an integration of complex industrial processes across Europe. Airbus consists of 1500 administrative and sales staff who have their headquarters near the Aerospatiale operation in Toulouse. The final assembly of the aircraft is currently carried out by Aerospatiale at Toulouse and DASA at Finkenwerder, Hamburg. All other tasks concerned with the development of the aircraft are carried out by the partners, in roughly equal proportions to their ownership of the project.

In October 1990, a new Aerospatiale plant was opened on a 130 acre site, after FF7 billion (£690 million) had been spent on preparing for the production of the A340 four engined long-range airliner, and A330 twin-engined, medium range jet. The centre piece of the development was a FF1 billion high technology assembly hall, which is partly robotized. This is designed to match the facilities which Boeing had in place in Seattle. The

DASA plant in Hamburg where the A321 and A319 were built was said to offer cost savings of $650 million by the year 2005.

The rules of Airbus mean that partners within Airbus cannot develop rival products, so that alternative consortia have to be either in smaller categories of aircraft, or be formed entirely from non-Airbus members. The precise dividing line between the class of jet that Airbus wishes to make and that which might be offered by rival consortium is uncertain.

The decision making structure of Airbus Industrie is based upon two levels. At the political level, the heads of state of the nations involved are frequently active in lobbying each other over key decisions, and progress on some issues is linked on the basis of either bilateral or on a multilateral agreement. What would be normal commercial decisions in other organizations, such as arrangements for fitting out and customization of aircraft, have often been decided upon by governments.

At the company level, since 1989 there has been a Supervisory Board, with five members, and an Executive Board with seven members. Each of the partners has a top level representative on each, and any of the partners has the power to veto a decision. The structure of Airbus is regarded as being very unwieldy, but the fact that the organization has been in business for over twenty years and the existence of a wide range of agreements and procedures, makes it difficult to reform.

Information about the finances of the Airbus project are limited, as the organization does not publish formal accounts. The sources of information tend to be the national governments, who release information because of the need to give information about public finances, or rivals of the Airbus, who complain about subsidy levels. Airbus is estimated to have received $13.5 billion in subsidies.

The pressure for reform

In 1993, Jean Pierson, who in the past showed some reluctance for reform, proposed a new structure based upon conventional ownership of assets and being able to award its own contracts. He proposed that it should no longer be registered as a *groupement d'intérêt économique* (GIE). This is a type of legal partnership, which need not declare results or pay corporate taxes, unless it so chooses. The existing structure was justified on the basis that the business was in its infancy, and needed help in its start up phase. However, the lack of a conventional structure has led to accusations from competitors that unfair subsidies are being given. Also suppliers, who are not part of the consortium, feel excluded. A conventional structure might give a better picture of the company's worth, and encourage operating efficiencies. In addition it might free the company from some of the political interference.

European collaboration in aircraft manufacture

Pierson felt that the existing structure had run to the end of its useful life. He believed that the company was too bureaucratic and decision making was too slow. There was unnecessary duplication of the research and development effort, and there were problems in rationalizing the overall process because of the differing social and labour regulations in the partner countries. The proposed new structure would move Airbus into being a public limited company, with an identity of its own. This independent identity would reinforce the view that the consortium had developed to the point where its reputation had outstripped that of its members.

Appendix C6.1   The Airbus family

Aircraft	No. of engines	Typical seating	Delivery from
A300-600	2	266	current
A310-300	2	220	current
A319	2	124	1995
A320	2	150	current
A321	2	186	1994
A330	2	335	current
A340	4	263-295	current

Source: *Financial Times*, 1 December 1993, p. 15

Appendix C6.2   The global commercial aircraft market

	1988	1989	1990	1991	1992	1993
Orders	1,058	1,833	1,236	482	458	209
Cancellations	9	36	58	143	138	262
Net intake	1,049	1,797	1,178	33	320	-53
Deliveries	511	506	570	822	789	490
Changes	+538	+1,291	+608	−483	−469	−543

Source: *Financial Times*, 1 December 1993, p. 15

Appendix C6.3 The order backlog of aircraft by manufacturer

	Backlog	Per cent	Value ($bn)	%
Boeing	1,259	54.7	87.5	56.9
Airbus	701	30.4	50.8	33.0
MDD	217	9.4	12.8	8.3
Others	127	4.6	2.9	1.8
Total	2,304	100.0	154.0	100.0

Source *Financial Times*, 1 December 1993, p. 15.

Appendix C6.4 Airbus: a history

1967

On 26 September British, French and German governments signed an agreement for the design of the A300. The go-ahead for production of a prototype was given provided three national carriers placed orders for a total of seventy-five aircraft.

1969

In March Britain announced its withdrawal from the A300 programme. The French and German governments agreed to go ahead with A300 production. By July, Hawker Siddeley Aviation (a forerunner of British Aerospace) signed a subcontract agreement for supply of wing boxes and responsibility for wing design.

1970

Airbus Industrie constituted with Aerospatiale and Deutsche Airbus as equal partners and the Netherlands as an associate member on the A300 programme.

1971

CASA of Spain became a full member of Airbus on 23rd December with a 2.4 per cent share.

1972

28 October: first flight of A300B.

1974

On 23 May the first A300B2 enters service with Air France.

European collaboration in aircraft manufacture

1978
In July the go ahead is given for the A310.

1979
British Aerospace becomes a full member on 1 January with a 20 per cent share. In April Belairbus became an associate member on the A310 programme.

1982
3 April: maiden flight of A310.

1983
In March the first A310-200s were delivered to Lufthansa and Swissair.

1984
On 1 March the then Secretary of State for Trade and Industry Norman Tebbit announced a £250 million launch aid for BAe participation in A320, 'repayable on terms designed to yield a return in real terms on the Government's investment.'

1987
On 22 February the A320 undertook its maiden flight.

On 14 May the then Secretary for Trade Paul Channon announced up to £450 million launch aid for BAe participation in A330/A340, 'fully repayable on terms designed to yield an acceptable return in real terms on the Government's investment'.

On 19 May French repayable launch aid of FF 4.86 billion and West German repayable grants of DM 2.9 billion were announced. It was reported in the press at this time that BAe had also put some £550 million of its own money into the programme. The A330/A340 programme was formally launched on 5 June.

1988
The first A320 was delivered to Air France on 26 March with British Airways receiving its first A320 on 31 March.

On 26 June an Air France A320 crashes at an air display at Halsheim in Eastern France; pilot error was blamed for the crash which killed three people (not including the pilot).

European Business

On 3 October came the death of Herr Franz Josef Strauss, Bavarian Prime Minister and Chairman of the Airbus Industrie Supervisory Board.

By 11 November total firm orders for the A300 and A310 pass the 500 mark.

On 17 November Dr Hans Friedrichs was appointed Chairman of Airbus Industrie.

1989
By February there had been 1000 firm orders for all types of Airbus.

On 1 April the new statutes for Airbus Industrie come into force. The main changes relate to the composition and size of the supervisory board, structure of senior management and establishment of an Executive Board.

On 10 June the 500th Airbus aircraft was delivered, it was an A320 for Northwest Airlines (the first of 100 ordered).

In August Airbus Industrie formed two new directorates – Administration (combining procurement and finance) and Transport (bringing operations and maintenance of Guppies in-house). Guppies are the strange looking aircraft which are used to transport the various parts of Airbus to Toulouse.

In October Mr Adam Brown, VP in charge of strategy, leaves Airbus on his recall to British Aerospace. (No reason is given for the recall.)

November – workers at BAe plants at Preston, Chester and Kingston upon Thames go on strike in support of a claim for a shorter working week. The strike at Chester directly affects the supply of components to the Airbus assembly line in Toulouse. The production of aircraft falls from a peak of 12 per month to 1.2 per month. The strike lasts 18 weeks, and Airbus loses £181 million in lost production.

1990
On 25 January the world's biggest airline Aeroflot of the Soviet Union, announces it is to purchase five A310-300 Airbuses for delivery between November 1991 and June 1992.

15 February – an Indian Airlines A-320 crashed just before landing at Bangalore airport. Ninety of the 146 people on board were killed in the crash. The first crash of an Airbus aircraft in service.

European collaboration in aircraft manufacture

1991
New orders for Airbus show a decline throughout the year.

1992
A report in February reveals that the A320 has the worst accident record of large passenger jets registered in Britain.

It was estimated on 7 March, that 10 per cent of the world's fleet of passenger aircraft were idle.

Airbus gain an order for $600 million for the Middle East.

8 November 1992 Northwest Airlines cancels 74 aircraft orders worth $3.5 billion.

1993
October – Hamburg tipped for the site to assemble the new super-jumbo.

Questions

1. Discuss the view that the decision to start assembly of Airbus in Hamburg has more to do with Airbus politics than sound business practice.
2. Assess the validity of Jean Pierson's claim that; 'Airbus has become a model for such ventures in the aerospace and other capital intensive industries.' *Financial Times* 8 June 1993 (Survey Aerospace page II).
3. Critically assess the problems associated with companies engaging in multiple alliances.
4. Is it now more appropriate for firms in the aerospace industry to think in terms of global rather than regional alliances?
5. Consider the case for Airbus retaining its present structure.

Case 7 The European plastics industry: responding to change

Debra Johnson

Introduction

This case examines in detail two of the major challenges facing the European plastics industry in the depth of the European recession in 1993: overcapacity and the increasing demands of environmental regulation.

The plastics industry has, for decades, followed a cycle of overcapacity, rationalization, boom, overinvestment followed by overcapacity again. This pattern is repeating itself in the 1990s. The industry is responding to the competitive challenge via a series of asset swaps, mergers and transnational alliances to reduce the number of players. These restructuring efforts are complicated by the increasing globalization of the plastics business; growing questions about European competitiveness; and an avalanche of legislation to control the impact of post-consumer plastic waste on the environment.

The relatively new environmental challenge raises the possibility of the reintroduction of trade barriers within Europe and places obligations on the plastics industry which it may not be able to meet. The second part of this case assesses the extent and nature of these new regulations and examines the problems which have arisen when one country, Germany, introduces laws which have serious spillover effects in other European countries. This section also examines the response of the European Community to the proliferation of national laws.

Introduction to the plastics industry

During the Second World War, commercial-scale plastics production replaced natural materials which were in short supply. Since then, as the versatility of plastic materials has become apparent, worldwide production and consumption of plastics have increased to over 90 million tonnes. Consumption growth has been over 7.5 per cent p.a. during the last quarter century and annual global plastic sales approached $200 billion at the beginning of the 1990s.

The European plastics industry: responding to change

Plastics have been successful because of the advantages they bring to their applications (Table C7.1).

Table C7.1 *Plastics – properties and applications*

Properties	Applications and Benefits
Lightweight	Transport and fuel cost savings
Electrical insulation	Wiring, switches, plugs, appliance housing, power tools and electronics
Optical/transparency	Packaging, lighting & lenses
Corrosion resistance	Irrigation, plumbing, boats, rain wear, pumps, valves
Chemical resistance	Fuel tanks
Mouldability	One-piece complex shapes – reduces tooling costs
Cost savings	Cheaper than many alternatives
Adaptability	Balance of properties easily altered by slight changes in processes or fillers and additives
Colouring ahead of use	Painting becomes unnecessary

In the broadest sense, the plastics industry includes not only those companies who produce the plastics materials but also those which transform these materials into finished or semi-finished products. The plastics materials producers are national or multinational oil and gas companies whereas the plastics processors, of which there are thousands in Western Europe, are mostly small and medium enterprises.

This case study deals primarily with the materials producers but the demand for plastics is a derived demand: technical and market developments in those sectors which consume plastics translate into demand changes for the materials. Plastic material producers have strong links with the energy industry which provides the basic feedstocks for plastic materials.

The plastics processors are the main link between the producer and the end-user. Few industries do not employ plastics in some form as an important input. Packaging, construction and the transport/automotive industries are the major end-use sectors for plastic materials with the electrical, electronics and houseware sectors also providing useful outlets (Table C7.2).

Table C7.2 *West European plastics consumption by sector (%)*

Sector	Spain	Ger	Fr	NL	It.	Belg.	UK
Construction	11	8	17	25	14	23	25
Packaging	34	16	28	29	41	31	33
Electronics/electrical	2	6	5	1	5	2	10
Transport	6	17	0	3	7	6	10
Agriculture	10	2	0	4	5	5	5
Furniture	6	1	5	1	6	1	3
Household	2	4	0	5	4	4	3
Others	29	46	45	32	18	28	11

Source: Plastic Waste Management Institute (Japan)

The term 'plastics' covers a heterogeneous group of materials with widely varying characteristics and properties: hundreds of plastics resins and thousands of different grades, each employing different additives and fillers, are produced commercially. The main categories of plastics are listed below.

1 *Commodity plastics:* low-price, high volume, relatively homogeneous products which are highly sensitive to changes in the supply–demand balance. The commodity plastics – polyethylene, polypropylene, polystyrene and PVC – account for over two thirds of all polymer sales.
2 *Engineering plastics:* engineering plastics have higher specifications than commodity plastics and are often 'engineered' for specific applications. Demand for engineering plastics has grown rapidly in recent years, but they are produced in smaller quantities than commodity polymers and consequently fetch prices which are four to five times higher than commodity polymers. Polycarbonate, polyamides, epoxy resins and polyacetals are examples of engineering plastics.

  The distinction between commodity and engineering polymers is not hard and fast. Technological improvements have extended the range of applications of commodity polymers and have brought them into competition with some engineering polymers in recent years.
3 *Advanced polymers:* at the higher end of the price–performance spectrum, plastic materials like liquid crystal polymers (LCPs), polyketones and polysulfone achieve standards of performance previously beyond the reach of plastics in terms of strength and chemical, radiation and temperature resistance. No more than a few thousand tons (compared to millions for the major commodity polymers) of these advanced polymers

The European plastics industry: responding to change

are produced and they can be priced up to one hundred times more highly than commodity plastics. In view of their high prices, these plastics are used in specialist applications in the aerospace, defence and electronic industries.
4 *Structural composites:* high levels of performance can also be achieved by reinforcing polymers with other materials. Such products are known as 'structural composites' and are used in aerospace and military applications and in high-tech sports equipment.

Challenges facing Europe's plastics industry

Western Europe is one of the three main plastics producing and consuming regions of the world: the others are North America and Japan (Figure C7.1).

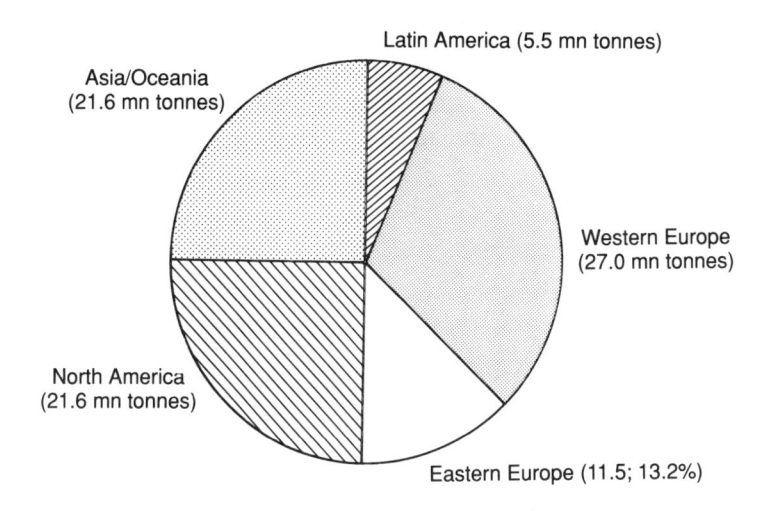

Figure C7.1 1991 world plastic consumption (million metric tons; percentage)

The plastics industry in Europe, and elsewhere, lurches from overcapacity to rationalization. The industry in Europe has undergone the full cycle during the last fifteen years. At the beginning of the 1980s, the European plastics industry was in a serious depression: excess capacity was hitting at company profits and a major rationalization programme was initiated.

As the European economy picked up from the mid-1980s, capacity utilization improved and prices and the financial situation of materials producers recovered. This improvement in industry performance encouraged manufacturers to plan major new capacity, especially for polyethylene and polypropylene. These capacity expansions, which occurred not only in Western Europe, but also in North and South America, the Middle East and the Far East, started to come onstream in 1991 and 1992, i.e. at precisely the time when the major consuming countries were bearing the brunt of recession, resulting in oversupply and lower prices and profits (see Table C7.3 and Figure C7.2).

Table C7.3 *West European market for major plastics ('000 tonnes)*

	Low density polyethylene	High density polyethylene	Polypropylene	Polystyrene	PVC
1987	4850	2365	2730	1500	4470
1988	5070	2618	3055	1658	4878
1989	5250	2720	3350	1720	4880
1990	5295	3046	3680	1820	5300
1991	5430	3090	3920	1791	4905
1992	5577	3197	4082	1788	5200

Source: Association of Plastics Manufacturers in Europe

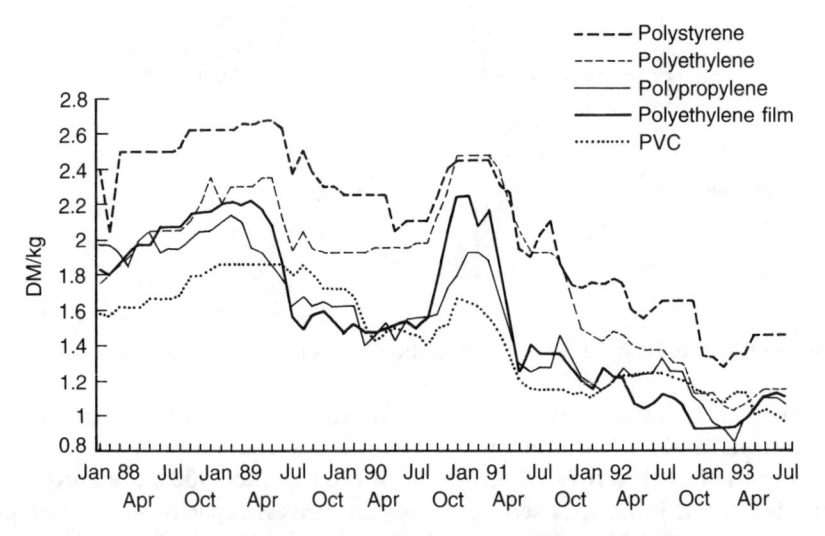

Figure C7.2 Representative European plastics prices (Deutschemarks per kilogramme) (source derived from *European Chemical News*)

In addition to these changes, the European plastics industry is facing a number of other challenges during the 1990s.

The European plastics industry: responding to change

The trade challenge

Typically, Western European plastics producers have satisfied the majority of domestic demand and exported their surplus production. However, a world market for plastics materials is developing as new producers from energy-rich and developing countries build up their plastics production capacities. Such developments threaten to upset the delicate market balance of recent decades.

The European plastics industry will be steadily pushed out of the domestic markets of the new producers who will provide stiff competition in Europe's other export markets. South Korea, for example, which has built up world-scale polyethylene, polystyrene and polypropylene capacity, is seeking to sell that part of its output which it cannot sell domestically in the rest of the Far East. European producers are also increasingly finding themselves under pressure in their domestic market from new producers.

The competitive challenge

Recession is heightening the concern about competitiveness in many European industries. The petrochemical and plastic industries are no exception, especially in view of the globalization of the industry described above. US polyethylene producers, for example, can exploit their cheaper ethylene feedstock costs to sell their product in Western European at prices competitive with those of the European industry despite additional freight, delivery and duty costs. Only the abnormally low prices prevailing in Western Europe prevented American producers from doing so in 1993. Producers from the Arabian Gulf states, which have feedstock prices of less than a third of European producers, can compete in Europe, even at low 1993 prices.

The technical challenge

In order to retain competitiveness, new applications and new specifications for plastics products are constantly sought and the European industry must provide technical leadership or, at minimum, keep abreast of technical developments within the industry.

The motor industry, for example, has proved a major source of new applications for plastic materials: on average over double the quantity of plastics is used in the production of a car in 1993 than in 1983. Many different plastics are utilized in the motor car and in a multitude of applications, including fuel tanks, bumpers, dashboards, roof linings, interior trim, wiring, upholstery, seat frames, body panels and a wide range of under-the-bonnet applications.

Environmental factors are affecting the use of plastics in motor cars: the lightness of plastics generates fuel savings but plastics components are being redesigned to reduce the number of plastics used and thereby facilitate recycling.

The environmental challenge

Throughout the industrialized world, the pressure for policies which protect the environment has moved from the political fringes to the mainstream since the mid-1980s. The plastics industry has been the target for a wide range of legislative initiatives to try to curb the adverse effects of plastics on the environment.

Plastics are frequently viewed as a symbol of the throw-away society and have been the focus of environmental legislation on the following waste management grounds:

1   toxicity and leachate in landfills;
2   shortage of landfill capacity;
3   incinerator emissions;
4   the possible migration of plastic material into food or medical products;
5   the non-degradable nature of most plastics;
6   the lack of plastics recycling compared to other materials like glass, paper and aluminium;
7   the excessive use of material in applications like packaging;
8   the use of non-renewable natural resources.

The legislation which has been passed to deal with some of these issues is affecting the costs of the European industry and the way it conducts itself. If the appropriate set of conditions prevail (i.e. high prices for the virgin material and availability of markets for the recycled product), the environmental legislation could result in changed fortunes for the producers of virgin plastic material. The policies in question are discussed in more detail below.

The industry's response

The crisis in the European plastics industry is the result of a combination of factors, including recession and overcapacity. The Association of Petrochemical Producers in Europe (APPE) has approached the European Commission with a programme of measures to resurrect the petrochemical industry. The APPE's proposals relate to a broad swathe of the chemical industry but could apply specifically to plastics. The APPE calls for a three-pronged approach to the crisis:

1   a support package;
2   voluntary action;
3   restructuring.

The European plastics industry: responding to change

Support package

The support package is intended to speed up and facilitate the industry restructuring process. The industry would like more rapid approval of mergers, joint ventures and proposals to share facilities. Financial help is also sought for the provision of basic infrastructure such as pipelines, for joint production facilities and research (e.g. into feedstock recycling) and for the funding of retraining and redundancies which will occur as the result of rationalization. The chemical industry also requests that it should not be hindered by the imposition of purely European energy taxes and environmental legislation and by unfair trading practices.

Voluntary action

Voluntary action is envisaged through the industry's Responsible Care programme which it has instituted to introduce ongoing improvements in environmental performance, continuing capital investment and research to improve competitiveness.

Restructuring

Restructuring involves the rationalization of productive capacity. Developments in the polypropylene market demonstrate the problems besetting the plastics industry and how it has responded.

During the 1980s, demand for polypropylene grew by almost 13 per cent per annum in Western Europe, largely as a result of its versatility and technological improvements. Rapid demand growth encouraged an increase in Western European production capacity of about 40 per cent in the first two years of the 1990s. Although significant, such expansions were relatively restrained compared to those in the Middle and Far East where capacity more than doubled during the same period, creating greater competition in important export markets.

Producers continue to be bullish about polypropylene compared to other plastics but the trend in demand growth is lower, even when the effect of the recession is discounted. Consequently, polypropylene prices, like those of other commodity prices, have tumbled as the tightness of supply has eased.

Profits of polypropylene producers have plummeted. The industry has responded to the crisis with rumours of mergers, restructuring and joint ventures. Not all of the rumours will come to fruition but some will, and by the mid-1990s there will be a smaller number of players in the European polypropylene field. In 1992, there were nineteen polypropylene producers in Europe – this could quickly fall to thirteen or fourteen.

Table C7.4 *1993 West European polypropylene capacity ('000 tonnes per year)*

Company	Capacity
Himont	745
BASF/ROW (BASF-Shell jv)	590
Shell	565
Hoechst	510
Neste	430
ÖMV	390
Montefina (Himont-Fina jv)	390
Appryl (BP-Atochem jv)	350
DSM	280
Solvay	260
Amoco	200
Statoil	200
Hüls	195
North Sea Petrochemical (Himont-Statoil jv)	180
Exxon	140
Repsol-Hoechst	135
Polychim	120
Repsol	80
Total	5760

Source: Derived from trade press

The motivations for individuals mergers and assets swaps vary. In early 1993, BASF doubled its polypropylene capacity at a stroke by acquiring ICI's 300 000 tonnes of polypropylene capacity. BASF gained a presence in the UK, Netherlands, Germany and Spain and elevated itself into the second position in the Western European polypropylene league alongside Hoechst and Shell and behind Himont (see Table C7.4) (the latter two companies are also in the throes of uniting their production capacity). ICI was heavily involved in the raffia-grade textile market with an emphasis on high volume, low price commodities. BASF, on the other hand, concentrated on higher value co-polymer products with outlets in film and thermoforming applications. ICI's polypropylene assets therefore complemented BASF's existing portfolio and strengthened its position in the market place.

Other producers welcomed BASF's acquisition because it represented a reduction in the number of players and there was the hope that fewer, larger companies would help stabilize the market and thereby strengthen prices. However, in view of ICI's recent modernization of its Wilton and Rozenburg

The European plastics industry: responding to change

plants, it was felt unlikely that the needed capacity rationalization would result from this particular deal.

The biggest deal to date has been the mid-1993 announcement of the merger of Neste and Statoil's polyolefins (polypropylene and polyethylene) in a 50–50 joint venture. Not only will the new company, which will come into being in early 1994, be the dominant polyolefin player in Western Europe (at least until Shell and Himont complete their deal), but it will also be a world leader in polyolefins, ranking fifth behind Exxon, Dow, Himont and Quantum. The new company will have polyethylene capacity of 1.4 million tonnes per annum and polypropylene capacity of 670 000 tonnes (see Table C7.5).

Table C7.5 *Neste/Statoil olefin/polyolefin capacity ('000 tonnes per year)*

	Ethylene	Propylene	PE	PP
Neste				
Porvoo	240	140	200	150
Antwerp	350	180	120	
Beringen			120	280
Sines	330	130	260	
Stenungsund			440	
Saudi				20
Malaysia				20
Total	920	450	1140	470
Statoil				
Stenungsund	400	190		
Noretyl	200	80		
Bamble			270	100
Antwerp		200		100
Total	600	470	270	200
Neste/Statoil	1520	920	1410	670

Source: Neste and Statoil

Neste of Finland is providing the majority of the assets and Norway's Statoil has paid Neste a substantial cash sum to correct the balance. This cash injection was a major attraction for Neste.

One of the major motivations behind the deal is to increase market share and the capability to invest in new technology. The new company has global ambitions and will strive to compete in the world as well as the European market. It will have manufacturing facilities in Belgium, Finland, France,

Germany, Norway, Portugal, Sweden and the United States. The new company is particularly strong in northern Europe and hopes its strong position there will act as a springboard for making inroads into world markets. Neste is also contributing its share of joint ventures in Saudi Arabia and Malaysia. This market power will weaken the competitive position of smaller producers.

As in the BASF/ICI deal, no capacity closures are envisaged as a result of the deal, thereby bringing into question the benefits of the deal to the European industry as a whole. From the point of view of the two companies involved, however, the deal brings certain advantages, including:

1. economies resulting from joint marketing and research and development;
2. improved feedstock positions: Statoil offers access to large reserves of natural gas in the North Sea – an important factor for Neste which has to replace the supplies of Russian crude oil which have disappeared since the disintegration of the Soviet Union;
3. better cracker balance: Statoil has a surplus of ethylene whereas Neste has been a major purchaser of ethylene. Both companies also have interests at the Stenungsund complex: Statoil's cracker already supplies Neste's polyolefin units but the deal will allow greater synergies to be gained.

Neither the BASF takeover of ICI's polypropylene assets nor the Neste–Statoil polyolefin merger involve capacity closures. Further deals have been mooted and cannot be ruled out if producers are to withstand the current tough competitive environment.

Environmental policies and the issues for industry

Environmental concerns have moved to the top of the political agenda in most industrialized countries. Plastics, which in Western Europe account for 7 per cent by weight and 20 per cent by volume of municipal solid waste (MSW), have provided a focus for this concern (Figure C7.2).

Landfill is the prominent disposal method (55%) in Western Europe, with incineration accounting for 30 per cent of waste disposal. Recycling accounts for 5-15 per cent of all waste disposal but plastics recycling rates, however, are much lower (Figure C7.3).

As landfill capacity is increasingly in tight supply and the bad press of incineration continues, legislation to reduce the quantity of plastic waste and to encourage reuse and recycling, especially of packaging, has proliferated throughout Europe. Increasingly, legislative attention is turning towards other sectors such as the automobile industry, household goods and electrical and electronic equipment. Germany and Denmark are leading the way in this respect.

The European plastics industry: responding to change

Governments can employ a range of policy instruments to solve their waste management problems. The more common instruments, each of which poses different problems for industry, include:

1 Recycling targets: recycling targets have proved most popular with many governments but the targets are often set at levels which are unrealistically high and within impossibly tight time frames. In the early 1990s, Western Europe had achieved a plastics recycling rate of 7–8%. As the German experience shows, account also needs to be taken of a country's recycling capacity and of the availability of markets for recycled goods (Table C7.6).

Table C7.6 *Some Western European recycling targets*

	Material	*Target (%)*	*Deadline*	*Comments*
Austria	Packaging	80		
Belgium	Bottles:			
	Plastics	70	1.1.98	Draft law
	Glass	80	1.1.98	
	Metals	80	1.1.98	
France	Packaging	77	2002	Incineration OK
Germany	Plastic	30	Jan '93	Incineration
	packaging	80	June '95	not OK
Italy	Bottles:			
	Plastic	40	1993	Incineration
	Glass	50	1993	OK
	Metal	50	1993	
Netherlands	All packaging	60	200	Voluntary
	Glass	80	2000	incineration
	Aluminium	75	2000	OK
	Paper/board	60	2000	
	Plastic	50	2000	
Sweden	Aluminium	90		
	PET bottles	90		
	Glass	70		
	Steel cans	70		
	Corrg. board	65		
	Paperboard	65		
	Other plastic packaging	65		
Switzerland	Bottles			
	Glass	90	1993	
	Metal	90	1993	
	Plastics	90	1993	
UK	Household waste	25	2000	Voluntary

Source: derived from trade press

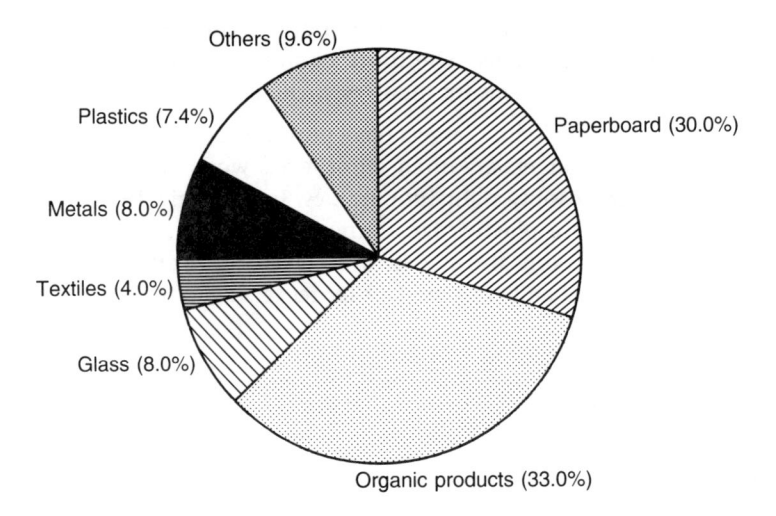

Figure C7.3 Composition of European municipal waste (source: Shell)

2 Landfill levies and landfill limits: such levies and limits are contemplated by Italy, the UK and the Netherlands for the purposes of encouraging the removal of waste disposal from landfill sites to other methods, including recycling.
3 Reusability targets.
4 Targets for percentage of recyclate in new products.
5 Procurement policies which favour recyclable products or products with recycled content: these policies are used to assist the creation of markets for recycled products.
6 Mandatory deposit schemes: used in Scandinavian countries, these schemes yield high recovery rates.
7 Material bans: PVC bans have been popular in Europe because of concern about the emissions from the incineration of PVC. Outright bans or measures to restrict PVC use are in operation or threatened in Austria, Belgium, several German länder, the Netherlands, Sweden and Switzerland. Attempts to limit PVC use throughout the EC have been made, so far unsuccessfully, through the Packaging Waste directive as it proceeds through the European Parliament.
8 Taxes on certain materials/products: taxes are used or proposed in several European countries to limit the consumption of plastics materials. These measures can be most effective – the European Commission has estimated that the introduction by Italy of a tax on plastic bags has resulted in a 40 per cent fall in the consumption of such bags.
9 Material and recyclability labelling: commonly used to facilitate recycling.

The European plastics industry: responding to change

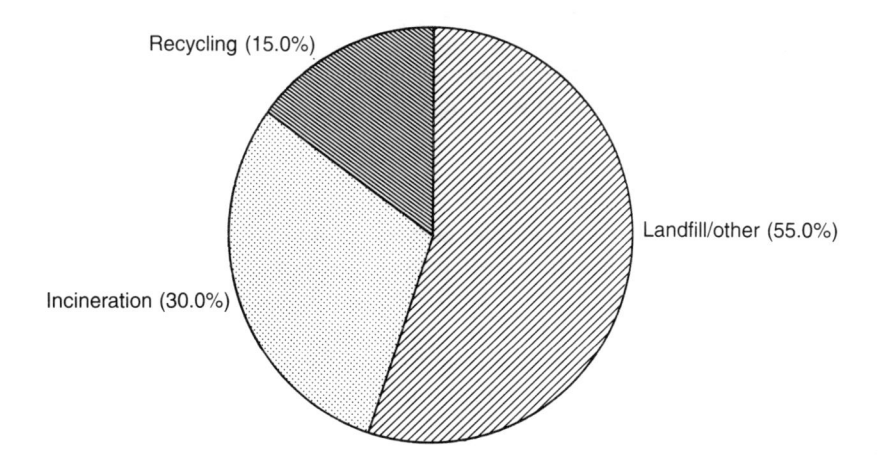

Figure C7.4 Disposal of European municipal waste

The proliferation of environmental regulation has important implications for the plastics industry and its end-users. The requirement for recycling is affecting choice of material and product design. Direct product bans have obvious consequences for producers of that material and are imposing additional costs on industry. The new rules also create potential trade barriers. Companies subject to tough legislation in their domestic market will find their costs higher than those of their rivals in major export markets. Companies trying to penetrate markets with higher environmental standards will have to develop different products specifically for these markets, again increasing costs and rendering products uncompetitive.

German recycling legislation

Germany's Packaging Ordinance, Europe's most ambitious and most controversial provision for the recycling of packaging waste, plainly demonstrates the problems which can arise from hasty introduction of recycling legislation.

The Ordinance contains the following provisions:

1 All packaging materials, except those with residues of hazardous materials, are covered by the Ordinance.
2 Targets for the collection of plastic packaging waste are 30 per cent by January 1993, rising to 80 per cent by June 1995.
3 Used packaging must be returned to manufacturers and distributors, preferably at the site where it was purchased.

4   The following mandatory deposits apply:
    (a)   50 pfennigs for liquid food containers of 0.2–1.5 litres;
    (b)   DM1 for such containers over 1.5 litres;
    (c)   DM2 for containers of washing, cleansing and emulsion agents over 2 kg;
5   Reuse has priority over recycling.
6   Incineration with energy recovery is not regarded as a form of recycling contrary to practice in some other European countries.
7   The Ordinance applied to transit packaging from 1 December 1991; to secondary packaging from 1 April 1992; and to sales packaging (e.g. containers and bottles or beverages, soap powder and cleaning products and items such as cutlery, dishes and other disposable products used by takeaway establishments or private households) from 1 January 1993.

Obligations to take back used packaging are set aside for manufacturers and distributors who belong to Duales System Deutschland (DSD). DSD is an umbrella body which organizes collection and sorting of consumer waste before selling it on for recycling. Members of DSD are entitled to mark their products with the Green Dot logo. The presence of the Green Dot implies that the packaging is recyclable and that the manufacturer or distributor has paid a fee to DSD. Segregated Green Dot waste must be recycled and not incinerated and all relevant collection and recycling targets must be met.

Europe's toughest recycling legislation encountered serious problems in its early years and has been roundly criticized by an impressive array of opponents. DSD was in severe logistical and financial difficulties (temporarily solved by cash injections and increased charges) by the summer of 1993.

The source of DSD's difficulties lay in the unexpected willingness of the German public to collect packaging waste for recycling. Unexpectedly large quantities of collected material plus insufficient recycling capacity created numerous problems.

Unable to cope with recycling at home, DSD exported its collected waste throughout the world: German waste with the Green Dot logo has been spotted as far afield as Indonesia (where it has subsequently been banned), China, South America and closer to home in Bulgaria, Hungary and the rest of the European Community.

In order to dispose of the waste, DSD offered financial incentives of up to DM600 per tonne to non-German recyclers to take the waste. This action unbalanced nascent recycling markets in several European countries. British recyclers, for example, accepted the German waste with the consequent collapse of prices for waste plastics collected in Britain (price falls of 60 per cent during the period 1989–1992 are reported) and the endangering of the

The European plastics industry: responding to change

viability of plastics waste recycling schemes which were only just getting underway in Britain. This pattern was repeated in France, the Netherlands and other European countries.

This situation led to a formal complaint from the UK to the European Commission on the grounds that the lack of adequate recycling capacity and unfair financial incentives in Germany have caused acute trade distortions and that unilateral action by one member state is causing serious disruptions in plastics and paper recycling throughout the rest of the Community. This action was supported by France, Spain, the Netherlands, Italy, Ireland and Luxembourg.

More general criticism of the Ordinance reflects many of the criticisms of ill-thought out recycling schemes. Critics claim the Ordnance:

1 pays insufficient attention to whether there is a market for the resulting recycled product;
2 sets recycling targets for all materials without due regard as to whether sufficient recycling capacity is available;
3 is based on dubious environmental and economic assumptions: the Ordinance focuses on recycling and ignores other options, such as incineration with energy recovery, which can sometimes be more environmentally appropriate;
4 breaches the Treaty of Rome by forcing exporters to Germany to devise special packaging arrangements for their products, thereby distorting cross-border trade and fragmenting the Single European Market;
5 undermines emerging recycling initiatives in other European countries;
6 infringes competition at home: the Federal Cartel Office is investigating complaints that DSD's nationwide recycling network restricts competition, and that DSD plans to start collection of sales packaging from commercial premises will inhibit the growth of other disposal companies;
7 discriminates against plastics through the DSD charging system – a situation which will be aggravated by the introduction of new charges from October 1993. The collection scheme has already affected material choice. DSD itself has estimated that plastics accounted for only 27 per cent of German packaging in 1992 compared with 40 per cent in 1990.

The majority of the legislation affecting plastic waste disposal in recent years has concerned packaging waste. However, the attention of the German government has turned to other sectors: the Environment Ministry estimates that one million metric tons of waste is generated in Germany each year from electronic equipment alone.

A proposed law contains provisions similar to those in the Packaging Ordinance and requires manufacturers of cars, household appliances, office equipment, industrial equipment and suppliers to the construction industry to take back and recycle their products. If the product is not made in Germany, the obligation to take back the product falls on the importer. The law also requires manufacturers and distributors to furnish the government with an annual list of parts that have been recovered.

Given the constraints which the proposals may impose on trade, the new Ordinances will encounter fierce opposition from Germany's trading partners, especially from within Europe, who will view this as a serious infringement of the principles of the Single European Market.

The European Community

The proliferation of national measures was in danger of fragmenting the single market and of distorting trade within the EC market and the wider European Economic Area (EEA) which came into effect in the summer of 1993. Accordingly, in 1992 the European Commission approved and published a draft directive on Packaging Waste (Com. 92 278). The Commission decided to act because it noted that:

1. only 18 per cent of the 50 million metric tons of packaging waste generated within the EC each year is recycled;
2. the proliferation of national measures was in danger of fragmenting the single market and of distorting trade within the EC market.

The main provisions of the draft Packaging Waste directive are:

1. 90 per cent by weight of packaging waste is to be recovered and 60 per cent by weight of each material in the waste stream is to be recycled within ten years of the directive coming into force. Incineration can be considered for the possible 30 per cent of packaging waste which is recovered but not recycled. Final disposal will be limited to the residues of collection and sorting and will be no more than 10 per cent by weight of packaging waste output. The targets will be reviewed within six years of implementation;
2. within five years, all packaging will carry approved harmonized labels which show recyclability and the nature of materials used. Harmonized markings are considered necessary to avoid trade barriers;
3. packaging will have to conform to 'essential requirements' before it can be used within the EC. Such requirements aim to ensure that the weight and volume of packaging is minimized; that it can be reused easily and that the presence of noxious metals and other hazardous chemicals is minimized;
4. economic instruments (i.e. taxes) may be used to raise funds to support national plans.

The European plastics industry: responding to change

The draft directive acknowledges the complexity of waste management issues and allows for changes in the preferences given to various waste management techniques if life cycle analysis, still in its early stages, shows existing assumptions about waste management to be misplaced.

Lobbying on this directive has been unusually intense with critics advocating:

1 greater emphasis on source reduction;
2 greater emphasis on reuse;
3 the removal of incineration as a form of recovery;
4 greater flexibility in relation to targets – poorer states want more time to achieve the directive's objectives;
5 the reduction of recycling targets;
6 individual targets for each material;
7 the right for states to set stiffer domestic targets than those set by the EC, leading to fears of trade distortion;
8 special treatment for developing countries who will find it difficult to fulfil their obligations under the directive because of inadequate technology, finance and even information about their obligations.

Whither the environment?

Environmental issues have moved extremely quickly in most industrialized countries from the political fringes to the political mainstream where they are expected to remain.

Key environmental issues for plastics producers, processors and end-users in the next few years include:

1 the spread of legislation to sectors apart from packaging which has, until now, borne the brunt of environmental and particularly recycling legislation;
2 market access: exporters must keep abreast of the latest environmental legal requirements affecting their products to ensure that they will not be barred from particular markets;
3 the evolution of virgin resin prices: virgin resin prices in Western Europe have plummeted in recent years. An extended period of low prices for new material endanger the survival of recycling schemes and recyclers;
4 technological change: technological change could alter the economic feasibility of environmental options. Improvements to material sorting equipment could improve the economics of recycling, for example, and the possibility of widespread, commercial feedstock recycling would alter the balance of the environmental debate altogether;
5 the effect on the demand for virgin resins if recycling rates are met.

Conclusions

The European plastics industry is accustomed to coping with the cycle of boom and bust. Its response to this challenge in the 1990s is complicated by the demands of environmental legislation; increasing competition from oil producers who have moved downstream who have an inherent feedstock cost advantage; and increasing technological development. In the past, plastics have replaced materials like glass and metal. Increasingly, improved technical specifications are leading to competition with materials with much higher performance and to competition between polymers. Against this background, industry restructuring, particularly the reduction of the number of manufacturers, is likely to continue.

Questions

1. Assess the balance of competitive forces facing the European plastics industry.
2. What are the main arguments for and against EC aid to the plastics industry?
3. What do European plastics producers hope to gain from their new alliances and mergers? Are their aspirations justified?
4. In view of the diversity of environmental regulation currently affecting the European plastic industry, assess the case for a unified European approach. How far will the EC's Packaging Waste directive successfully address the waste problem?
5. What are the main implications of the rush of waste disposal legislation for plastic material producers?

Case 8   The European car market

David Gray and Gary Cook

Introduction

Western Europe is the largest market for cars in the world. With stagnation in the US market, a rising Yen, protectionist noises from European politicians, and untapped demand in the East, Europe in the late 1980s, was seen by US and Japanese car producers as an important base offering an accessible, growing market.

The complexion of the European car market changed during the early 1990s. Europe became a battleground upon which a number of weaker producers lost their independence. The present slump in the car sales is leaving producers with excess capacity. This is compounded by production facilities, ordered when the market was buoyant, now coming on stream. Car manufacturers who reached for the eastern European grail found it to be a poisoned challis as the market slumped and labour costs rose. But the most feared spectre is that of the three Japanese European transplants as they gear up to full production.

This case study charts how the most important players are responding to this adverse combination of factors.

The European car market

After a decade of buoyant sales, the European car market plunged into a deep and damaging recession during the first half of 1993 (Figure C8.1). 1984–89 were particularly favourable years for car demand in Western Europe. Sales soared from 10.17 million vehicles to 13.47 million over this period.

Between 1989 and 1992 sales stabilized at around 13.5 million units, but beneath this apparent calm considerable volatility was experienced in different national markets. In the UK, an economy ravaged by recession in the early 1990s car sales slumped from a peak of 2.3 million in 1989 to 1.549 million in 1991, a decline of over 30 per cent. However, Germany at this time was experiencing a post-unification boom and car sales in former East Germany alone rose to 730 000 vehicles in 1991, taking the total for Germany as a whole to 4.2 million compared with 3 million a year earlier. East Germany is effectively a new market for 'western' car producers. The old East German Ostmark has been converted into Deutsche marks at an incredibly generous exchange rate, giving the people of East Germany a vast increase in their purchasing power and access to material possessions on a scale undreamed of only a few years ago. The rapid expansion of East German car demand in the early years of the decade allowed car manufacturers to maintain record sales in the continent as a whole.

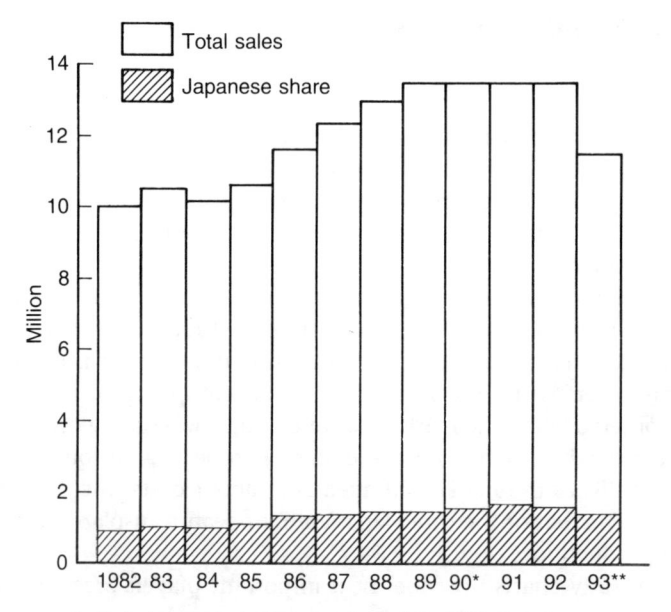

Figure C8.1 West European car sales (source: *Financial Times*, 17 June 1993)

The post-unification boom, however, was short-lived and during 1993 all but one of the major national car markets of Western Europe began to decline. The exception was the UK where sales began to rebound from the depths of recession (Table C8.1).

Overall car sales in Western Europe plunged 17.7 per cent during the first half of 1993 compared with a year earlier – a fall in units sold of over 1 million. At any point in time such a severe downturn in demand would be a major problem for European car producers, but this particular recession arrived at a time of recent and continuing investment in capacity which was taking place on a massive scale. The recession greatly intensified the competitive pressures already felt by car producers and heightened awareness of the threat to European Manufacturers posed by the Japanese car industry. Europe has truly become the battleground of the world motor industry in the 1990s.

The European car market

Table C8.1 *Western European new car registrations*

	Volume January-July 1993 units	Volume change (%) on a year earlier
Germany	2,016,000	−20.6
Italy	1,241,000	−23.6
UK	874,000	+9.1
France	1,007,000	−17.1
Spain	467,000	−27.7

Source: industry estimates; *Financial Times*, 15 June 1993.

Europe's position within the world car market

The world market for cars in 1992 stood at 34 million vehicle units. Approximately 39 per cent of this was accounted for by sales in Western Europe, a sales volume of 13.39 million cars. The European Community economies alone absorbed sales of 12.48 million units (Figures C8.2, C8.3).. These figures dwarf even the massive US and Japanese markets with sales of 8.44 million and 4.58 million cars respectively.

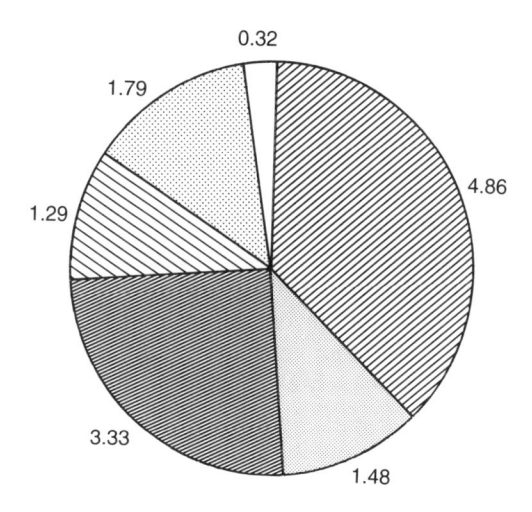

Figure C8.2 EC car production (millions), 1992 (source: *Financial Times*, 9 September 1993)

229

European Business

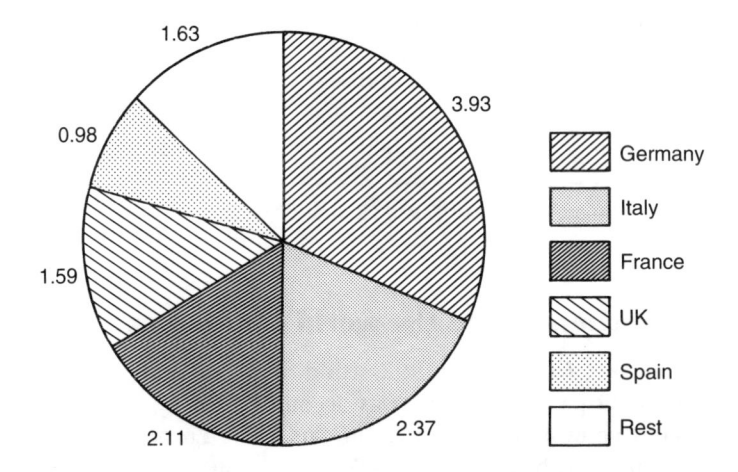

Figure C8.3 EC car sales (millions), 1992 (source: *Financial Times*, 9 September 1993)

Because of its huge scale, success in the Western European car market has been increasingly seen as a necessary condition for success on a world stage for most of the industry's key players. This conclusion is powerfully reinforced by an examination of past trends and future markets prospects (Figure C8.4).

Both Japan and Europe have seen spectacular growth in car sales in the latter half of the twentieth century, while the USA and Canada have stagnated, Japan's growth of nearly 5 million units since 1960 represents an astonishing rate of expansion, but falls short of absolute growth in Western Europe of 9 million units during the same period.

Forecasts of future growth must be treated with caution, but Europe is generally regarded as a more favourable market for expansion in the late 1990s than Japan. The automotive analyser, DRI, point to recent decline in the Japanese market (in the early 1990s) and predict sales of only 5.1 million units by 1996. By the same date sales in Europe are predicted to recover more sharply and reach over 14.5 million. Japan is viewed as a mature market with limited scope for expansion, while Europe contains a number of countries and regions ripe for expansion. These can be particularly found in the Mediterranean periphery of the EC. Eastern Europe is also seen as a major opportunity for future car market expansion.

The European car market

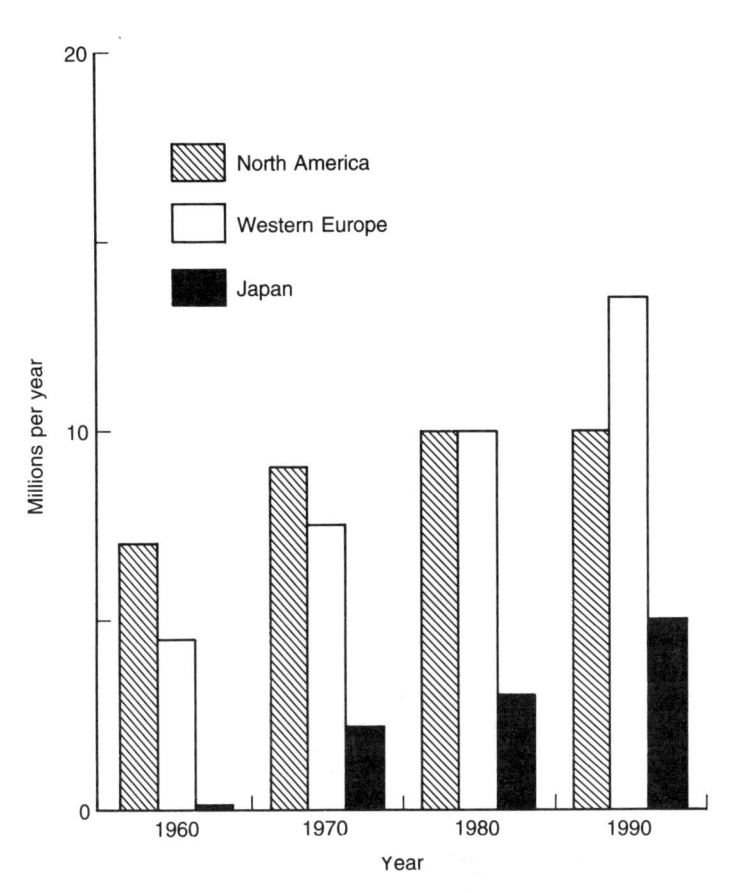

Figure C8.4 Car sales (source: *Automotive News*, various issues)

European car market – the major players

The largest car market in the world has attracted interest from most of the major producers. European demand is satisfied principally by European, North American and Japanese car manufacturers, with smaller volumes supplied by South Korean and Malaysian companies (Figure C8.5).

In terms of market share, six manufacturers dominate: Volkswagen, General Motors, PSA Peugeot-Citroën, Fiat and Renault. However as we see the Japanese share is increasing and their expansion is much feared by European and North American competitors. Japanese manufacturers are seen as a growing threat to European car makers, including Ford and GM's European operations. For the US manufacturers this is seen as a threat to the continued profitability and success which they have historically enjoyed.

European Business

1984

- GM 11%
- VW 12%
- REN 11%
- FORD 13%
- FIAT 13%
- JAP 10%
- OTHER 18%
- PEUG 12%

1992

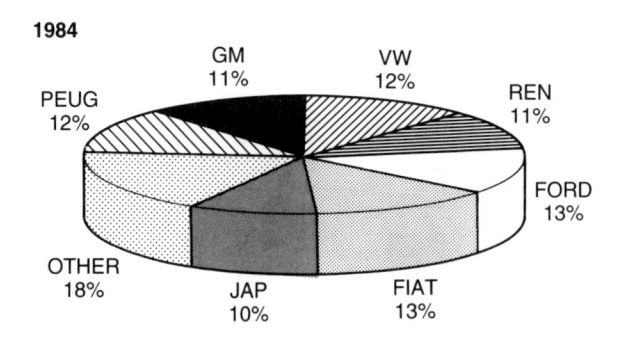

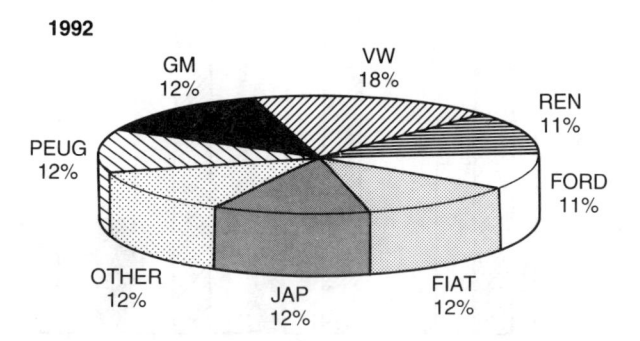

- GM 12%
- VW 18%
- REN 11%
- FORD 11%
- FIAT 12%
- JAP 12%
- OTHER 12%
- PEUG 12%

Between 1984 and 1992 VW acquired Skoda and SEAT, Ford acquired Jaguar, Fiat acquired Alfa Romeo, Ferrari and Maserati and sold SEAT.

Figure C8.5 European car market share, 1984; 1992 (source: *Financial Times*, 17 June 1993; 28 June 1993)

For the European car manufacturers it strikes at the heart of their home market. Also, because the Japanese threat to their sales and profits is also a threat to jobs and prosperity in the home base industrial heartlands.

A comparison of the profitability of each of the big six can be made using the chart shown in Figure C8.6. Each business reports its results in the currency of the home base (Ford $, VW Deutsche marks, Fiat Lira etc.). In order to facilitate comparison the results of these businesses from 1988–92 have been converted into ECUs. This is an appropriate measure to use in such a comparison of producers serving the European Market. Greater use of

The European car market

the ECU in financial analysis can be expected if Economic and Monetary Union in Europe progresses. One practical reason for expressing profits in ECUs is that the exchange rates against the ECU tend to fluctuate less strongly than they would if an individual currency (such as the pound sterling) was selected. In order to assist in the interpretation of the chart, ECU exchange rates are given for the central year in the series, 1990.

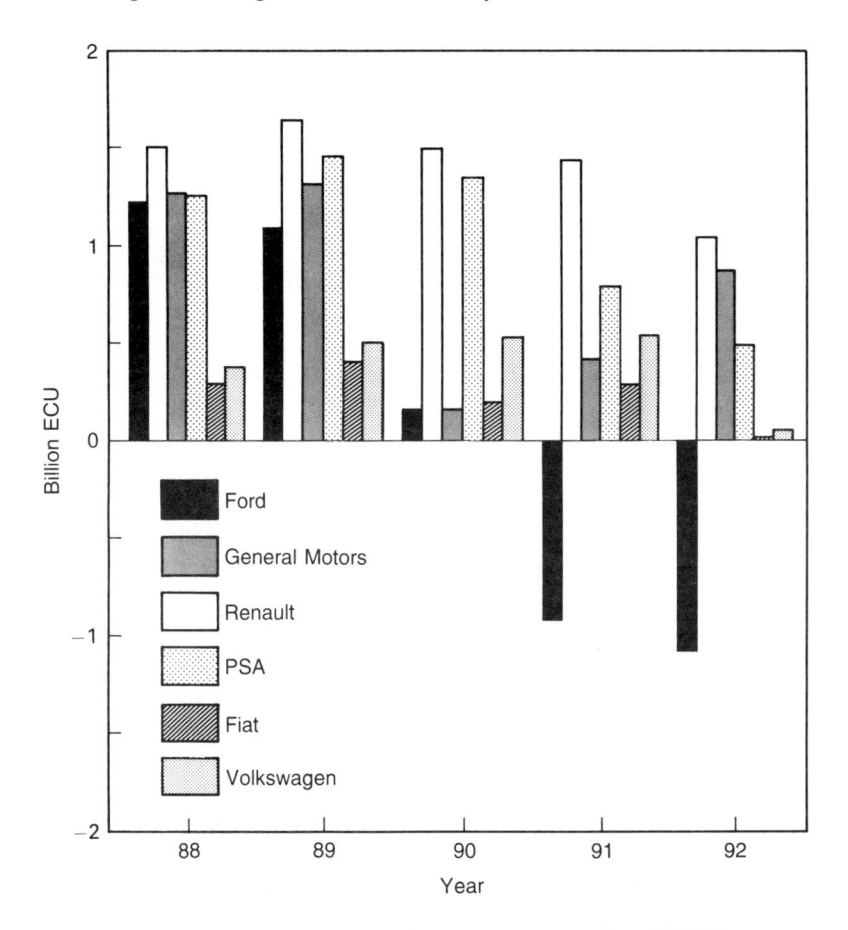

1990 Exchange rate (1 ECU =): $ 1.27, Ff 6.91, L 1521.9, DM 2.06

Figure C8.6 Net profit – 'big six' producers (source: *Datastream International Financial Statistics Yearbook*, IMF 1992)

Taking the European car industry as a whole, the squeeze on profits is very striking indeed. Net profits for the whole of the six taken together in 1989 were 6.38 billion ECU. By 1992 profits had shrunk by 78 per cent to 1.39

billion ECU – an alarming situation given the continuing heavy investment by these businesses in new capacity (much of it located in Eastern Europe).

German car manufacturers face high labour costs in the home market (see Figure C8.7). The German car worker also works a relatively few number of

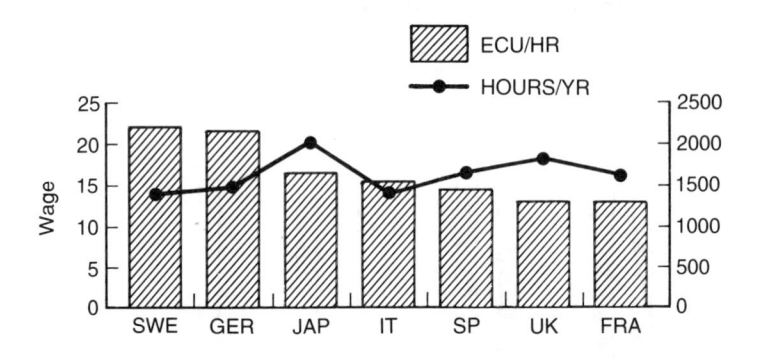

Figure C8.7 Hours worked per year and wage rate (ECU per hour) in 1991 (data source: *Financial Times*, 20 February 1992; 10 June 1993)

hours. These are important indices, as around 70 per cent of the cost of a German-built car is accounted for by the labour. The traditional means of off-setting this disadvantage is through greater productivity growth. During the 1980s, German car companies increased their productivity by 2 per cent per year while French, British and Spanish producers saw a 5–6 per cent rise.

Location strategies

In recent years the major European car producers have been much more committed to manufacturing located in their home base country than the major US car makers – Ford and GM. Furthermore, where the Europeans have diversified in forms of production location this has been overwhelmingly into other European locations – initially Western Europe, but more recently Eastern Europe as well (Figure C8.8).

The contrast with Japanese manufacturers is also striking. During the 1980s they invested heavily in US and Canadian factories, from which, by the end of the decade, they produced 25 per cent of the North American output of 5.36 million cars in eight plants in the USA and three in Canada. The major European producers have not invested in North America. Indeed, VW and Renault have closed their plants in the USA, though, as noted earlier, BMW, a smaller player has decided to locate some of its production in South Carolina to reduce labour costs and reduce exposure to the fluctuating value of the dollar.

The European car market

General Motors
Total production
5.5 million cars

(Segments: United States, Canada, West Germany, United Kingdom, Spain, Brazil, Australia, Mexico)

Volkswagen
Total production
2.7 million cars

(Segments: West Germany, Spain, Brazil, Mexico, Argentina)

Nissan
Total production
2.3 million cars

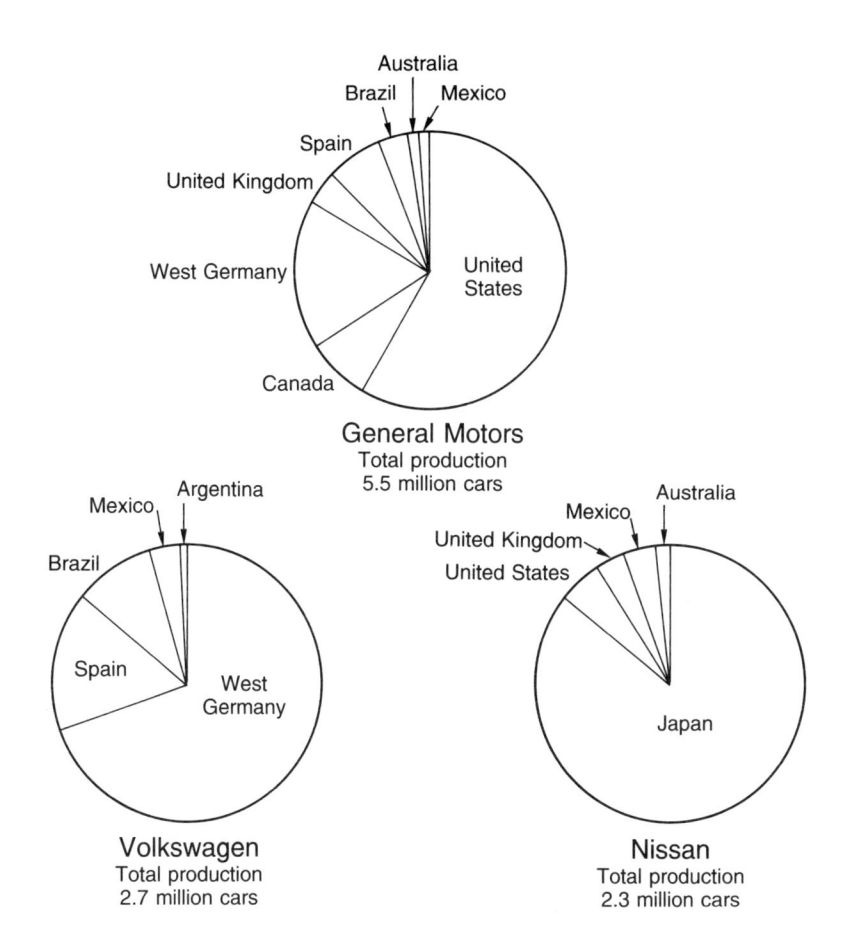

(Segments: Japan, United States, United Kingdom, Mexico, Australia)

Figure C8.8 Location diversification of US, European and Japanese motor manufacturers (source: Dicken, *Global Shift*)

Competition from Japan

A major ingredient which has heightened competitive pressures and squeezed profit margins in European car manufacturing has been the impact of import penetration from Japan into the European Market and the arrival of Japanese manufacturers locating production for the first time in Europe.

In 1963 when the Japanese car industry was still in its infancy, net exports (exports – imports) stood at a mere 22 000 vehicles. By 1982 Japanese net exports had climbed to 4.4 million. Exports represented 57.1 per cent of total production. Europe, after the USA, has been the second big market area absorbing this expansion. As a share of European new car sales, Japanese manufacturers had captured 12 per cent of the total market by January – November 1992. Industry experts including those at the Economist Intelligence Unit predict that 20 per cent of the European market will fall to the Japanese by the year 2000. Much of this growth is likely to be based on increasing output from 'transplant' factories in the UK and other European countries. These transplants are factories constructed overseas as a result of Japanese direct investment in other economies (mainly in the USA, Canada and Europe). The idea behind them is to transplant Japanese technology, production methods, labour practices and managerial expertise, in order to achieve levels of productivity and build-quality previously found only in Japan itself.

Lean production

Lean production is a concept closely associated with Toyota and Japanese manufacturing methods. It is a broad heading covering a number of different concepts closely related to the application of flexible production techniques. The traditional Fordist mode or mass assembly line production, involving a large number of semi-skilled workers, operating with capital designed to produce a large number of identical units so that the cost of each one was low, is the backbone of scale economies. One major drawback to mass production is its inflexibility. For example, once a production line is set up to produce one model the costs and time involved in altering that design are huge.

This mass production mode had a number of characteristic features. The car factory held a considerable level of stocks. These were maintained to ensure that the assembly line could be continually fed. Mass production also had a defect problem. The system of mass production could compete in the area of cost not quality control with 'craft', low volume, production. Quality control would occur at the end of the production line.

Suppliers were played off against each other to achieve a low price for the component parts. This supplier relationship was organized to suit the assembler. The car producer also made some of the parts and bought in others. Friedman (1977) argued that some suppliers were used to hold the excess capacity that the assembler would face in the event of a downturn in trade. The assembler could manufacture much of its production in-house, but this dual system would allow the assembler to maintain an operating level of around full capacity even in a downturn.

Lean production, by contrast, uses similar elements but in a different way. Lean production covers just-in-time inventory, human resource, production, and defect management. This form of production is far more economical with time, space and resources than mass production. The most well-known aspect of lean production is just-in-time supply. This is where the target inventory level held by the assembler is drastically reduced, which will release working capital, space and labour to be allocated elsewhere. The suppliers are expected to supply what is needed at very short notice. Nissan, in Sunderland, can order, say, carpets for the Micra and forty-two minutes later, they are being fitted to the car. This reliance upon a network of suppliers is dependent on good relations. Indeed, the new thinking places the suppliers on a much more important plain. The supplier is more likely to be expert in his field than the assembler and so should play a role in the research and development of new components. An adversarial relationship was typically adopted by companies under a mass production system: the assembler would play one supplier off against another in an effort to extract the lowest price. This is replaced by a more co-operative style where a recognition of mutual dependency leads to information sharing and joint product development. We would see key supplier/assembler collaboration in R and D. This not only uses under-utilized expertise but it also leads to a sharing of R&D costs. Indeed car companies view the component suppliers as a key source of competitive advantage. They produce better and cheaper components and this suggests that the more one can buy-in the more competitive the car.

Secondly, the number of defective parts and general quality control is of a different order. The Japanese operate at an order of 100 times better at not producing defects. For every 10 000 components produced, the Lean Production Benchmarking Project found that the Japanese produce 2.5 and the average British component firm 250 defective units.

The quality control mainly occurs on, not off, the assembly line. Mercedes, for example, operating under a mass production system, were found to be spending a third of total assembly 'effort' in fixing problems that occurred on the production line, after the car was built. Lean production requires operatives to correct the car during the production process.

Thirdly, the type and size of the labour force are again different to mass production labour. The watch-word is flexibility. The worker needs to be continually trained to adapt to the requirements of the job. The (flexible) technology that the worker is operating can be easily altered to suit the whims of the market. The workforce must be able to adjust the specifications of the process and correct problems on the line implying the need for better educated and more able operatives than under mass production. This flexibility is also a cause for concern for trade unions. Union demarcation agreements are, by their nature, incompatible with this mode of production. Workers function in teams following the production of a car increasing the range of tasks asked of the employee, lengthening the time between repeating the same operation from a few minutes to hours. A compliant, non militant and docile workforce is essential for this system to prove productive. Lean production may not suit the European working style. If there is a stoppage, as Renault discovered in 1991, at any stage of the chain of supply/assembly, the lean nature will lead to a cessation of production within days.

Quality circles and empowerment are also associated with lean production. Workers can be given more scope to manage their own work time and indicate where they think a process could be improved, rather than a distant manager dictating all key decisions, such as the number of permitted occasions that a worker can visit the lavatory. The management structure can be 'de-layered' as many of the decisions they traditionally took are now made on the shop floor. The workforce is then more involved in the success of the company and may become more contented and so more productive.

Another related concept is simultaneous (or concurrent) engineering. As the term implies, this is a move away from sequential engineering where a development project is passed from department to department in a strict order. Any alterations that are deemed necessary further down the line must be sent back to the earliest stage affected by these changes and the process begins again. The simultaneous version employs a multi-disciplined team to develop a car together, reducing the 'time to market'. The team stay with the design from the target market and price identification to the prototype. Any solutions to enforced changes or compromises that may arise can be negotiated by the team together, so avoiding the problems of departments defending their own interest or the department pigeon-hole problem. European car producer's average time to market is 63 months compared with a Japanese time of 43 months in 1991, but this is falling. To achieve this form of engineering the team should be in constant contact.

Product churning is the practice of placing new, updated, versions of the product on the market in a short space of time. This process enables the churner to put the latest technology into the new car, differentiating it from the competition. To churn, a company must be able to design a new product and/or easily alter the specifications of the existing product and get it to market before its rivals. This new version will have a short life as a newer variant will be replacing it with even better features. Although this can prove an expensive way to compete, it does enhance the reputation of the assembler as one providing a quality service. For example, the introduction of air bags would enhance the reputation for safety consciousness.

The MIT study that provided the information for 'The Machine that Changed the World' identified some key measures which would indicate the likely relative prosperity of car companies. The most important of these is the productivity figure total direct man-hours associated with producing a car, or hours per car. This encompasses body welding, painting and assembly of a car. The Japanese operate at a level of efficiency that leads to a cost/price advantage over their European rivals. Beyond this, they also have a quality advantage. The strategies that car producers have adopted to cope with their relative deficiencies are various.

Other key measures they use include defects per hundred cars, design lead times and assembler inventory days. Womack, Jones and Roos (1990) found that the average Japanese car producer in Japan in 1989 had figures of 17 hours per car, 60 defects per 100 cars, 46 months' design lead time and 0.2 day's worth of inventories. The equivalent figures for European volume car producer plants in Europe were 36, 97, 57 and 2. These figures were standardized for a vehicle of a certain size and options, to give some meaningful comparison.

The average figures for the luxury European car producers of Jaguar, Rover, Audi, Saab, Volvo, BMW, and Mercedes were 57 hours per car and 77 defects per 100 cars; worse than the Japanese figures of 17 and 34 and much less productive than the volume producers. It also took the Europeans 60 months to develop a new luxury car.

Lean production does have one major weakness. The capital that presents such a flexible production process, is so costly that it is inflexible as far as volume is concerned. Lean, implies no fat, and so almost no scope for cost-cutting in a downturn in market demand. The factory must be working at close to full capacity to enable the assembler to recoup sufficient revenue to meet the higher capital costs.

Transplant factories

In recent years the UK has been the favoured location for Japanese inward investment, particularly in the car industry. Nissan has located on a 750 acre site at Washington, in the north east of England. Nissan constructed an assembly plant capable of producing 300 000 cars and engines a year. The target output for 1993 was around 270 000 Primeras and Micras supporting 4 600 employees. It had been keen to boost this target but the economic climate meant that this was abandoned and the revised output was set at 246 000. In addition, at Cranfield in Bedfordshire, Nissan has located its European Technology centre, responsible for research and development. Nissan also have two plants in Spain. Nissan Motor Iberica produces up to 30 000 Serena people carriers and a Nissan–Ford joint venture produces up to 50 000 Terrano/Ford Mavericks. Nissan wish to reduced the number of suppliers with whom it deals at each plant and, in the longer term, it wishes to encourage more component firms to supply both the UK and Spanish plants. At present only 37 of their 198 UK suppliers comply with this request.

European Business

Toyota, the largest of Japan's car manufacturers, has located its main European production facility at Burnaston, near Derby in the east Midlands. From this location, car assembly began in December 1992. Engines are built at Deeside in Wales. Initial design capacity was for 100 000 vehicles. Overall, employment was expected to reach 3 300 plus another 15 600 jobs being created as a result of the multiplier effects, when output (mainly of Carina Es) reaches the 200 000 mark in the late 1990s.

Honda, based at Swindon in Wiltshire, began production in October 1992, and intends to build 100 000 cars by the mid-1990s, employing 2000 workers. This output and employment is in addition to Rover's in whom they have a 20 per cent stake. At least 66 per cent of the output from each of the UK Japanese car producers is destined for Europe; around 88 per cent of the 179 000 unit output from Sunderland went abroad in 1992.

Isuzu has also formed a joint venture in the UK with General Motors to produce four-wheel drive Vauxhall/Opel Fronteras.

Elsewhere in Europe, the Japanese car manufacturers have also established an important presence. Suzuki operates in Spain and Hungary. In the former country Suzuki originally had two joint ventures. It is working with Santana to build a four-wheel drive leisure utility vehicle with a capacity of 80 000 units. It also had a joint venture to manufacture 150 000 small cars with SEAT who have since left the partnership.

Suzuki also build small cars in Esztergorm near Budapest where, at full capacity in 1995, 50 000 Swifts will roll off the assembly line.

A joint venture between the Dutch government, Mitsubishi and Volvo has been set up in the Netherlands to produce the Volvo 400 family saloon series. It is also charged with developing its replacement by 1995/6.

The Japanese car builders are facing a double squeeze. The recession in the car industry has reduced the demand for cars and stiffened the resolve of the protectionist lobbies in Europe and the US. The second pressure is the rising Yen. This reduced the profit margin on exports. The big Japanese car producers have the capability to reduce their exposure to the rising Yen by increasing output in their overseas plants. Honda is to substitute US production of Civics and Accords for imports. Honda has also approached Rover to increase production of the Accord. Under the present agreement Rover was to produce progressively fewer Concertos as production was shifted to Swindon in 1994. Now Honda wish to boost Rover's contribution to 50 000 Accords from last year's 32 000 Concertos. Also Toyota announced, in August 1993, a plan to build a second model (the Corrolla), adding a further 100 000 vehicles to its production capacity, and an unspecified number of extra jobs to its UK payroll.

By 1999, Japanese companies are likely to be building between 1.2 and 1.7 million cars in Europe, in addition to any direct imports.

The European car market

General Motors (GM)

The American car giant, General Motors, produces cars in Europe under three marques. Vauxhall cars are built in the UK for that market and Opel cars are built throughout the rest of Europe. GM also took a 50 per cent stake in the up-market Swedish car maker, Saab, in 1989. GM, the largest car maker in the world, has been adjusting to huge losses, particularly in the US, involving a programme to shut twenty-one US plants by the mid-1990s with a loss of 74 000 jobs (20 000 white and 54 000 blue collar), while relocating capacity to the European market. Its best selling cars are the Astra and Cavalier.

GM have been opening and expanding capacity in eastern Europe. East Germany has recently benefited from Opel's new factory at Eisenach. The project cost an estimate DM1.27billion of which state aid provided DM260million. It operates with 1200 workers, producing 125 000 cars in 1992/3, at 83 per cent capacity. It conforms to the general characteristics of lean production, involving just-in-time inventory management, flexible, non-demarcated workers and employing only 20 per cent of the normal number of staff for that output. It employs ten skilled maintenance staff in the body shop per shift compared with 300 at Opel's Bochum plant. A car is produced in 18.3 hours. It has a two-hour stock of parts compared with two days in other GM plants. It also can produce seven vehicle variants on the same production line. Due to over capacity elsewhere, this flexibility is left unexploited, as the plant at Eisenach will be left with building the Corsa/Nova along with Opel's Spanish Zaragoza plant. This small car is to compete in the Uno and Fiesta and took a record 36 months to develop.

GM has been attracted to Szentgotthard in Hungary, where it will spend $300 million on building an engine plant and a car factory capable of producing 35 000 Astra cars.

GM has agreed to work with FSO, the Polish car maker, to build 10 000 Opel Astras in Warsaw. The investment of around $75 million will eventually provide GM with a 33 000 capacity. These levels of output are not significant by GM standards, but Fiat, GM and VW have been pressing the Polish state for excise tax reductions as a reward for their financial commitment.

Although eastern Europe appears to offer GM favourable opportunities the company has not abandoned the west. They have chosen an existing site at Kaiserslautern for a DM500m diesel engine plant in west Germany, which recently lost the battle with Ellesmere Port for GM Europe's main petrol V6 engine plant. The workforce has agreed to operate in a more 'lean' or flexible manner. They have consented to lower absentee rates and to maintaining production during shift change-overs. Management tiers at the plant have been reduced from five to four.

GM have also built an engine plant at Ellesmere Port, which will become the sole supplier of V6 engines for its European operations. It has an absenteeism rate of 5 per cent, half that of its German counterpart. Other UK plants can also boast advantages over their equivalents in Germany. The Cavalier/ Vectra built in Luton and Russelsheim was DM750 (before Black Wednesday) cheaper to build in the former location. The Astra made in Bochum (as well as Antwerp) and Ellesmere Port cost DM900 (after Black Wednesday) more to build in Germany. Indeed the number of hours per car built in the Bochum is thirty and twenty-five at Ellesmere Port. These figures suggest that the UK plants are among the lowest cost plants in Europe. GM UK have a 15 per cent cost advantage over the rest of GM Europe's other factories. Up until the Ellesmere Port investment, GM were gradually withdrawing from the UK, absorbing losses for around twenty years until the late 1980s.

GM has been forced to cut the number of workers in its European car and light vehicle operations by 7830 or 8.6 per cent in 1993 in response to a forecast of a 17 per cent decline in the market.

GM acquired Saab in the late 1980s in a bid to purchase a European up-market car builder. They bought in to the company as its home market and key overseas market, the US, weakened drastically. It moved from a profitable car producer to a big loss maker. Saab lost SKr2.7billion in 1992 which, in part, is a result of the poor productivity of the main Trollhattan plant where it takes fifty-seven hours to build a car. GM's improvement programme started from a worse position when, three years before, Saab spent 110 hours producing the 9000. They have also reduced Saab's workforce by 45 per cent to 9200 and halved its break-even point to 80 000 units. The cost-cutting programme also involved the sharing of development costs and components with GM. It will exchange gear boxes for V6 engines from GM's Ellesmere Port factory. The new Saab 900 replaces the fourteen-year-old 900 and that succeeded a model that lasted 11 years. It will take thirty-five hours to make and has many similar components, chassis and running gear to the Vauxhall Cavalier.

Ford

Ford is a US-based company but almost all of the Ford cars sold in Europe are built there. They principally operate under their own marque but they also own Jaguar and 99 per cent of Aston Martin. Ford of Europe made a loss of $1.3billion in 1992 which, apart from a $400 million charge for redundancies, is almost entirely attributed to its British connection. Ford of Britain (all operations) made a pre-tax loss of £353million for 1992 following £935million in 1991. These losses are on the heels of a decline from record results in 1988 which follow the same pattern as Ford of Europe's results. The results also reflect the under-utilization of capacity which was only 62 per

The European car market

cent in 1992. Ford's 93 000 European workforce is to be reduced by 10 000, with 2500 of the 31 000 UK workers to go in 1993. The Merseyside plant at Halewood or the Essex plant of Dagenham of Ford's twenty-four car plants in Europe is the most likely to close in any European rationalization. The latter plant, for example, requires 27 per cent more man-hours to produce a Fiesta compared with its sister plant in Cologne. Ford have fallen from first to fifth largest European market share from 1984–92. They have also lost the top spot in the UK fleet market to Vauxhall despite offering higher discounts.

By contrast, GM in the UK has been breaking records. Vauxhall has been ticking over at full capacity, increasing output by 15 per cent and operating profit doubled (to £269million and pre-tax profit increase by 69 per cent to £224m). Over the period 1988-92 the workforce at GM of Britain has remained around 11 000 whilst output has increased by 50 per cent to 300 000 vehicles. GM Europe made a net profit of $1.2billion, which is more impressive if one takes into account the SAAB losses of $270million, problems at Lotus, the esoteric British car builder whom they subsequently have sold, and the Ford loss.

Ford have recently been involved in constructing two new engine plants; one is at Bridgend producing 50 000 V8 engines and the other in Valencia, Spain, assembling 550 000 smaller engines 1–1.4 litre beginning in 1995. Thus they aim to centralize engine production to achieve greater economies.

Ford has secured some manufacturing capability in eastern Europe since mid-1992. It has recently acquired Autopol, the Czech component manufacturer, and is also negotiating a deal to build a seat cover factory in Plonsk, Poland that will displace 490 UK jobs. Ford also has a presence in Hungary, producing fuel pumps, ignition coils and other car components, at Szekesfehervar, near Budapest. It has recently announced an increase in its investment by another 21 per cent ($18million), which has been rewarded by the rules of tariff application on imported vans (of 18%) into Hungary in practice exempting only the Ford Transit. These acquisitions appear to be part of a strategy to locate some capacity in the emerging eastern European states as well as increasing its ability to produce parts in Europe.

Ford is aiming for a 'world car' that can be sold in all key markets. The Mondeo, which was largely designed in Germany and the UK and took sixty-six months to develop, represents the fulfilment of a shift in strategy. This is the first model designed to be sold in both the north American and European markets. The factory capacity, in Genk, Belgium, is 440 000/year and its sister factory in Kansas City can produce 250 000/year. The Gent facility has 200 suppliers compared with the 400+ traditionally used, using just-in-time delivery, which was supported by fourteen suppliers setting up within 30km, so that no stocks of these parts need be held in the assembly plant.

The Mondeo programme has led to some changes at Ford's engineering division. They have more faithfully followed simultaneous engineering practices and reformed their relationship with their suppliers. Now they have a longer term R&D relationship with their key suppliers and will reduce the number of suppliers for their European operation from just over 1000 in 1988 to 600 by 1995, while reducing the component prices by 10 per cent. The target lead design time has also been reduced to four years.

The heavy loss maker Jaguar, bought in 1989 at a cost of £1.6billion when it was 'worth' £250million, has received a large injection of capital and a new boss. Nick Scheele, who was working in Ford's Mexico plant, which was described by the MIT team as amongst the best in the world, is now at Jaguar. Since its takeover, Jaguar has shed 40 per cent of its workforce; down to 6481 at the end of 1992. An injection of £700million is being spent on developing a new range of Jaguars. The XJ6 saloon will be replaced by the X300 and launched in 1994. The replacement of the XJS will be the X100, to be launched in 1996, and a smaller sporty saloon, to compete against the BMW 5-series, code named X200 scheduled for the late 1990s.

Ford have adopted two interesting features. First, the AJ26 family of engines developed by, and for, Jaguar will be built in Ford's Bridgend engine plant, not in Coventry by Jaguar. Secondly, the X200 could be built in Ford's factory in Cologne or in the US or both as X200 is being considered one of the next Ford world cars, providing the 'platform' of the car is interchangeable with other Ford models. This would require a 50-60 per cent commonality of parts while using Jaguar styling and appearance.

Volkswagen (VW)

The Volkswagen group is the largest European car maker. The cluster of companies that makes up this group are Volkswagen, Audi, SEAT and Skoda. The first two companies are native of Germany, with Audi the marque in the luxury car market. SEAT is a Spanish based company and Skoda is a Czech car builder. Its best selling models are the Jetta and the Golf.

The VW group's after tax profits fell 87 per cent in 1992 to DM147million which led to a radical company shake-up. The dividend payout was cut from DM11 to DM2 and the supervisory board appointed Piëch as chairman. When he took up his post in January 1993, Piëch faced, at least with some operations, a break-even capacity of close to 100 per cent. His first undertaking was a job cutting programme over five years to reduce the group's workforce. The VW division are to be slimmed by dramatic proportions. The actual number increases as the depth of the recession is becoming apparent. The group's total labour force stood at 273 000 in 1992. The VW division is set to slim from 130 000 to 72 000 by 1995. SEAT is set to lose 40 per cent of its workforce and Audi 10 per cent. The full extent of the restructuring is not yet clear.

The European car market

VW has a problem of low productivity, low level of bought-in parts (for cars made in Germany), high cost labour and a very high break-even point. It took thirty to thirty-two hours at the VW Golf factory at Wolfsburg to produce a car; the Nissan plant in Sunderland took 10.5 hours to produce the Micra in 1993. The Sunderland plant had a 75 per cent rate of bought-in parts as a proportion of a car's operating costs; VW operation had a figure below 40.

VW are introducing a hierarchy of responsible suppliers where VW only deal with the top tier, which will be responsible for subordinate suppliers. The example given by Piëch was an Audi dashboard and instrument panel. The old system involved twenty-two suppliers producing components for assembly by VW. The new system involves twenty-one supplying the first tier company and it produces the dashboard. This logistical partner system echoes Toyota which operates with 220 first tier suppliers. The VW division of the group is aiming to reduce the number of direct suppliers from 1500 to 200 by the end of the decade. VW also wish to specialize in their core competencies and import the expertise from outside suppliers. VW will concentrate on gear boxes, body-work and painting and the rest will be bought in. This is coupled with a move to the standardization of components across model ranges. Such items as complete brake units should be able to be installed into as many models as possible. For example there are twelve different cigarette lighter designs when only one or two are needed. In the longer term VW wish to be able to 'construct the whole model range on a single construction set'.

Porsche, the German luxury car maker, which is facing major loss of sales of 50 per cent+ in the first half of 1993, is to collaborate with Audi to produce an up-market Audi-badged car. Not only will this stabilize Porsche's income but also assist Audi to move up-market. The Audi/Porsche venture will be a Porsche-built model based on the Audi Avant S2. It is significant that the family that controls Porsche have in their number the chairman of the VW group, Piëch; Porsche is one of the few remaining independent producers without a large parent.

Eastern Europe has opened up opportunities for cost cutting moves. VW were quick to see the advantage of a low wage area with growing market potential. The Czech republics have about the same wage level as Poland, that is 10 per cent of that in west Germany, but have the advantage of many areas where German is spoken. Skoda, which is 31 per cent (eventually 70 per cent) owned by Volkswagen, is hoping to raise capacity of its Mlada Boleslav plant to 450 000, and VW has purchased the old state owned company BAZ with a 30 000 cars and 300 000 gearbox capacity at Bratislava.

VW also has a plant at Mosel in east Germany that should eventually churn out 250 000 cars a year. This is being put on hold at the second stage of the project. The east German labour cost advantage is to be eroded within five years as the IG Metall trade union brings wages up from 70 per cent to level with the rest of Germany.

Audi is to build an engine plant in Gyor, in western Hungary. This expansion appears to be part of a strategy to move out of Germany, where labour costs are six to ten times higher, as they also announced, in late 1992, a reduction of 10 per cent of the workforce. This cut is likely to fall heavily on the west German Ingolstadt plant, which also produces engines.

SEAT was also another target for expansion. A factory at Martorell, Spain, with a capacity of 1500 cars per day, cost £1.4billion (Pta244billion), is run by an ex-manager of Nissan's Sunderland Plant. It was opened in early 1993 to build a larger version of the Ibiza model.

VW have been hit by the prolonged downturn in the car market and are cutting back on output, investment and the workforce. VW have been forced to cut back on its investment programme for its group. VW have been reining back on a number of joint ventures. It was operating a joint venture with Suzuki to develop a mini-car and with SMH, the Swiss watchmaker, in the design of an electric, up-market city car, but both have been dissolved in an effort to restore VW profits. This leaves the Chio as VW's small car project.

VW have also apologized to the Czech Government for the cancellation of a 20 per cent tranche of a promized DM7billion investment in Skoda. Piëch suggested that efficiencies made the loan unnecessary. At the same time VW have been forced into injecting DM1.5billion into SEAT to offset an expected poor performance in 1993, losing DM1.2bn, which should significantly affect the VW group's overall loss. Indeed, the problems at SEAT are so severe that the old Barcelona plant is to close.

Mercedes

The car division of Mercedes-Benz is part of the Daimler-Benz industrial group that collectively contributes 4 per cent of the GDP of the old West Germany. Mercedes-Benz is the symbol of post war German industrial success and is the world leader in the production of heavy trucks and buses. In line with the other German car producers, Mercedes have been squeezed by the downturn in trade in Germany and elsewhere. Mercedes, which was operating at 80 per cent of the 600 000 capacity in 1992, was not happy to discover that the Japanese car producers had a 35 per cent cost advantage over Mercedes. Of this, only 10 per cent is related to regional specific attributes as cheap finance and the greater number of hours worked by the Japanese. The rest must be related to German inefficiencies.

Mercedes have adopted a number of strategies to tackle this stiff competition. In keeping with the other German motor manufacturers, Mercedes are to shed 37 400 from 222 500 German vehicle workforce by 1995.

The European car market

They have also opened a factory designed to use the latest techniques to compete with the Japanese. The plant at Rastatt, inaugurated in 1992 will have a capacity of 90 000 by 1996, and is using a teamworking system of production. Ten to fifteen workers operate around a body-shell, assembling the car using easy access fixing points. Responsibility for organizing holiday rotas, mending tools and equipment, and resolving minor production problems has been pushed down to the factory floor.

Mercedes will also centralize its vehicle design, development and engineering operation at Sindelfingen and Stuttgart, from the present eighteen sites. Mercedes intend to reduce the number of parts that have to be assembled, the first-tier suppliers offering completed units, which Mercedes will test.

They have been developing three new ranges of Mercedes cars. A smaller car below the 190 series to be a new Class A commuter car (like the BMW Z13) called the Vision A 93, a people-carrier, like the Renault Espace, and a four-wheel drive to go with the existing three ranges. This reflects the vision of the new form of competition of the chief executive, Helmut Werner. He believes that the market is moving away from emphasizing the engine size to one which involves 'vehicle concepts'. This includes both the role of the car, what it is made of (e.g. aluminium) and its propulsion unit (such as a diesel engine).

They were looking for a site for a 200 000 capacity plant for the production of their new A-Class range. The four short-listed sites were in the UK, Germany, France and the Czech republic. The chosen site was at Rastatt, where the luxury E-class cars are assembled. One could suggest that Mercedes were sabre rattling to extract concessions from a German workforce keen to retrieve some of the job losses.

The multi-purpose, or people-carrier, vehicle is to be built in Vitoria in Spain, where at present it produces vans. The target capacity is 60 000 units, which will be launched in 1994/5.

Mercedes have recognized that the traditional engineering excellence is proving to be too expensive. Indeed, Werner has identified this very problem. He intends to shift the company away from 'over-engineered luxury cars' that are priced out of the market. He wants to reduce the life-cycle of a Mercedes from eleven to eight years; reduce the development time from fifty-seven to forty-four months and expand the product range to serve all sectors of the luxury market. The over-engineering with a cost plus price made a Mercedes car very expensive. In future, a vehicle will be priced according to what the consumer wants to pay, or target priced. The price will be determined first to appeal to the target market and then the car's costs adjusted to suit.

The most recent example of the success of the implementation of the change of strategy is the replacement of the old 190 series with the new C-class. The director of production, Vohringer, reported that it took forty months to develop; productivity is up by 15-25 per cent partly as a result of greater use of robots, but also teamworking has been introduced; the car takes ten hours less to build than the old 45 hr rate; two management layers have been removed, leaving four; suppliers, working more closely with Mercedes, supply more complete units such as electrical harnesses, on a just-in-time basis; the proportion of bought in parts has increased to 52 per cent from 58 per cent. The net result is a reduced cost disadvantage compared with the Japanese in this class of 15 per cent compared with 25 per cent with the old model.

Rover

Rover was bought by British Aerospace in August 1988 when it was privatized by the Thatcher Government; Honda acquired a 20 per cent stake eighteen months later. It was the mass car producer of British Leyland, and host to some of the worst industrial practices in the car industry. It was, and remains, a parochial car producer, assembling all its 380 000 units in 1992 in Britain. This puts it below BMW and Mercedes at around 500 000 units.

In the five years since privatization Rover has implemented a £215m investment at Cowley, which has a capacity of 110 000 units/year, agreed new working practices with a slimmed down workforce and introduced three new cars.

The plant at Cowley houses the new-look Rover. In 1992 they managed to achieve an agreement from the 30 000 strong union membership at the Rover group to adopt Japanese style working practices, including removing all distinctions between blue and white collar workers and clocking on. In the two years preceding 1993 almost a quarter of the workforce was laid off. The new agreement included a promise of 'jobs-for-life' and Rover has since introduced an extra shift at the Cowley plant, creating 300 new jobs.

The new range of Rover cars has been jointly developed by Rover and Honda, who have their own versions of each vehicle. The 200/400 series is based on the chassis of the Honda model, the Concerto. The executive Rover 800 series is the partner model of the Legend. The most recent addition, the 600 series, is very similar to the Honda Accord. Even the old range, including the Metro, has a Honda floorplan (chassis) and most have a Swindon-made engine. The benefits of collaboration for Rover are huge. The cost saving over the actual development cost for Rover of £200 million from joint product creation of the 600 series is estimated to be £15 million.

As a result of the investment in the Cowley plant and the adoption of flexible working patterns, Rover has managed to reduce its breakeven point from 560 000 to 440 000 units in five years. It has shifted from being a

The European car market

volume, to an up market niche, producer, pitching the 600 series against the BMW 3 series, expanding its sales force in Germany and revamping the old MG marque. Rover also possesses the Land Rover/Range Rover marque, which is small but very profitable part of the Rover group. An expanding US market for these type of vehicles is likely to be caught in the Japanese US trade dispute and be subject to a ten-fold increase in utility-vehicle import tax to 25 per cent.

The change in quality of the Rover product permitted them to offer a thirty day money back guarantee if-not-satisfied in May 1993. This followed a similar move by Jaguar, who also experienced a subsequent increase in sales, and has since been copied by Ford. Rover appears to have slipped off the reputation for shoddy workmanship and militant workforce that it acquired while it was part of BL.

This does not mean all in the garden is rosy. The return on capital is low and the productivity is poor. The Rover productivity at Cowley will be around fourteen cars per man per year in 1992. This compares favourably with the BL rate of ten, which was the worst in Europe, but it certainly needed to be improved to compete with its part owner.

By August 1993 Rover could be sold without BAe having to repay the incentives offered by the government when BAe took over. On 31 January 1994 BMW bought BAe's stake in Rover for £800m. BMW had been interested in Rover for some time. In taking all of BAe's stake, BMW, like Mercedes, was thinking of expanding its range of cars but, unlike its German competitor, it purchased rather than designed its new models. Rover has the premier four-wheel-drive utility vehicle marque in Europe (Land Rover) plus a sports label (MG) and small car technology (the Mini and Mini Metro). Beyond these advantages, Rover has a lower cost production base, access to the British cheap and effective component suppliers and is now immersed in Japanese working practices and technology.

BMW had embarked on a programme to design a car smaller than the 3 series, a utility vehicle as well as sports car to compete with the Mazda MX-5. The Rover acquisition will reduce the development costs and time as the Rover buy-out appears an astute purchase that provides BMW with these new cars. Where they compete, the 800 and 600 look vulnerable as they directly compete with BMW 3 and 5 series, but Rover is weak in Germany and strong in the UK, which complements BMW. A joint marketing programme would share overheads and a greater geographically spread sales network would be mutually beneficial, particularly assisting Land Rover's assault on the US. The replacement of the 600 will not be required for some time and the joint replacement programme for the Concerto and 200/400 is due to be completed in 1995. The 800 has no replacement programme in place and this is the car most directly in competition with BMW.

The BMW link up gives the new luxury car company a capacity of over 1 million cars. If Honda remain closely linked with Rover, as they still retain a 20 per cent equity holding, the Honda–BMW–Rover group has a great potential to exploit the economies associated with large volume, while offering the consumer a range of quality marques across all the key luxury markets.

The French connection

There are two major car producers that originate in France, Renault and Peugeot-Citroen. Renault is a heavily unionized, state owned vehicle builder which has been recently transformed into an efficient unit to be privatized. It builds the Clio, the 19 and the Espace. Peugeot produce the 106 and the 205, while Citroen's successful cars include the AX and BX. In 1992 Peugeot, including Citroen, produced 1.8million units and Renault built 1.7million vehicles, which, between them, made up over a quarter of the output of European producers. Renault and Peugeot have been consistent profit makers since 1987. All the major players have felt the market decline since about 1989/90, which has reduced profits, but Renault's profits actually rose. Fiat, VW and Ford have been hit badly over this period with Ford free-falling into loss. Fiat and VW made comparatively little profit in 1992 and they were joined by Renault in making losses in early 1993. GM and Peugeot were affected but remained relatively healthy in 1992 with the former, as far as profits are concerned, the most robust in Europe.

The French motor industry is probably the most healthy in Europe. In the past five years they have moved towards Japanese style techniques of production. Renault and Peugeot are adopting simultaneous designing techniques to reduce the time-to-market. Renault aim to improve its time to market to under four years from present estimated average time of four to five years. It is now working with the Peugeot and Citroen design teams under the same roof and this recent move should bear fruit in 1994. At a time when all car builders are making deep incisions into their labour costs, Peugeot is losing around 4000 and Renault, 2250 workers from their home operations.

As with Mercedes, Peugeot and Renault have altered the quality control to on-the-line rather than after the car was built, which has allowed Peugeot to close all of its refinishing shops. Teamworking has been introduced.

The French assemblers have altered their relationship with their suppliers. They have reduced the number of direct suppliers. In 1991 Renault had about 1100 component suppliers; they wish to reduce this number to 6-700 and Peugeot has reduced theirs from 1700 to 740 in eight years. The smaller suppliers have become second or third tier. The proportion of bought-in parts (Peugeot 60 per cent and Renault 67 per cent) for both companies is

The European car market

high by European standards and they operate just-in-time stock management, enabling Peugeot to reduce its stockholdings by eight days to four.

This is not to say things could not be better. The production line is operational 70 per cent of the time at Peugeot and 75 per cent at Renault which compares unfavourably with a Japanese rate of 85 per cent. The French car worker is relatively untrained and old. The average age at Renault's main plant at Flins is forty-five compared with forty at Rover and twenty-eight at Nissan's Washington plant. Renault increased their productivity from 10.4 in 1985 to 16 cars/man/year in 1991. This compares favourably with VW's rate of 12, but Opel operates at a rate of seventeen and the world's leading (Japanese) rate is twenty. Piëch estimates that the French car makers have a 20 per cent cost advantage over VW whereas the Japanese have a 25–30 per cent advantage.

Volvo

In the mid to late 1980s Volvo was one of the most profitable car producers in the world. This profit melted away in the 1990s as hugh losses led to the decision to shut two of its three factories in Sweden in a massive rationalization programme. Volvo suffers from huge operating losses of SKr2.25billion in 1992 and is in need of some assistance.

Renault and Volvo have agreed to share engines, gearboxes, chassis and axle assembly, R&D, as well as purchasing. In the long run they wish to use a common outside supplier for 80 per cent of purchases; at present this covers only 15 per cent of purchases. They are to jointly develop a replacement for the Volvo 850, which is only a year old. The project will follow a similar pattern to that of the Peugeot 605 and Citroen XM which have a common platform, engine and gearbox, but have different styling and finish. Volvo is also working with Mitsubishi and the Dutch government in a joint venture in Holland to build up to 200 000 Volvo 400 cars and to develop its replacement by the mid 1990s.

Volvo's automotive operation and Renault were to merge by the first day of 1994 to form one of the world's top twenty industrial groups. Like Renault, Volvo is a large truck builder but unlike Renault, is solely an up-market-niche car producer. They had cooperated and held shares in each other's operations for three years. The merged company would have been weighed 65-35 in favour of Renault. Unfortunately, Swedish shareholders saw this as a poor deal. They were unable to assess the worth of Renault and were likely to vote against it when the senior management forced the main Swedish protagonist, Pehr Gyllenhammer, Volvo's executive chairman, to resign by demanding the merger proposal be dropped.

251

This merger had been described as the first of the mega-mergers in a rationalization of European vehicle industry. To gain advantages beyond cooperation the two companies can merge operations. This may provide scope for greater economies in the commercial vehicle division than the car operations. In the case of cars, Renault and Volvo complement rather than compete with each other; their trucks directly compete. It was thought that Renault would acquire an up-market badge and Volvo would, in return, receive the capital injection that Renault would have provided the funds to develop new cars, but the costs of rationalization would fall more heavily on Volvo.

Fiat

The Fiat Auto group includes all the major Italian car producers. Its parent company is the largest industrial group in Italy, accounting for over 3 per cent of Italian GNP, including Iveco, its truck/commercial vehicle division. The car division encompasses the marques of Fiat, Alfa Romeo, Maserati, Lancia and Ferrari, which is almost all Italian output. Most of its production and key market lie in the home market where, historically, it has received preferential treatment from the state. This protection is being withdrawn as the EC moves towards a single market, and permits unfettered Japanese access to her markets by the year 2000. Although the Japanese are restricted to 38 800 by a recent EC/Japanese agreement (i.e. a voluntary export agreement) there appears to be some confusion as to whether this includes transplants in Europe. Fiat cars have been losing their share of the home market, from 60-44 per cent in four years to 1992. By contrast, Nissan have increased their share by over 50 per cent in 1992, admittedly from a low base, but they are European under local content rules and so the British and Spanish made Japanese cars cannot be subject to the old voluntary export restraint. This follows a large increase from the 44 000 quota in 1990.

Analysts identify the model range as being a major problem. The Fiat Uno and Lancia Thema are almost ten years old. The Fiat range has been subject to the criticism that they appear similar. This is a likely outcome of the widespread sharing of platforms and components. Also, Fiat specialize in the relatively competitive smaller car sector, building the Uno, Panda and Tipo, which has a low profit margin.

Fiat has also been dogged by high Italian inflation, which would translate into automatic wage increases through the 'scala mobile' indexation system. After negotiation, this was relinquished across Italy in July 1992. Fiat also had to contend with the high non-wage charges as a proportion of wage cost. For every one Lira paid in wages an Italian employer pays 1.15 Lira on top in social charges. Having disposed of SEAT in the mid-1980s, Fiat was left producing all of their output in the home market and so their competitive position was largely determined by the associated costs. One strategy adopted to address the cost issue was the construction of the showpiece factory at Cassino, built in the 1970s, designed to use robots rather than workers. It has been suggested that this plant was built to demonstrate to unions how vulnerable they could be. Dan Jones (of the MIT report) argues that this factory is only efficient at full capacity. This means that to offset downturns in trade another factory must duplicate the production of Tipos and carry the fluctuations of demand while its sister Cassino factory continues at full throttle. Thus, they have removed one fixed cost (labour) and taken on another (high interest payments).

Fiat have embarked on a L40 000bn investment programme which addresses the car and light commercial vehicle range and how they are produced. They intend producing eighteen new models, open new production facilities in south Italy, and in eastern Europe, while closing factories in the north. The scale of the programme is forcing Fiat to borrow heavily and to sell of other parts of the Fiat conglomerate. They acquired a standby loan facility of L2 000bn in July 1993, sold Telettra telecommunications in 1991 and called for the largest rights issue in Italian history.

A car plant at Melfi and an engine plant at Pratola Serra are being built in the Mezzogiorno region. These are part of a L12 000bn programme of Fiat expenditure in the depressed region, and have been awarded L4884bn in regional aid. The Melfi car plant represents Fiat's shift in production and management techniques. The greenfield site will operate a teamworking system, with workers maintaining their own equipment. The average age of the workforce will be around 26 compared with Fiat's average of 46. A 450 000 unit capacity is to be available in late 1994, about a year after the plant opens. The Fiat Punto, the replacement of the Uno, has been designed by a multi-disciplined team in thirty-six months, twelve months faster than the Fiat norm. It will be built at Melfi, using just-in-time supply management from the first-tier suppliers, located on site. Fiat are placing great reliance upon the success of the Punto to turn the Fiat fortunes around.

The Cinquecento is built in Poland in collaboration with Poland's largest car producer, FSM. It was on sale in August 1993 at a price of £5400 in the budget city car class aimed at both the (25 per cent) eastern and (75 per cent) western consumer. Fiat spent £155m in acquiring a 90 per cent stake in a new company, Fiat Auto Poland with Poland's FSM car group. Fiat acquired two factories at Bialsko Biala, one of which produces 240 000 Cinquecentos a year; the other is being prepared for another model. Polish labour costs are one-fifth Italian at around £200 a month, which gives Fiat some return on their investment which they would not get in the west. The scale of Fiat's promised commitment there is £2billion. This is to be reduced as the European Bank for Reconstruction and Development is negotiating to buy a 5 per cent stake.

Fiat also planned to build a huge factory at Yelabuga in Russia with a capacity of 600 000 units, but since the break up of the old Soviet Union all plans concerning the plant are on ice and in its place the old Lada Togliatti operation, producing 300 000 cars was to be used. This too is on the shelf.

European protectionism

Faced with the threat posed by the Japanese, we have seen that the European car manufacturers have initiated a variety of commercial responses, involving revised production strategies, alliances between larger and smaller producers, and the adaptation of a whole host of Japanese business methods. In addition to all this, European car makers are challenging Japanese encroachment into the European market through political lobbying at the level of national governments, and through the institutions of the European Community.

Much of the political debate revolves around a 1991 agreement between the European Commission and the Japanese government known as the 'Elements of Consensus'. Under this agreement, which came into force in January 1993, there would be 'no restrictions' on Japanese investment in Europe, or the free circulation of its cars within the Community. This part of the agreement was particularly important to the continued development of Japanese transplants and joint ventures with other manufacturers in Europe. During these negotiations the British government argued strongly that output from the Nissan, Toyota and Honda factories in Britain would be regarded as European and not Japanese.

In return, Japan undertook to avoid 'market disruption by direct exports from Japan' and to monitor the level of these exports until the end of 1999 – after which they would have unrestricted access to the European market. The transitional period of seven years from 1992 to 2000 was to allow EC car makers to adjust towards adequate levels of competitiveness.

From the outset this agreement was greeted with hostility by European car producers, and the pressure to renegotiate its terms has mounted. The timing of its introduction in 1993, as demand for new cars in Europe slumped, could hardly have been worse.

Pressure from the motor industry, and politicians within the EC and national government lead to tough negotiations with the Japanese Ministry of International Trade and Industry (MITI) which resulted in a quota of 1 089 000 cars and light vehicles being established in April for total Japanese export to the European Community. As agreed in 1991, this would exclude output from the Japanese transplant factories. The aim was to stabilize Japan's share of the European market at 1992 levels. Unfortunately the EC negotiators had not anticipated the scale of the slump in European car sales (down 17.7 per cent in the first half of 1993). A new round of talks began later in the year and MITI reluctantly agreed to reduce direct exports to 980 000 (17.6 per cent less than in 1992).

Even this revised agreement failed to quell the growing chorus of criticism from the European car makers over the 1991 agreement and its interpretation. Assuming that the Commission's forecasts for car demand for the whole of 1993 was accurate, the new arrangement gave Japanese exporters 8.6 per cent of the EC market in 1993. However, the rapidly rising output of transplant factories could take this to 12.5 per cent, compared with 11.3 per cent in 1992.

Jaques Calvert, Chairman of Peugeot Citroen, described the deal as 'unacceptable and suicidal for the European car industry'. He has argued for continued protection after 1999, tougher annual quotas up to this date, and the carrying forward of excess sales above these quotas to apply in later years.

The Association of European Automobile Constructors has also argued in favour of tougher quotas to restrict the overall Japanese market share (including transplant output) to 11.3 per cent, its 1992 level. This appears to breach the spirit of the 1991 Elements of Consensus, but indicates clearly the stand most car manufacturers would like their governments and the EC to make.

Even Ford is reported to be campaigning for tougher controls on the Japanese expansion, insisting on quotas which are exactly in line with actual developments in the European market. On the subject of transplant factories, however, Ford and General Motors are on more shaky ground, for their European operations are the result of earlier transplants from their American parent companies.

Japan and 'fortress Europe'

It is clear that (in addition to the issues of cost, and a rising value of the yen) Japanese car makers developed transplant factories, first in North America and later in Europe, to help overcome hostility and protectionism against their expansion. Such global strategy has particular importance in Europe, identified earlier as a key battleground for all of the key players. The expansion of the EC to include more countries and the eventual possibility of Economic and Monetary Union have made access to the EC market a key issue for the Japanese car producers. During the early 1990s their strategy, heavily supported by the British Government appeared successful. Instead of being shut out of an increasingly restricted market, the prospects for liberalization seemed bright, and the nightmare scenario of Europe as a fortress keeping out Japanese exports seemed to recede. However, the coincidence of deep European recession in 1992/3 and the prospect of accelerated expansion of Japanese transplants have threatened to destroy the consensus which appeared to be within reach of policy makers in both the EC and Japan as they turn to the aid of their respective motor industries.

Discussion

The European car producers plus the US transplants are having to adapt to two forces. The downturn in the car market is a short term difficulty, the spectre of the Japanese is a more permanent problem. The alternative packages adopted by each car company to cope with these problems have many themes. The most common feature relates to the assembler/supplier relationship. VW has greatly benefited from a change in the purchasing strategy. Piëch has been quick to see the major advantage of employing a system that could lower costs at almost no sacrifice to VW. Following a Japanese hierarchical supply structure not only reduces the number of component makers one deals with, it also allows for suppliers to produce more complete component units.

The shift towards a more 'lean' form of production is being pursued by almost all the producers. Whether the European worker/employer relationship is conducive to such a form of production is open to question. Renault have experienced the problems of stoppages in October 1991 when operating lean production. In a period of job cuts, those that remain are likely to be compliant. Once the market improves, the degree of commitment and compliance may change.

Some are locating in low cost areas while often hunting for subsidies or tax exemptions. The move east was based on cost and market growth assumptions which would have changed. East German wages are programmed to rise, market growth in eastern Europe is forecast to be negative this year (1993) and much of the old Soviet bloc is politically unstable.

Piëch has head-hunted a number of staff to run his plants with some experience of lean production. The manager of the GM Eisenach plant was poached by Piëch and SEAT has an ex-Nissan manager at its head, and Jose Lopez, the GM head of purchasing, is now at Volkswagen.

Despite announcing massive job losses, car companies like VW, Ford and Mercedes do not make workers redundant; they reduce the labour force by natural wastage. The German companies provide their workers with perks such as Christmas bonuses or paid leave to visits spas. The German attitude to the employee is akin to the Japanese jobs-for-life and part of the consensus that German post-war success was built on. Indeed the VW

The European car market

worker receives the highest rate of pay for the job. If Piëch is to turn VW around much of the benevolent employer attitude must change.

GM in the US also offer excellent conditions of service. They have an agreement with the UAW union to call back workers laid off for thirty-six months to work indefinitely on full pay regardless of the necessity. Both VW and GM have reduced the retirement age as a way of reducing the workforce. The former to fifty-five and the latter to fifty-three. The offer of these favourable conditions is related to the militant union UAW active in the car industry. One of the great appeals of a greenfield site is the scope to employ young, non-unionized workers.

Perhaps the most interesting finding from the US was the level of inefficiency in car building. An Economic Policy Institute report found the 'big three' had a cost advantage over the Japanese, and were the lowest cost producers in the world, assisted by a 27 per cent cost advantage on the components industry. When health care, pensions and operating at 62 per cent capacity (significantly behind the 95 per cent of the Japanese) were taken into account, the Japanese became the lowest cost producer.

GM instituted lean production techniques in the production of the Saturn. It has been so successful they are not being built quickly enough to meet demand and have a high level of consumer satisfaction, only bettered by the Lexus and Infiniti.

The consumer can sit back and reap the benefits of the misfortunes of bloated car companies. All the big car producers have reduced their UK dealers' margins, commonly from 16 to 10 per cent; many have improved their warranties. Rover and Ford have introduced money-back-if-not-satisfied within thirty days. Mercedes is producing a C-class with 20 per cent better value per DM. As you will have noticed, car builders are planning to open new factories during a period of stagnation in the Euro-market. Over the period 1992-4 the European vehicle makers will add an extra 1.5 million capacity while Japanese will move towards a 1.2 million capacity by the end of the decade. It is estimated that the excess capacity in the market will be of the order of 4 million cars in 1993. It appears that the winner from this added competition will be the consumer. He/she will purchase a better quality car at a cheaper price.

The need to address long term internal problems, for at least some of the producers, is long overdue. Perhaps the oncoming train of the Japanese is the reason for a radical change in the way cars are produced in Europe. It appears that the American car builders are fighting back in their own backyard.

Bibliography

Friedman A. L. (1977) *Industry and Labour: Class Struggle at Work and Monopoly Capitalism*. Macmillan.

Womack, J. Jones, D. and Roos, D. (1990) *The Machine that Changed the World*. Rawson Associates (MIT report)

Questions

1 Identify the major strategies recently adopted by the various car producers in Europe.
2 Assess the possible ways of reducing the costs of producing a car. What implications would each have for the choice of workforce, suppliers and location?
   Analyse the changing relationship between major car companies and their component suppliers. Is this change necessary to be competitive?
4 Assess the nature of the environmental forces present in the car sector occupied by VW.
5 Conduct a SWOT analysis of VW within the European car market.
6 Using Porter's 'Five Forces' model, assess the balance of 'competitive forces' that exists in the European car market occupied by a car producer of your choice.

Case 9 Satellite broadcasting: a missed opportunity for the SEM?

Campbell McPherson and Lesley Twomey

Introduction

In this case study, the development of satellite television within the SEM, and the role of the European Commission will be considered. This will include taking an overview of technical standards and EC involvement in their commercial exploitation. The case study will also consider the EC's role in the development of a common standard for the whole European Community and comment on how far the EC has been successful in developing such a standard. The second section of the study will be concerned with common access and the issues involved in the ability of EC nationals to access programmes broadcast by satellite on an equal basis.

First, it is necessary to outline the nature of the television market, as a background to the development of the satellite broadcasting market, as well as the potential benefits of such a development.

The benefits of satellite broadcasting

Television is, in itself, an extremely powerful form of communication and entertainment across Europe, even though there is some evidence that in certain countries such as Britain, television is becoming marginally less popular, especially amongst teenagers[1].

In the 'new world' of the Single Market, the development of satellite television opens the opportunity to disregard national frontiers, as companies and advertisers strive to exploit this freer, wider market. From this perspective, it would, therefore, appear likely that television will have a powerful role in the development of the Single European Market (SEM).

Certainly, in economic terms, policy justifications for the SEM by the European Community have traditionally relied heavily on the benefits to be gained from increased economies of scale and from increases in competition, as national barriers fell; this was the main argument for the SEM propounded in the Cecchini Report[2].

Some of the benefits to be gained are immediately apparent. Satellite broadcasting offers enormous potential for trans-European advertising and programming. Language differences can be instantaneously resolved through the transmission of different languages on different audio sub-carriers [refer to the Appendix for a glossary of technical terms].

For the European Commission, there would also appear to be a certain logic in the promotion of trans-frontier broadcasting within the SEM. Such developments should help to encourage international understanding, facilitate language acquisition, and, not least, to foster the ongoing momentum of the Single European Market. In addition, satellite transmissions erode national controls over broadcasting and, therefore, constitute a small part of the process in which sovereignty flows from the nation state to Brussels.

The economic importance of satellite broadcasting should also not be neglected as a factor; satellite television is an important part of contemporary, domestic consumer expenditure. For the United Kingdom, for example, industry figures indicate that some 2.8 million households in this country have satellite receiver systems. To this figure must be added those households which can access satellite through cable links. This represents an investment in reception equipment alone of an estimated £550 million, based on historical and current costs of basic reception equipment. Projected on the same basis throughout the EC, these figures would suggest an expenditure of several billion pounds across the Member States. The satellite television industry is, thus, far from being an insubstantial economic factor.

Satellite television and radio are also extremely cost-effective from the broadcaster's perspective. A single transponder [Appendix] on an Astra satellite[3] may be received across all of Western Europe and far into Eastern Europe. Such a satellite would cost around $50 million excluding launch costs, but costs could be shared by a number of broadcasters using different transponders. By comparison, to provide the United Kingdom alone with a network of television transmitters doing the same job would currently cost approximately $100 million just for the transmission masts. This figure would be amplified many-fold across twenty or thirty States. It does need to be noted, however, that terrestrial television has substantial advantages in certain respects. First, a huge investment already exists in terrestrial equipment, while consumers have to actively decide to purchase satellite dishes to receive broadcasts. This clearly makes investment into satellites more uncertain. In addition, while satellites are generally designed for a life of around nine years, television masts can serve for up to fifty years. This once again has implications for long-term costs. However, despite these reservations, for new companies entering the television broadcasting market with pan-European interests, satellite direct broadcasting has obvious economic benefits.

Satellite television can, therefore, be seen as important, both for its contribution to the SEM and because of its future technological and

Satellite broadcasting: a missed opportunity for the SEM?

economic importance. It would therefore appear to be an area in which the European Commission should have been pro-active. Within the context of the Single European Market, satellite direct broadcasting looks as though it should constitute the perfect SEM.

Developments in satellite technology

No study considering the future of satellite television within the concept of the SEM, and the role of the European Commission, can fail to take account of recent technological developments. This is inevitable, given that the main barriers to the creation of the SEM were identified by Cecchini[4] as consisting of: physical barriers, technical barriers and fiscal barriers.

The reception of satellite television is, generally speaking, subject to neither physical nor fiscal barriers. Technical barriers do, however, have relevance to satellite reception. According to Cecchini, technical barriers include 'meeting divergent national product standards, technical regulations and conflicting business laws'[5]. Moreover, satellite broadcasting barriers were specifically identified by Cecchini as a problem area in this context[6].

It is clear, then, that some action would be required, in order to overcome these technical barriers and create a SEM for satellite television. It is necessary to note, at this point, that this process is not, necessarily, totally under the control of the European Commission. Intergovernmental organizations, generally working within a United Nations framework have set some technical standards and been involved in some of the decisions taken. One consequence of the process is that satellites have historically been separated from each other in space (see Figure C9.1). For the typical consumer on the ground, this meant that their satellite dish was pointed at one satellite, and the number of channels they could receive was therefore limited to the number of transponders on that one satellite. The 'market size' of each satellite was limited by technical and financial constraints. For example, a British viewer might have been interested in receiving programmes from Astra 1A/1B or from Marcopolo 1/2. Such a viewer would have been either limited by the alignment of his/her satellite dish to reception of one set of broadcasts only, or faced with an investment of some £1500 for a motorized system to enable reception of both.

Recent technical developments have resulted in the possibility of parking a number of satellites so close to each other that, from the perspective of the consumer, they appear as one. For the typical British consumer, this development has been reflected in the increased number of channels offered by BSKYB, such as Sky One and Sky Sport, on the Astra system. This currently consists of three co-located satellites, as shown on Figure C9.2, with perhaps three more to be added.

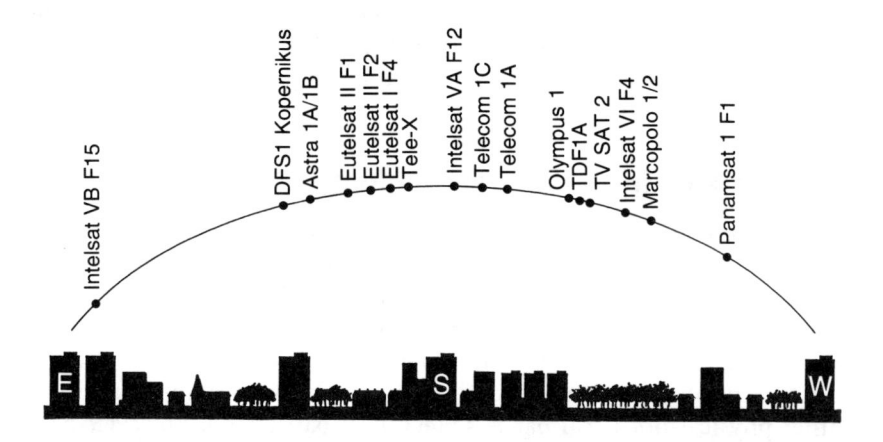

Figure C9.1 Position of major TV communication satellites in orbit November 1991 (source: *What Satellite*, December 1991, p. 125)[7]

Such developments would theoretically permit the location of all programmes for the EC area to be transmitted from co-located satellites in the foreseeable future. This would not, however, solve the problem of technical standards.

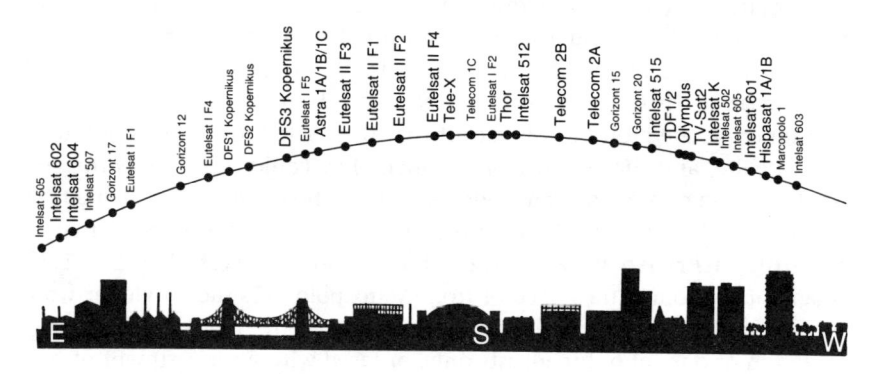

Figure C9.2 Major and minor TV communication satellites in orbit December 1993 (source: *What Satellite*, December 1993, p. 155)[8]

Progress toward a common standard

It must be said that national television systems have tended not to permit the full business exploitation of the SEM. In themselves, national television systems reflect the fragmentation of Europe into nation states, with broad

Satellite broadcasting: a missed opportunity for the SEM?

differences in policy concerning the content and timing of programmes as well as the nature and extent of advertising. However, satellite television also inherited a number of differences in technical standards which reflected the historical link between terrestrial television and the nation state. These differences centred upon the visual and audio transmission systems used, the most apparent of which was the use of PAL in countries such as Britain and Germany and of Secam in France and much of Eastern Europe.

It would not have been impossible to overcome these differences. Relatively inexpensive additions, probably in the order of £20 to £30, to the design of new television sets would have resulted in the progressive replacement of old 'national' sets with modern ones capable of dealing with multiple standards.

Such a solution was not followed. This was because of the historical evolution of the industry and its protagonists. First, satellite communications are regulated by national governments working within inter-governmental and United Nations agreements. Hence, in the European context, many of the early developments in satellite transmission standards were made by the European Telecommunications Union (ETU), working within technical regulations established by the United Nations' International Telecommunications Union (ITU). As the ITU was concerned with technical standards without much concern for common standards, regional groupings such as the ETU continued to use a range of national visual and audio standards on their Eutelsat satellites. Secondly, the French also used their own standard on their Telecom satellites. Thirdly, these satellites, in effect state-owned, were joined by the launch of satellites belonging to private companies. The most important of these is the Luxembourg-based Société Européenne des Satellites (SES), which owns the Astra satellites. This company effectively dominates European satellite broadcasting. Though operating under licence from the Luxembourg government, SES is an overtly commercial organization with trans-European share ownership and a keen eye on the market rather than issues of European or state policy.

It did, however, appear until quite recently that European partners might work towards a common standard. Satellite television's growing popularity in the 1980s coincided with a growing awareness of the decline in Europe's electronic base, in the face of fierce Japanese competition. The potential importance of satellite in the future as part of the 'media super highway' was also a factor. The Commission was persuaded by the Dutch electronics national champion Philips, and its French counterpart, Thomson, that the development of a new European standard for satellite transmissions would not only provide a boost to the industry and give it entry to subsequent technologies, but would also wrong-foot the Americans and Japanese. More importantly, as the former Spanish Minister of Trade and Industry, Joan

Majó predicted in 1991, if European industry failed to capitalize on HDTV, then the European consumer electronics industry could disappear in the next ten years. 'Si Europa no es capaz de desarrollar la alta definición, la industria electrónica de consumo podrá desaparecer en 10 años'[9].

Because of these considerations, an EC decision was taken to concentrate upon the development of a new standard, which would not only produce larger, better pictures, but which would also be capable of carrying substantial amounts of additional data. This data could be used for computer systems, interactive communications, such as home shopping and for the development of virtual reality systems. The aim was that 'wide-screen television would act as the foundation for a whole range of advanced electronic services, irrespective of the technology and standard used'[10].

The agreed new standard, known as D2-Mac[see Appendix], was perceived as an interim standard in the development of true High Definition Television (HDTV). In 1986, the Commission proposed, and the Council of Ministers agreed, a directive (86/529/EEC) which established D2-Mac as the legal norm for future satellite transmission, and this Directive was renewed in 1989 (89 / 337 / EEC).

The initial Directive was extremely restrictive in nature, and attempted to create the parameters for a satellite SEM not only by insisting that all future satellite programmes be transmitted in D2-Mac, but that all future large televisions (over 22") and their ancillary equipment should be D2-Mac compatible. The framework thus appeared to have been created for the development of a common standard within the EC. As late as January 1993, satellite owners were promised an increase in D2-Mac programme hours by Télé Satellite. 'La chaîne publique a introduit des programmes en 16/9, programmes qui avec son arrivée sur Télécom 2A (en D2Mac également) deviennent de plus en plus nombreux'[11].

By the summer of 1993, this policy had been abandoned, for a number of reasons. The first major breach in the Commission's policy occurred in the UK. Here, British Sky Broadcasting (BSB) had launched its programmes, in 1988, using a MAC variant. Numerous households were soon decorated by the distinctive squarial dish characteristic of BSB. However there were problems both in supplying the equipment to meet the demand for BSB and in the cost differential between its rival in the market, Sky, which broadcast from the Astra satellite.

Sky had decided, for commercial reasons, to broadcast using the traditional Pal format. It was able to do this by exploiting a legal loophole, relating to transmission powers, contained in the 1986 Directive. The result of this was that Sky was able to supply reception equipment both more rapidly and at a lower price, thanks in part to a deal with Alan Sugar's Amstrad Corporation. Both BSB and Sky suffered severe financial losses, as

Satellite broadcasting: a missed opportunity for the SEM?

they failed to attract both revenue and sufficient audiences. Eventually, in 1990, the two companies merged to form BSKYB, but Sky's more powerful financial base, the price-advantage it enjoyed in equipment and its ability to more successfully penetrate the British market ensured that its technology and satellite formed the basis for the new company. Sky's success was a near mortal blow to the EC's policy, and the debâcle over systems cost industry and consumers dearly: Thomson alone had to write off some $38 million[12] worth of DMAC dishes (squarials) in 1991, while Citizens Advice Bureaux and the letters pages of media magazines were bombarded by irate purchasers of the obsolescent British Satellite Broadcasting equipment. Not only did many thousands experience inconvenience and costs, despite the eventual agreement of the newly-merged company BSKYB to provide new receivers or free subscriptions, but the uncertainty engendered by these developments doubtless slowed the development of the UK satellite market.

In the meantime, the Sky debâcle had served to gravely weaken the Commission's policy. This was further weakened, in late 1991, when the Franco–German–Dutch axis, which had been driving the policy, collapsed. This was partly the result of national interests developing an alternative technology. The Germans, for example, had developed yet another possible standard, called Pal+ which could be used for both terrestrial and space transmissions. The collapse of the potential common standard was also an indication of the growing rift between the broadcasters, whose interests lay in the continuation of Pal\Secam broadcasts, and the television industry whose interests lay with D2-Mac.

The British Government has also been active in opposing continued subsidies for both D2-Mac transmissions and for research, and, throughout 1992 and early l993, a Dutch auction developed in the Council of Ministers meetings dealing with communications. The proposed subsidy for D2-Mac was pushed down from 800 mecu (million ECU) in December 199l, through 750 mecu to 'a figure around 400 MECU'[13] by the summer of 1993.

In the meantime, events had overtaken D2-Mac. Philips and Thomson had been playing safe by pushing for the development of D2-Mac in Europe while encouraging the development of digital television[see Appendix] in the United States, where the two companies had also been working together. As the delay and confusion in Europe resulted in any possible advantage from early market entry being dissipated, the two lost interest in D2-Mac. By July 1993, following trials in the United States, it was agreed that digital transmission system would be the future norm, and, during the summer of 1993, the European Commission announced that it would no longer finance research and development for D2-Mac, though subsidies for ongoing broadcasting in the standard would continue.

Moreover, market forces helped to destroy D2-Mac. While the Commission had created a legal framework for D2-Mac transmissions, manufacturers did not have the equipment ready for the market. There was actually considerable reluctance on the part of television manufacturers to become involved with D2-Mac, because it could not be used for terrestrial broadcasts and involved additional costs. There was also understandable consumer reluctance to even consider purchasing unproven technology.

Some ten years after the D2-Mac standard was first mooted as a European norm, and about six years after technical standards for satellite television were identified as a problem by Cecchini, there is clearly no single standard for satellite television. If anything the situation is becoming more complex as Pal and Secam have been joined by D2-Mac or similar systems, and as digital transmissions in both picture and sound have increased. Indeed digital transmission is gaining ground, as it is expected that the first satellite to broadcast primarily digital programmes will be Astra E, which is due for launch in 1995.

What is certainly apparent is that consumers are again likely to suffer from the failure to develop clear, consistent policies. While in 1991, only 170 000 European households had DMac receivers[14], a conservative estimate would suggest that the figure, by the end of 1993, is closer to 250 000. A central point for the additional expenditure involved in buying Mac, as opposed to the Pal/Secam system, would suggest that this has involved at least £200 x 250 000 or some £5 million which has already been spent on satellite receivers and additional equipment intended to receive D2\Mac. French consumers have already been involved in considerable outlay in this respect. In January 1993, customers were being advised to change their TDF dish for a bigger Télécom 2A dish if they owned a 16\9 television. 'Si vous recevez Canal+ en D2Mac sur TDF (vous êtes environ 45.000!) et si vous possédez un téléviseur 16\9, il est nécessaire de modifier votre installation de réception et votre abonnement'[15]. While D2\Mac transmissions are likely to continue for several years, in view of the fact that the old BSB satellite has been renamed Thor I and relocated to serve the Scandinavian market with DMAC, consumers who have bought such equipment will find themselves increasingly restricted in their access to the communications market.

It should be noted that such instability may prove highly negative for the consumer electronics market as a whole. Some consumers may be dissuaded from making further purchases in new technology, as a result of losses incurred in past purchases, or because of the spread of rumour concerning others who have lost money in this way. This may be significant in the light of earlier comments in this case study, concerning the potential contribution of satellite television to Europe's technical and economic development.

To create a SEM in satellite television would, then, require a common transmission and reception standard. In addition to the technical commonality, a common policy on the content of programmes related also to the time of showing, a common policy on advertising and a common policy on copyright would be necessary. Linked to all of these factors would also be the ability of EC inhabitants to gain access to programmes on a common basis.

Access to programmes for all Europeans

Not only is the development of a common standard necessary to ensure that satellite television realizes its economic potential but also a policy enabling Europeans to access broadcasts on an equal basis needs to be developed. The programme content of terrestrial television has been, so far, controlled by the national government of the sovereign state. There were, therefore, and continue to be, widely differing attitudes toward the content of programmes. In addition, the fragmentation of broadcasting along broadly national lines, meant that the selling and copyrighting of programmes tended to follow the same pattern. While satellite television offers the technical potential to break down such national divisions, this may run counter to the interests of large film companies which can make larger profits by selling the rights to a film to twelve national television channels than to one satellite operator. It is easy to see why the satellite television market could become increasingly fragmented, as a consequence of these political and economic considerations.

If the issue of state policy towards satellite television is considered, it immediately becomes evident that broadcasting poses severe problems for the nation state. In part, such problems may stem from the global nature of the industry. To give an example, a programme received in Britain may, for example, consist of an American film, sold to a German company to transmit to Austria, and be transmitted via satellite in international space by a Luxembourg-based company which has large French, German and Italian shareholders. The viewer may, thus, be at a considerable distance from this process. S\he may indeed have no legal right to view the programme. In this situation, it is uncertain which set of laws operate. An example of the multi-state nature of broadcasting is the German company Pro-7, which broadcasts mainly American films via the Luxembourg-owned Astra satellite.

Moreover, a serious question concerning the right of the state to restrict programmes had already been raised by a European Court of Justice ruling in the 1980s. The case of Bond van Adverteerders and others versus the State of the Netherlands, the Dutch Government asked if it could legally ban Dutch companies from advertising on television programmes broadcast from outside of Holland, but targeted on Holland as a way of avoiding Dutch Government restrictions on television advertising. The Court ruled that trans-frontier broadcasts were a 'service' under Articles 59 and 60 of the Treaty of Rome, and any ban would, therefore, be illegal as a restriction of inter-Community trade and counter to the development of the common market. Moreover, the Court ruled that any measures taken at a domestic level to prevent such trans-frontier broadcasts had to be proportional, that is to say, reasonable.

It was to ensure such a common market in television services, with particular reference to satellite broadcasting, that the Commission proposed common standards for broadcasting during the 1980s. While these had already included restrictions on the advertising of tobacco and alcohol, the main interest for broadcasters lies in the 1989 Directive 89/L 29123, which committed the Community to the free reception of programmes. Essentially, this prohibited member states from preventing satellite television reception, though, equally, Article 22 of the Directive gave Governments the right and duty to control broadcasts containing incitement to hatred on the grounds of race, religion or nationality. Importantly, the same article provided the power to restrict programmes in order to protect minors.

An interesting example of the potential contradictions inherent in this situation can be seen in the UK government's reaction to programmes it did not wish to be received in Britain. By the autumn of 1992, the government had become extremely concerned over transmissions by a channel calling itself initially *Red Hot Dutch*, and subsequently *Continental Television*, which was broadcasting highly explicit sexual material. Despite the title, the company was actually based in Manchester and used largely American programme materials. These were transmitted via a transponder which the company leased from the Danish Telecommunications service. Given that the Danish authorities were not prepared to prevent transmission, there did not appear to be any obvious way of preventing transmissions.

The Heritage Secretary, Peter Brooke, eventually decided to ban Continental and, in order to do so the British Government finally decided to make it illegal to advertise the programmes and/or publicize the sale of the decoder and smart card needed to receive it. After Continental's appeal against these measures failed in the British courts, the company decided to appeal to the European Court of Justice in Luxembourg. The case is likely to be heard in 1995. Meanwhile, it has decided to move its operations to Holland, selling decoders and smart cards from there, while advertising via the satellite. Fortunately, the British Government was not forced to attempt to prevent the entry of decoders and smart cards into Britain, since the Danish Post Office stopped Continental's transmissions. Business practice prevailed in the Post Office action: the company had not paid its fees. Any such attempt at prevention of movement of goods into Britain from a Member State, would have raised fundamental legal issues.

Satellite broadcasting: a missed opportunity for the SEM?

On a more general level, the Commission has failed to develop an SEM for satellite transmissions because it has not acted to prevent the practice of signing agreements which permitted programmes to be shown in a particular region of Europe. As noted earlier, the owners of film copyrights are likely to increase their revenue if they can sell programme rights to a scattering of companies, in competition with each other. It is in the interests of both copyright holder and broadcasters to restrict the area over which the programme is seen.

In order to limit programme viewing by geographical area, the supply of smart cards and 'legal' decoders also has to be geographically limited. This market fragmentation is obvious from contractual statements, such as those restricting the use of Sky outside Britain and the Republic of Ireland: 'Use of the viewing card outside of this geographical area is strictly prohibited'[16]. Equally, French broadcasters such as Canal Plus refuse to provide smart cards to addresses outside France, while one of the most sought-after channels, Filmnet, restricts issue of its decoders to the Benelux area.

Copyright matters also impinge on non-profit orientated satellite transmissions. For example, RAI, the Italian national Radio and Television company, broadcasts two domestic programmes, RAI uno and RAI Due on Eutelsat F2. These programmes are targeted for non-commercial, political, social and cultural reasons on the Italian communities scattered throughout Europe. While a substantial range of domestically-produced programmes are not encrypted [see Appendix], American and other foreign films as well as certain other programmes, such as documentaries of British or foreign provenance, are encrypted.

A natural result of this has been the sale of pirate decoders and smart cards. These claim to be able to break the encryption and may sell for as much as 300 per cent or 400 per cent more than the official cards. Ironically, the industry itself is now beginning to realize that this carve-up of the market is becoming counter-productive, in that American companies, attempting to enter the satellite television industry in the European Community, are finding themselves excluded by their own pre-existent copyright and geographical exclusion agreements. One of the major barriers to the USA Network's launch of the proposed science-fiction, Sci-Fi, channel on Astra, was that Paramount, one of the partners in the USA Network, has already sold the geographical rights to Star Trek Mark I, II and III to Sky.

Conclusion

As this case study has indicated, the EC has been generally unsuccessful in developing common technical standards, since, despite the economic, social and political importance of satellite television, indicated earlier, satellite broadcasting operates within a legal framework which is far from established and in which uncertainty is a prime characteristic.

The conclusions of this case study have implications for both consumers and producers. There are clear lines of progress for the development of both trans-European advertising and for greater inter-cultural understanding. Technical developments, the logic of a coherent single market and the economic potential of the industry required the development of policies which would permit the pan-European reception of programmes without technical or legal barriers. This, indeed seemed to be the main thrust of the European Commission's proposals and directives on trans-frontier broadcasting.

Diagrammatically the satellite broadcasting sector might have been viewed thus:

Broadcasting system	Sound system	Encryption	Technical and copyright geo-market
Unified[17]	Unified	Unified	EC and EEA

Because of differences in the nature of the market and the failure to develop a coherent and enforceable policy within the Community, the reality in 1993 is:

Video format[18]	Sound system[19]	Encryption	Technical and copyright geo-market
D/2-Mac	Various	Eurocrypt	Scandinavia, France and scattered
SECAM	J17	Syster	France, Spain
PAL	50 us	Videocrypt	UK, Ireland
	Panda		Scattered
		Discret	Italian communities
		Save	UK, Ireland
		Crypt	Holland
		Satbox	mixed

The failure to develop a full trans-Community policy has, thus, resulted in a situation in which the market is fragmented by differing technological standards and uncertainty. It is also fragmented by the deliberate use of

Satellite broadcasting: a missed opportunity for the SEM?

technology to restrict reception for copyright reasons. Fragmentation is also a result of legal measures intended to impose national standards on transmissions, as the case of Continental Television shows. The market is characterized by technical instability resulting from the mis-match between market forces and attempts to control the reception process if not the broadcasting process.

In the light of current developments, the state of the satellite broadcasting industry, by 1997, is likely to be:

Video format	Sound system	Encryption	Main geo-market
D2-Mac	Various	Eurocrypt	Scandinavia, France
Pal	50 us	Videocrypt	UK, Ireland, Benelux
Secam	50 us/J17	Syster	France, Spain
Digital	Digital	Unknown	UK and scattered

From a comparison of these tables, showing the ideal, the actual and the future situations, it can be seen that, whatever the success of the Single European Market in other areas, the Community has failed, to date, to develop a single market for satellite television. In addition, copyright restrictions on broadcasting appear likely to continue and with them, a continued loss of business opportunities in the satellite broadcasting SEM.

Appendix   Technical glossary

Audio sub-carriers

In addition to the visual signal, television programmes require an audio signal for the sound. By using different frequencies for the audio signal, it is possible to have a range of languages accompanying the same picture. For example, Sell-a-vision on the Astra satellite has the following audio sub-carriers: English at 7.02 megahertz (Mhz), German at 6.50 and 7.20 Mhz, French at 7.56 mhz and Dutch at 7.38 Mhz.

Transponder

This is an antenna that re-broadcasts signals from a satellite to Earth. Normally not all transponders on a satellite would be in use, so that back-up can be provided in the event of systems failure.

Encryption

This is the process by which pictures are rendered non-viewable. Reversing the process requires the payment of a fee to cover access to the appropriate technology to unscramble the picture.

D2-Mac

There are a number of variants of Mac which represent different stages in the development of the technology. D2\Mac systems can operate in both D2-Mac and D-Mac.

Digital Systems

These systems provide higher quality sound and pictures than traditional (analogue) systems. Digital sound is already familair to many consumers in the form of CD systems.

References

1. Evidence for this trend can be drawn from the 1991 Census.
2. Cecchini, P. (1988) *1992: The Benefits of a Single Market* (Wildwood House).
3. The Astra satellite is frequently used in Britain because it carries Sky programmes.
4. *Op. cit.*, p. 4.
5. *Ibid.*, p. 4.
6. *Ibid.*, p. 48.
7. *What Satellite*, December 1991, p. 125. This diagram is reproduced by kind permission of *What Satellite TV*
8. *What Satellite*, December 1993, p. 155. This diagram has been reproduced by kind permission of *What Satellite TV* It should be noted that Marcopolo has been re-named Thor and moved to serve the Scandinavian market rather than the United Kingdom. It is also interesting that Olympus I no longer exists. It was apparently destroyed by a meteor in October 1993.
9. *El País, Negocios*, 4 August 1991, p. 1.
10. *The Week in Europe*, London, 18 March 1993.
11. *Télé Satellite*, January 1993, p. 47.
12. *The Economist*, 16 March 1991.
13. *The Week in Europe*, 13 May 1993.
14. *The Economist*, 15 March 1991.
15. *Télé Satellite*, January 1993, p. 62.
16. Sky Subscription Agreements, August 1993.
17. Unification of the broadcasting system disregards the comparatively small technical problems inherent in the co-existing, current terrestrial systems, based on PAL and SECAM. As noted earlier, it would have been easy to have engineered out these problems.
18. This categorization of the standards currently in use in Europe disregards the B-Mac standard used in Europe by the United States Armed Forces Radio and television.

Satellite broadcasting: a missed opportunity for the SEM?

19 50 us and Panda audio are essentially compatible. J17 de-emphasis is required for certain transmissions in order to avoid the harsh sounds which would otherwise occur.

Questions

1 Satellite broadcasting appeared to have the potential to develop within the SEM. What factors operated in its favour?

2 To what extent was a common technical standard developed and why did such a common standard ultimately fail to materialize?

3 What EC directives affected satellite broadcasting and what effect did they have on it?

Index

Aerospace industry, 6, 192
  American share, 197–8
  competition, 197
  European share, 198–200
  global market, 203, 204
  political links, 195–7
Aerospatiale, 200
African–Caribbean–Pacific (ACP) states, 82, 87
Airbus Industrie consortium:
  aircraft table, 203
  history, 204–7
  make-up, 200–1
  reform proposals, 202–3
  structure, 201–2
Aircraft, market demand, 6, 194–5
Airline industry, 192–4
Aktiengesellschaft (AG), 141–2
Alonso, Juan F Biones, 60, 61
Anti-absorption measures, 78
Anti-competitive measures, *see* Competition, control of
Anti-dumping measures, 77
Association Agreements, 80, 81
Association of European Automobile Constructors, 255
Association of Petrochemical Producers in Europe (APPE), 214

Banana regime, 79, 87–8
Bangemann proposals, 151–2
Barriers:
  fiscal, 41–2
  physical, 40
  technical, 40–1
BASF/ICI deal, 216
BAT case (1987), 56
Belgium, steel industry, 165
Blair House Agreement, EC–US Accord, 84, 91
Boeing, 197–8
Braun, Fernand, 158, 159
Braun Plan, 158–9, 165, 169–71
Bretton Woods System, 67

British Aerospace (BAe), 200
  sweeteners case, 65
British Petroleum, eco-auditing, 120
British Sky Broadcasting (BSB), 264–5
British Standard BS 5750, quality assurance, 126, 129–30, 131
British Standard BS 7750, environmental management systems, 126–7, 131
BSN (food group), 60–1
Bureau of European Consumers (BUEC), 43

Car market, 7
  background, 227–8
  European protectionism, 254–5
  global, 229–30
  Japanese competition, 235–6, 239–40, 252, 254–6
  major manufacturers, 231–4
  manufacturers' location strategies, 234
  review, 256–7
CASA (aircraft manufacturer), 201
Cassis de Dijon case (1979), 41
Cecchini Report (1988), 38–40, 52, 259, 261
CEN, *see* European Committee for Standardization
CENELEC, *see* European Committee for Electrotechnical Standardization
Central Europe, trade with, 83
Chemical Industries Association (CIA), 127–8
Chemical industry, eco–auditing, 124–6
City Code on Takeovers and Mergers, 148
Coal industry:
  background, 95
  EC role, 99–103
  market size, 96–7
  producers, 103–13
  rationalization, 97–9
  regional problems, 102
  state aid, 99–100
Cockerill Sambre, 165

Index

Cohesion Fund, 50
Committee of Permanent Representatives (COREPER), 22
Committee of the Regions (CoR), 14, 31
Committee of Transport Unions in the Community, (ITF-ICFTU), 18
Common Agricultural Policy (CAP), 18, 34
  MacSharry reforms, 86
  and world trade, 86
Common Commercial Policy (CCP), 67, 73
  challenges to, 85–8
  common external tariff, 36, 73, 75–6
  common procedures, 76
  evaluation, 73
  and GATT, 85
  legal basis, 74
  objectives, 75
  principle of parallel powers, 75
  reasons for, 74
  supranational character, 84–5
  trading rules, 76–9
Common Customs Tariff (CCT), 36, 73
Common external tariff (CET), 36, 73, 75–6
Common Foreign and Security Policy (CFSP), 12, 73
Common markets, establishing, 37
Communication satellites, *see* Satellite broadcasting; Satellite technology
Competition, 37
  control of, 52–3
Concentration with a Community Dimension (CCD), 57–8
Concentration regulation, 52–3
'Concert party' (takeovers), 143
Concurrent engineering, 239
Consten & Grundig case (1964), 54–5
Consultation procedures, EP, 24
Consumer needs, 43
Continental AG, merger proposals, 145–7
Continental Can case (1973), 56
Cooperation Agreements, 80, 81
Copyright protection, 47
Corporacion de la Siderurgica Integral (CSI), 166–7
Corporate culture, UK business, 147
Council of the Union, *see* European Council
Countervailing duties, 77

Court of Auditors, 14, 29–30
Court of First Instance, 14, 28–9
Customer service targets, 44
Customs unions, 36, 73

D2-Mac (television standard), 264–6
D'Avignon plan, 154, 155–7, 160, 168
De Havilland/Aerospatial/Alenia case (1992), 59
Debt finance, German business, 141
Decision-making models, 3
Decisions, EC, 15
'Defence pool' (takeovers), 143
Denmark, eco-auditing, 128–9
Deutsche Aerospace (DASA), 200–1
Developing world, *see* African–Caribbean–Pacific (ACP) states
Dillon Round, GATT talks, 76
Directives, EC, 15
Directorate-Generals (DG), 17
Duales System Deutschland (DSD), 222–4
Duty free sales, 41–2
Dyestuffs case (1972), 54

Eastern Europe, trade with, 83
Eco-auditing, 120–2
  chemical industry, 124–6
  cycle, 138
  Denmark, 128–9
  EC initiative, 123
  logo, 134
  in United Kingdom, 130–1
  voluntary and mandatory, 134–5
Eco-labelling scheme, 119
ECOFIN (Ministers of Finance), 20
Economic development, deprived areas, 66
Economic integration, EC:
  framework for, 36–7
  larger market benefits, 37–9
  process, 35–6
  progress towards, 39–40
Economic and Monetary Union (EMU), 34
Economic power, 38
Economic and Social Committee (ECOSOC), 14, 30–1
Economic union, establishing, 37
Economies of scale, 37
Elements of Consensus

Index

(European/Japanese agreement), 254–5
Elf Autochem/Rohm & Haas case (1992), 63
Environmental Action Programme (EAP), Fifth, 118–19
Environmental issues, plastics producers and users, 225
Environmental legislation, 214
Environmental Management and Audit Scheme (EMAS), 5, 115, 119–20, 135–7
  benefits 127–8
  components, 116
  environmental statement, 131–3
  progress, 123–4
  in United Kingdom, 130–1
Euro Disney, 6
  background, 177–8
  competition, 187–8
  corporate structure, 179–81
  cultural diversity, 189–90
  finance package, 181–2
  lack of success, 188–9
  share price movements, 186–7
  site performance, 182–6
  site selection, 178–9
European Aerospace Industry Council (EAIC), 197
European Atomic Agency (EURATOM), 13
European Bank for Reconstruction and Development (EBRD), 14
European Central Bank, 14
European Centre for the Development of Vocational Training, 15
European Coal and Steel Community (ECSC), 13, 95, 99, 154
  Consultative Committee, 14, 31
European Commission, 12, 17–19
  compliance enforcement, 47–8
  Packaging Waste draft directive, 224–5
European Committee for Electro-technical Standardization (CENELEC), 41
European Committee for Standardization (CEN), 41
European Community (EC), 11–12
  areas of compliance, 16
  budget, 19
  decision making process, 31–3

Environmental Policy, 115, 117
  framework, 12–15
  and global trading economy, 67–72
  international agreements, 79–84
  legal instruments, 15
  preferential agreements, 72
  principle of subsidiarity, 16
  unique international role, 73
  see also under names of constituent institutions
European Council, 12, 21–2
  presidency role, 20
European Court of Justice (ECJ), 12, 15, 20–9
  complaints procedure, 48
European Currency Units (ECUs), 232–4
European Economic Area (EEA), 1, 28, 81–2
European Economic Community (EEC), 11, 13
European Environment Agency, 14
European Free Trade Area (EFTA), 1, 12, 28, 35, 70–1
European Investment Bank (EIB), 14, 29
  network funding, 50
European Monetary Institute (EMI), 14
European Monetary System (EMS), 1, 43
European Organization for Testing and Certification (EOTC), 45
European Parliament (EP), 12
  Budgetary Authority, 25
  contacting members, 25–6
  election of members, 22–3
  environmental policy making, 117
  powers, 23–5
  role, 26
  seat allocations, 23, 24
European Political Cooperation (EPC), 73
European Telecommunications Union (ETU), 263
European Toy Directive, 45
European Trade Union Confederation (ETUC), 18
European Union, *see* Treaty on European Union (TEU)
European Work Health and Safety Agency, 14
EUROPOL Drugs Agency, 14
Exchange Rate Mechanism (ERM), collapse, 43

277

Index

Excise duties, alcohol and tobacco, 42
Expansion process, EC, 35
External trade, 70–1

Fiat, 252–4
Financial institutions, UK business, 147–8
Flachglas/Vegla case (1992), 62
Flexibility, labour force, 237–8
Ford, 242–4
'Fortress Europe', 71, 86
Foundation for Training (agency), 14
France, coal industry, 103–6
Free trade development, 79–84

General Agreement on Tariffs and Trade (GATT), 19, 67, 68, 76
  Dillon Round, 76
  Kennedy Round, 76
  MFN clause, 79
  Tokyo Round, 76
  Uruguay Round, 2, 85, 87, 90–1
General Motors (GM), 241–2, 243
General Objectives for Steel-1995 (GOS–95) report, 154, 155
Germany:
  coal industry, 106–9
  Packaging Ordinance, 221–4
  steel industry, 162–5
Global trading economy, 67–72

High Definition Television (HDTV), 264
Honda, 240, 248

ILVA, 165–6
Industry restructuring, 66
Infrastructure coordination, 49–50
Intermills case (1984), 65
Internal energy market (IEM), 101
International agreements, 79–84
International Airtransport Association (Iata), 193
International Bank for Reconstruction and Development (IBRD), 67
International Monetary Fund (IMF), 67
International Telecommunications Union (ITU), UN, 263
Isuzu, 240
Italy, steel industry, 165–6

Japanese competition, car market, 235–6, 239–40, 252, 254–6

Joint ventures, merger regulation, 62–4
Judicial and Home Affairs Policy, 12
Kennedy Round, GATT talks, 76
Kloeckner Stahl, 162, 163
Krupp-Hoesch, 163

Lean production (manufacturing mode), 236–9
Legal compliance, 16
Legitimate interests (merger proposals), 59
Lomé Conventions, 82, 87

Maastricht Treaty, *see* Treaty on European Union (TEU)
McDonnell Douglas (MDD), 198
Management board, German business, 144
Management role, UK business, 148
Medicines Evaluation Agency, 14
Mercedes-Benz, 246–8
Merger Control Regulation, 52–3, 56–7
  application, 59–61
  CCD reviews, 64
  joint ventures, 62–4
  procedure, 58
  scope, 57–9
Milan Summit, 52
Monopolies and Mergers Commission (MMC), 150
Most Favoured Nation (MFN) clause, GATT, 79
Multi-Fibre Agreement (MFA), 84
Multilateral Steel Agreement (MSA), 159

National Accreditation Council for Certification Bodies (NACCB), 133
National laws, importance of, 49
Natural disaster effects, 65
Neste/Statoil deal, 217–18
Nestlé/, merger proposals, 149–51
Nestlé/Perrier case (1992), 60–1
Networks, trans-European, 49–50
New Commercial Policy Instrument, 78
Nissan, 239
Non-discrimination principle, 79
Non-tariff barriers, 38, 52
Norsk Hydra, eco-auditing, 123

Opinions, EC, 15

278

Index

Organization for European Cooperation and Development (OECD), 19

Packaging Waste, EC Draft Directive, 224–5
Pal/Secam (television standard), 265–6
Payments system, cross border, 43–4
Peugeot-Citroen, 250–1
PHARE (reconstruction programme), 19
Pierson, Jean, 202–3
Pilkington, eco-auditing, 121–2
Pirelli, merger proposals, 145–7
Plant Breeder's Rights Office, 15
Plastics industry, 6
  background, 208–10
  capacity rationalization, 215–18
  challenges, 211–14
  environmental issues and policies, 218–25
  materials categories, 210–11
  restructuring support package, 215
  voluntary action, 215
Polypropylene market, 215–16
Practical compliance, 16
Price differentials, 44–5
Product churning, 238
Public pressure, pollution incidents, 125–6

Qualified majority voting (QMV), 21
Quality control, 238–9
Quinine Cartel case (1969), 54
Quota agreements, *see* Voluntary Export Agreements (VERs)

RECHAR (coal initiative), 103
Recommendations, EC, 15
Recycling, *see* Waste management recycling
Regional trading arrangements, 87
Regulations, EC, 15
  No 4064/89 (mergers), *see* Merger Control Regulation
'Reinforcing the Effectiveness of the Internal Market' (Commission Report 1993), 35
Renault, 250–1, 252
Responsible Care Initiative, 126–7
Rhone Poulenc/SNIA case, 63–4
Road network, 50

Rover, 248–50
Rowntree, merger proposals, 149–51
Royalties, 47
Rules of Origin, 76

Saarstahl, 163
Safeguard measures, 77
Satellite broadcasting:
  benefits, 259–60
  programme access, 267–9
  review, 269–71
  technical glossary, 271–2
  technology, 261–2
  television standards, 262–7
SCA (Sociétés en commandite par actions), 181
Schengen Agreement, 40
Schengen Information System, 40
Services sector, 43
Share ownership:
  German business, 142, 143
  identification, 144–5, 149
  UK business, 148–9
Shell, eco-auditing, 121
Single European Act 1986, 14, 21, 117
Single European Market (SEM), *see* Single Market
Single Market, 71
  1992 campaign achievements, 1, 42, 50–1
  compliance enforcement, 47–8
  fiscal barriers removal, 41–2
  new trade obstacles, 48–9
  physical barriers removal, 40
  post-1992 aims, 34–5
  programme gaps, 43–5
  role of television, 259–60
  second stage, 46–7
  technical barriers removal, 40–1
Single Market Compliance Unit, 48
Sky Broadcasting, 264–5
Social Chapter, 33
Société Européenne des Satellites (SES), 263
Solid fuels, *see* Coal industry
Spain:
  coal industry, 109–10
  steel industry, 166–7
STABEX support measures, 82
Standards, common, 45

279

Index

State aids, 64–5
  aerospace industry, 196–7
  coal industry, 99–100
  Treaty requirements, 65–6
State Aids Code, 154
Steel industry:
  Belgium, 165
  Braun proposals, 169–71
  effective capacity table, 173
  employees table, 175
  Germany, 162–5
  Italy, 165–6
  overcapacity, 160–7
  production table, 173, 174
  reorganization, 168–9
  restructuring, 153
    Eurofer proposals, 157
    Industry Council proposals, 158
  Spain, 166–7
  special status in EC, 154–9
Steetly/Tarmac case (1992), 59
Structural composites (plastics), 211
Subsidiarity principle, 16, 117–18
Subsidies, government, 65, 77
Supervisory board, German business, 144
Surveillance measures, 77
Sutherland Report (1992), 35, 46
Suzuki, 240
SWOT analysis, 3
SYSMIN support measures, 82

Takeovers:
  contested, 5, 140–1
    German business, 144–5
    structural barriers, 141–2, 147–8
    technical barriers, 142–5, 148–9
    UK business, 147–51
Tariff barriers, 36
  removal, 38
Technical Councils, 20
Television standards, satellite technology, 262–7
Thyssen, 162
Tokyo Round, GATT talks, 76
Tourism, importance, 6, 176–7
Toyota, 240
Trade associations, 32
Trade and Cooperation Agreements, 80, 81
Trade creation, 36–7
Trade diversion, 36–7

Trade Mark Office, 14
Trans-European networks, development, 49–50
Transparency principle, 79
Transplant factories, 239–40
Treaty on European Union (TEU), 11–12, 13, 39, 73, 117
  principle of subsidiarity, 16, 117–18
  Social Chapter, 33
Treaty of Paris, 99, 100, 154–5
Treaty of Rome 1958, 11, 14, 100
  Article 85 (anti-competitive agreements), 54–5
    block exemptions, 55
  Article 86 (monopolistic behaviour), 55–6
  Common Commercial Policy, 74
  European Investment Bank, 14, 29

Union of Industries in Europe (UNICE), 18
United Brands case (1978), 55–6
United Kingdom:
  coal industry, 111–13
  Environmental Management and Audit Scheme (EMAS), 130–1
Uruguay Round, GATT talks, 85, 87, 90–1
Users Charter (proposed), 44
Usinor Sacilor (SOLLAC), 168–9

Value added tax (VAT), 41
Van Miert, Karel, 64–5
Volkswagen (VW), 244–6
Voluntary Export Restraints (VERs), 77, 78, 156
Volvo, 251–2
Vondran, Ruprecht, 163–4
Voting systems, EP, 22–3

Waste management, 218–25
  German legislation, 221–4
  recycling, 219
World Bank, *see* International Bank for Reconstruction and Development (IBRD)
World Trade, 70–2
World Trade Organization (WTO), 85

Yaounde Conventions, 82